Wildly impressive teaching, remarkable research, unquestionable enlightenment. Startup Evolution Curve is by far the most concise framework for startups that I've ever read on the subject. Donatas covers everything needed to ensure not only success and scale but also the ability to do it over and over again. Every entrepreneur should have a copy of this book.

Germaine Moody,

Serial Entrepreneur, Author & Investor (USA)

Startup Evolution Curve is an amazing marketing manual that provides startup founders a step by step methodology to enlarge and sharpen their vision in a meaningful and useful way. Mixing a strong academic theoretical vision with solid experience, Donatas Jonikas is definitely an author "out of the curve"... I rate this book as a must have for every smart and dedicated entrepreneur!

Alex Quirino,

Founder/MP at Berks Capital Alliance (UK), Partner/CEO at Golden Dragon Holdings (HK), Mentor for the Stanford University Technology Entrepreneurship Online Course

Donatas' book is like an IKEA guide for building your next startup. Startup Evolution Curve is a detailed, comprehensive, understandable, and - most important - deeply practical instruction handbook. Every piece of information is based on more than 1,000 different practices, processes, routines, and tips from existing startups. That makes it a must-read when launching your next big thing.

Michal Tomek,

Co-founder & Editor at Slovak STARTUP

This book is a great way to rehearse some of the crucial elements that you need to align in order to have a successful business. Think about it like a roadmap that will guide you to the most important stages in your startup: 1. Feasibility Study, 2. Hypotheses and Experiments, 3. Fundraising, 4. Product Launch and the very hot topic of 5. Growth Hacking. Donatas has gathered together the essentials that I would love to have received from my entrepreneurship classes in high school and during my Business University degree.

Startup Evolution Curve is in the same league with The Four Steps to the Epiphany by Steve Blank and The Art of Start by Guy Kawasaki. I would recommend Startup Evolution Curve to startup enthusiasts, first time or serial entrepreneurs, and even to my own kids!

Denis Todirica,

Start-up Chile Entrepreneur. Forbes 30 under 30

Startup Evolution Curve is a masterpiece of practical, actionable, and easy-to-follow steps to turn an idea into a profitable and scalable business. Donatas has provided would-be entrepreneurs with a blueprint for building a business, along with some excellent templates and tools to help you during the journey. I am very impressed with the depth of the research, the range of examples and case studies, and the honesty and sincerity with which Donatas provides advice and guidance. This is a must-read for anyone thinking of starting a business or growing an existing business.

Debra Partridge,

Owner PearTree Consulting (USA)

I know how challenging it is to build a successful startup (I've already developed three). There are always more bad experiences and issues than truly exciting moments, but the result of all of the pitfalls is learning. If I could have read this book before creating my first startup, I would have avoided many pitfalls and tons of frustration. My philosophy is to always be coached and this book is full of guidance, not only for the early stage entrepreneurs but also for the already successful ones. None of the books will keep you from failure, but this one will definitely help you make better decisions.

Ariel Mizrahi,

Serial Entrepreneur & Mentor at StartupMexico (Mexico)

I don't know any book that sums up better the startup evolution and growth than the Startup Evolution Curve by Dr. Donatas Jonikas: The question isn't only what you should do; it's what and when you should do. So, if you are early stage startup founder and already have some innovative ideas, this is one of the most thought-provoking books you should give a try in 2017. Also, if you are looking for in-depth advice about topics such as business feasibility, market experiments, fundraising, product launch, and growth hacking, then this book is again an excellent choice to look for ideas and a different perspective.

Velimir Tasic,

Entrepreneurship Leader at garagErasmus,
Co-founder of ESAA entrepreneurship incubator (Singapore)

Dr. Jonikas combines academic research, observations from studying hundreds of startups, and personal experience to craft a solid framework for taking a new venture from idea stage through solid growth. His advice includes both what should be done, and what mistakes to avoid. He also references a variety of online tools that might be missing from other "how to" books, even a year or two old. It's a solid reference book for experienced entrepreneurs and a valuable roadmap for first-time founders. It's organized in a way that allows readers to jump into the sections of particular interest, so it isn't necessary to start at the beginning. It is well worth the read!

Akira Hirai,

Managing Director at Cayenne Consulting, LLC (USA)

If you are looking for foundations of how to build an innovative business, here it is! Startup Evolution Curve is like a textbook with essential checkup points. Secondly, it's easy to read. Donatas goes straight to the point without any idle talk. I am sure anyone who will start reading this book will just "swallow" it!

Alexander Soloveicik,

Serial Entrepreneur & Advisor at Silicon Valley Real Ventures (USA)

I believe this book does a great job educating the reader about the building phases of a startup from both a theoretical and practical perspective. I found the startup case studies to be extremely useful as it shed light on real life examples. Entrepreneurs, business owners, students in business schools, and anyone thinking of building an innovative business could benefit from this book.

Nunzio Presta,

Founder & CEO at BizON Marketplace (USA)

Startup Evolution Curve is like a startup MBA in 325 pages.

Tarmo Virki,

Founder of CoFounder Magazine (Estonia/Finland)

Startup Evolution Curve presents a clear scenario to facilitate understanding of the complexities of marketing in the early stages of high potential scalable ventures. This is most valuable information for MBA students and entrepreneurs. Donatas shares important strategies for identifying the business model, and in particular, offers the value proposition in contrast with "cool features," which lead to considerable distractors in our world.

Katherina Kuschel, Ph.D.

Researcher at Lazaridis School of Business & Economics (Canada)

Startup Evolution Curve is unique as it is based on real data about 1,000 companies. It reaches beyond plain facts by giving advice, templates, and real-life examples. The book covers the whole process of creating a successful startup, from the initial feasibility research to managing company growth. It is an excellent read for entrepreneurs.

Boyan Yankov, PhD

Co-founder of Web Motion Ltd (Bulgaria)

Nice structure, great research, and a solid foundation for startup founders who want to understand the details. I think every university student should read it!

Mark Tuttle,

Co-founder & CEO at Cryptografx Security Solutions (UK)

It's a practical combination and synthesis of old and new practices in terms of startup and business. Startup founders can surely find a complete journey in order to manage a startup, from creating business models based on ideas to developing funding approaches and metrics for new businesses.

Giorgio Ferrari,

Co-founder & Startup Mentor at quo·d (Italy)

Startup Evolution Curve is a wonderfully practical guide for both young founders and experienced entrepreneurs engaged in startups. I found it a very pleasant read, which creates an impression of not just a manual for those involved in startup development, but more of a hands-on guide empowered with real-life case studies, useful templates to be applied in individual startup business strategies and research activities, as well as suggestions of the modern tools to be used. It feels like the author has considered the most common questions startup founders come across and provided a set of recommendations for them to be easily managed.

Yuliya Tsimokhava,

Content manager at VCEE Startups (Belarus)

Startup Evolution Curve perfectly embodies all that is essential to becoming the definitive business manual: essential analysis; lean method; hands-on approach. Using an iterative and closed-loop process, with tons of visual and practical takeaways, it is highly recommended for startup practitioners. And, as a seasoned business, we will want to keep it on our working desk - because it just goes straight to the point.

Alberto Ratti,

Co-Founder BIBA Venture Partners (Spain)

It's an engaging book for all startups. The author has put across a lot of case studies which helps in understanding how it was implemented in a particular case. I recommend startups to learn and more importantly implement the strategies outlined in this book.

Arjun S Meda,
Startup Catalyst & Entrepreneurship Community Builder (India)

A very thoroughly researched and, what is more important, personally lived through must read for start-ups and prosperity seekers. Donatas provides us with useful tools to support our creativity and execution process, which is critical especially at the time of growth and expansion. If you want to achieve virality and brand affinity, I highly recommend it.

Anna Hejka,
Serial Entrepreneur & Founder of VC/PE funds (Poland)

The Startup Evolution Curve is filled to the brim with useful tools and insights presented in a very structured way. Simply a great guide for first-time and serial entrepreneurs alike.

Andy Cars,
Lean Startup Coach, Founder of Lean Ventures (Sweden)

Startup Evolution Curve reveals must-know essentials and strategies for early-stage startup founders. You just need to read it and implement recommendations relevant to your case step-by-step. Actually, it is helpful not only for young startups. Even though *InnMind* is in its growth stage, the book helped us to take a step back and dive deeper into our current situation as well as defining the most essential milestones of our growth strategy.

It is impressive how Donatas collected all the essentials and must know's for startups in one, easy-to-read book! I highly recommend Startup Evolution Curve to every startup founder from idea to the growth stage as a Bible of a startup journey.

Nelli Orlova,
Co-founder & CEO at InnMind (Switzerland)

Donatas gives a clear and concise guide to any entrepreneur or startup wanting success. No stone is left unturned. I just wish I had access to such a great resource in my early days as an entrepreneur. It would have saved me a lot of wasted time and energy.

Tom Payani,
Sales Psychology & NLP Trainer (Spain)

I remember talking to Donatas at an event in Vilnius in March 2016. This book was just an idea in a few simple words. I'm delighted to see this final product delivered. I hope this book will be an inspiration for many to turn words into action. This informative guide can take a startup at least one step forward to increase the probability of success and I highly recommend it!

Donatas Smailys,

CEO at KTU Startup Space (Lithuania)

All entrepreneurs dream of building a successful business. Startup Evolution Curve is undoubtedly a guide and a mandatory reading that will help us to follow the path we idealized at the beginning of our entrepreneurial journey.

Carlos Rubinstein,

Founder & CEO at Talentix (Brazil)

Startup Evolution Curve is one the greatest books I have read, one that not only wisely and realistically touches some of the most intricate pain-points of startups, but also offers an equally wise, simplified, and detailed solution. A good thing about this book is that it opens your mind to different possibilities and perspectives. Therefore, I would love to refer it to every startup, aspirant, businessman, and student I know.

Karan Rajani,

Startup Advisor. Business Columnist @Yo! Success (India)

I firmly believe that each and every person who wants to become successful and financially self-sustainable should read this book. It's a practical road map for entrepreneurs who want to improve their life by doing what they love. Startup Evolution Curve is a great and comprehensive guide for understanding the world of startup business.

Andrew Funk,

Serial Entrepreneur & President of #HomelessEntrepreneur (Spain)

This is one of the most insightful, practical and scientifically-developed resources into the complex world of startup marketing. The action-based blueprints, charts and to-do lists make it a necessary resource on the desk of all founders and marketers. Highly recommend for anyone building a startup in 2017.

Abdo Magdy,

Group CEO at EGY Enterprises Ltd (UK/Egypt)

The book is definitely helpful in getting right to the point insights on the practical issues of the startups growth and development. Aha moments are collected frequently by the novice reader and valuable notes often recorded for future reference. You can focus solely on a priority topic and still get immersive advice supported by the author's latest research. Hope Donatas shall expand exponentially his followers base after the book reaches the target audience.

Merab Labadze,

Innovative Educator & Technology Promoter at Innovative Education Foundation (Georgia)

Dr. Donatas Jonikas did a great extensive research to more than 1400 startups and found out good pointers to get you from an idea to a scaling business. We're especially charmed about the testing frameworks and tools he suggests within this book, that will help you test the riskiest assumptions of your startup and your startup marketing strategy.

Stephan Botz,

Serial Entrepreneur, Investment Manager at EPIC Seedfund & Co-Founder of BW Ventures

A solid book combining actionable strategies and insights from the trenches of entrepreneurship. If you plan to start a business this book will give you a big shortcut from theory to implementation.

Carl Allen,

Serial Entrepreneur, Investor & Founder of Ninja Acquisitions (UK)

Startup Evolution Curve is a must-read material for any entrepreneur who is thinking big. If you are planning to turn your ideas into a profitable company, this book is for you. As an entrepreneur, and entrepreneurship teacher in one of the best business schools in Argentina, I would say this book contains all the information any startup needs that is usually not explained in college. You don't have to reinvent the wheel - Startup Evolution Curve helps avoiding common mistakes and shows shortcuts to success. If you want to improve your learning curve, save your time and money, don't miss this book!

Damian Lopo,

Founder & Director at Newlink Capital (Argentina)

Special thanks to:

- Andrius Tamosaitis for the cover design and creative approach.
- Debra Partridge for copy editing, proofreading, and making this book easy to read.
- Amit Dey for book interior and ebook formatting.
- SlideModel for sharing their awesome design templates to illustrate this book.

Here is a gift for you!

Thank you for reading this book. *Startup Evolution Curve* is based on my analysis of 1,447 surveys of startup founders and more than 500 in-depth interviews with successful startups all over the world. This was a significant undertaking! But I've also gathered, created, and updated a set of templates that will help you save time and stay focused while embarking on your own startup marketing tasks. I've found these templates extremely useful in my consulting practice with different startups and you are welcome to download them for FREE at www.EvolutionCurve.com/templates.

Please leave your review

I would be sincerely grateful if you would review this book on Amazon. It will help other startup founders to better understand what they could learn from this book. Please share what you've found most valuable in this book and to whom you would recommend it. Thank you in advance!

My most sincere thanks go to my dear wife Dovile for her support and understanding during this journey of discovery and creativity.

Table of Contents

Warning: read this first!

Many people have innovative business ideas or even actual inventions, but they never start a business simply because they don't know how. Even if they do start a business, most startups fail and the founders find themselves asking "Why...?" Unfortunately, it's not enough to just have an innovative idea to start a successful business. It's not even about finding the money, either. Angel investors, venture capital funds, and even crowdfunding platforms receive many requests from early stage startups every day, but most of those requests are unpolished, unprepared, and lacking in sufficient proof of a viable business model. Sadly, even the greatest and most promising ideas quite often don't receive sufficient attention and interest from potential investors, just because the founders didn't know how or what to prepare.

Not surprisingly, there is no magic trick or one-size-fits-all methodology to skyrocket your startup and I can't provide you with one either. But the good news is that you are reading *Startup Evolution Curve*, a startup marketing manual on how to transform your innovative ideas into a profitable and scalable business. Consistently applying this methodology step by step will help you attract suitable investors and create a self-sustainable, profitable business. This methodology is built not just on theory, but on the best practices of hundreds of successful startups all around the world.

I wrote this book for entrepreneurs starting their own innovative business, early stage startup founders, and investors looking for promising innovative startups. The methodology shows you step by step how you can achieve three main goals:

- Secure your first sales and ensure that you have something that can become a profitable and scalable business.
- For founders, find the most suitable investors, and for investors, objectively evaluate which startups are worth investing in.
- Identify business growth possibilities and employ a growth hacking mindset to accelerate your growth at the right time and in the right way.

This is not a theoretical textbook that is difficult to implement and boring to read. This is a simple and actionable manual that will open your eyes to how you can improve the development of your startup. It will provide you with many "Aha!" moments. *Startup Evolution Curve* is the result of long-term practical and analytical work based on real world research.

I've been working as a Chief Marketing Officer (CMO), board member, and marketing consultant for more than 10 years. During the time, I've helped to develop and successfully implement marketing strategies in more than 50 companies in different countries. Marketing theory is useful as background knowledge, but when you have a real business, you need clear and actionable guidelines for what to do next, especially if you are a startup and already have a painful cash burn rate.

- To enhance my knowledge of startup marketing, I've recently read dozens of books and over 100 scientific articles about various aspects of startup development. I've attended more than 30 live seminars and conferences on start-up and innovation topics. I've watched an uncountable number of webinars and videos concerning startup marketing. Most of them are focused just on particular aspects of startup development. That's not necessarily a bad thing, but it takes too much time if you want to have an overall understanding of how innovative ideas are transformed into a profitable and scalable business. That's how I came up with the idea of writing a book that would be a step-by-step marketing manual for early stage startups.

- With a doctoral degree in economics, I couldn't resist the temptation to verify the *Startup Evolution Curve* methodology by conducting research that took me more than eight months. The result is that each step and task in this manual is based not only on my personal experience and a solid theoretical approach but also on practical evidence from my worldwide research. To prepare to write this book, I surveyed 1,447 startup founders all around the world and conducted nearly 500 in-depth interviews with founders who achieved significant results or had painful lessons to share.

Conducting the research also helped confirm that this book is needed and inspired me to continue the work. Soon after launching the survey, I started receiving personal messages from startup founders validating both the survey and my instinct that the book is needed:

- "Finally had time to sit down and do your survey. Some pretty deep stuff going on in there."

- "I really liked the kind of questions you have raised. It seems you're going deep in the startup metrics and analysis."

- "I have completed the survey and it did make me think more deeply about what to focus on and improve in the business."

- "I like very much the way you put together the critical questions to every entrepreneur."

- "I've finished your startup survey and I realized how much more work has to be done."

- "Nice survey, made me think about few things (especially in marketing domain) that I didn't think about - or maybe don't have the skill sets to do it."
- "I've gone through your test and understood that I have almost nothing prepared for marketing and growing my projects! I will definitely try to learn more in this field!"

If you want to find investors for your startup or if you are developing a startup business on your own, this book is a shortcut. This startup marketing manual will give you a significant boost to your business, save you time, and help you to avoid painful mistakes. The concept of *Startup Evolution Curve* has five stages with seven lessons (or tasks to be done) in each. So, you have in your hands a comprehensive book with 35 lessons on startup marketing. Each lesson explains:

- What should be done and why it is needed
- Actionable steps and how to do it
- Real case startup examples
- Useful templates for download and references for further reading

I obviously don't know your business in detail, but this book will give you insights on how to improve your startup and achieve better results. You don't even have to read the whole book from start to finish. Review those chapters that might be most relevant to your situation and use what you find most helpful for your business. My mission is to help startup entrepreneurs and early stage startups to build their business faster. And if you need just a few pieces of what I want to share, so be it! I'll be happy for you no matter how much you learn from this book!

"Marketing and innovation produce results; all the rest are costs."

P. Drucker

Let's start by looking at how startup marketing helps bring innovative ideas into reality and create a profitable business. But one thing you must remember: it's not enough just to have the knowledge. You must take action to make the vision become a reality and I'll gladly guide you on taking that action. Come on! Let's build your profitable and scalable business!

Save time! Read this book and download useful templates from www.EvolutionCurve.com to make your startup grow faster.

Increasing the chance of
your startup's success

The research of 1,000 startups worldwide

WHAT EXACTLY IS A STARTUP?

According to Steve Blank and Bob Dorf (2014), a startup is a temporary organization in search of a scalable, repeatable, and profitable business model. Neil Blumenthal proposed that a startup is a company working to solve a problem where the solution is not obvious and success is not guaranteed. Others say that only a technology business which is based on one main product or service and has a fast growth possibility activated by great teamwork and venture capital investment should be called startup.

These days, you will hear that nearly any new business can be called a startup. To me, the most acceptable definition was given by Paul Graham who said that, *"A startup is a company designed to grow fast. Being newly founded does not in itself make a company a startup. Nor is it necessary for a startup to work on technology, or take venture funding, or have some sort of "exit." The only essential thing is growth. Everything else we associate with startups follows from growth."* I would also add that a true startup is always involved in some kind of innovation. The innovation can be in technology, new products or services, new methods of production, new cost structures or pricing, a new business model, new funding ideas, and many other possible innovations.

But how much can a startup grow and still be called a startup? Alex Wilhelm (2014) in his article on TechCrunch proposed a term sheet for startup definition. If the company has or is any of the following, it can no longer be called a startup but rather should be treated as just another technology company either hunting for or actively avoiding an IPO:

- $50 million revenue run rate in 12 months
- 100 or more employees
- $500 million or more worth

Because there is little agreement on the definition of what constitutes a startup, it is instead helpful to classify startups into five categories in accordance with the main purpose for which they were established or initiated:

- **The small business startup** is associated with a fact that the vast majority of so-called startups never grow past the small business stage. So, if the founder just wants to run his own business and earn enough money to feed his family, it should be classified as a small business startup.

- **The lifestyle startup** is very similar to the small business startup, but in this case, the founder pursues his passion (does what he loves) and finds a way to earn money through it.

- **The buyable startup** is a new phenomenon wherein a startup is founded with the main purpose of being sold to a third party in return for a handsome amount of profit. The low cost of developing web or mobile apps allows startup founders to fund the business by their own savings, credit cards, or by raising small amounts of risk capital (usually less than $1 million). These startups are happy to be purchased by larger companies that often seek to acquire the talent as much as the business itself.

- **The scalable startup** is vastly different from the small business startup despite the fact that both have very humble beginnings. A scalable startup usually has a simple but powerful concept and believes that it can change the world. In most cases, these startups are looking for financial investors to help make their vision come true.

- **The social startup** is driven by a powerful cause rather than by profit. But just because social entrepreneurs are fighting for a cause doesn't mean that they are any less passionate about success or interested in making a profit. Unlike traditional startup companies, the goal of most social startups is to make the world a better place. However, there are some social startups that strive for wealth creation for a specific targeted group.

I used these same five categories when I conducted my research. My initial goal was to survey 1,000 startups, but I actually collected more than 1,500 responses, of which only 1,447 were qualified. I refer to this research in the book as my "global research on startups."

THE PURPOSE AND SCOPE OF THE RESEARCH

The idea to conduct this research was born during the Investor Day conference organized by VCEE Startups where I was giving a speech. I've been thinking about writing a practical manual on startup marketing for quite a while and this conference was a good opportunity to determine if my book idea had a market fit. At the end of my lecture, I introduced the book mock-up and a link where conference attendees could freely download a set of practical templates used in startup marketing. The audience got interested and started asking about the book content and where it could be purchased. That was a great motivation for me and the volume of template downloads during and after the event confirmed that topic is really worthy of a book.

After receiving such nice praise for my book idea, my elation soon returned to normal when one startup founder asked me directly, "Why should we believe in what you are telling us? How do we know that these steps are mandatory to build a profitable and scalable business?" Ouch! What a question! Somebody doubted me! I don't recall exactly how I replied, but I began answering it in my mind with something like, "Because I have more than 10 years in marketing and I know it from my experience." "Because I've developed and helped to successfully implement marketing strategies for more than 50 companies in different countries." "Because I have Ph.D. and I read countless numbers of scientific articles and books on these topics." But, so what? I said myself to stop trying to justify myself! Actually, I realized that it was a great question, even if I didn't like it. You also shouldn't take it personally if somebody doubts or critiques your ideas. It is your ideas that are being questioned, not you personally. For me, it became obvious that I must have a solid answer to this question.

Fortunately, David Goldsmith was in the room. As a global entrepreneur and a best-selling author, he confirmed that I made some really good points about startup marketing, but it would be good for me to have more validation or proof. Did you know that he interviewed 2,000 companies to write his New York Times best-selling book *Paid to Think*? His research is one of the reasons why his book became so highly valuable for entrepreneurs. I was amazed by the scope and depth of his research and he told me that I should do that, too! I agreed that it would be awesome to conduct that kind of research, but I didn't want to take a few years. I wanted to do it in few months.

Another guy came up to me during the coffee break and said he knew of many consultants and mentors who have built one or a couple of successful startups who were now teaching others. But he described his startup situation as very different, and he was not sure if he should listen to them. Then I had an *Aha!* moment. What if I gather knowledge and collect best practices from 1,000 startups all over the world? What if I could somehow test these methodologies on 1,000 startups before putting them in the book? Thanks to those guys for asking right questions, and to David Goldsmith for the inspiration, I designed a two-stage research project (Table 1).

Table 1. Goal structure of global research on startups

Survey & statistical analysis (1,447 responses)		In-depth interviews & case studies (nearly 500 interviews)
To check if startup business development methodologies are used in practice?	YES	How do particular methodologies contribute to startup success?
		Are these methodologies used correctly and effectively?
	NO	Why are these methodologies not used in practice?
		Do startups understand the essence and purpose of methodologies?

The general purpose of the research was to check what has worked well and what seasoned startup founders would do differently in their next venture. The survey was run for quantitative statistical research, while in-depth interviews and case studies were used for qualitative analysis. I have prepared the survey based on the five stages of startup development and have included methodologies and concepts recommended by theoretical literature and by well-known startup development experts. Classification of the startup development stages still remains complicated and ambiguous because not every startup can clearly say which development stage they are in. Therefore, the survey had five descriptive questions for the startup founders to self-assess on a scale from one to ten how close they are to one or another benchmark. It allowed me to identify the development stage of each startup and to check if they know and use the methodologies which are recommended for each particular stage. The in-depth interviews allowed me to go deeper into each individual situation, to analyze how a particular methodology contributed to the startup's success, and determine if the founders correctly understand and use them in practice. In addition, I was searching for any shortcuts in the development of a startup and checking to see if there might be a pattern among them that proved that using the same methodologies was an efficient way of starting a business.

I started the survey without a review by a native English-speaking business person and that was a mistake. I did a pilot survey (about 30 responses from my network), but most of the responses were provided by non-native English-speaking business people and it didn't occur to me to change it. The good news was that soon after launching the survey publicly (up to 50 responses), I started getting comments in my email, in Linkedin, and even on Facebook. A few people told me that they couldn't give the answer they wanted or spotted a spelling mistake. Here is what I did to resolve the issue:

1. I made all questions not mandatory, so if somebody couldn't find a suitable answer, they check none of them. I didn't include blank responses in the survey results.

2. I created a comment field below each question to get feedback from respondents in case there was an issue or additional information was needed. I did this after I had already received around 100 responses. Some of the respondents provided additional insights, while some of them were just funny, and some were not valuable at all. But, generally, there were no major complaints about not understanding the questions in the survey.

3. I added clarification or corrected spelling mistakes as I received them from respondents. As far as I remember, I got helpful advice from four or five native English-speaking people. The most helpful was a guy from Toronto.

4. During Skype interviews with the startups who wanted to be a case study, I double-checked their answers and dug deeper. They confirmed that making the questions not mandatory was a good idea. After that, none of my Skype interviewees reported having misunderstood any questions. If there were any confusing questions or answers, they were usually left blank or the respondents included additional comments in the comments field. Therefore I was able to filter out unreliable responses.

The survey ran for five months (151 days to be exact) from May 2, 2016 to September 29, 2016 and the in-depth interviews took an additional couple of months. My sincere thanks to *InnMind*, Startup Chile, Innovare Platform, Slovak Startup, VCEE Startups, and many other organizations, numerous social network groups (like "On Startups" and "A startup specialist group" on Linkedin), and all entrepreneur-minded people who helped to spread the news about the research.

Figure 1. Scope of the research

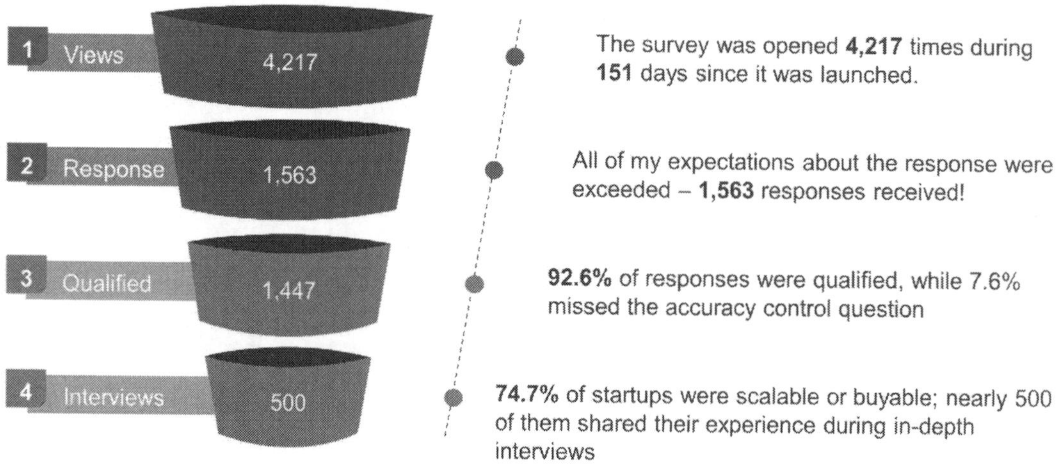

The survey was opened **4,217** times during **151** days since it was launched.

All of my expectations about the response were exceeded – **1,563** responses received!

92.6% of responses were qualified, while 7.6% missed the accuracy control question

74.7% of startups were scalable or buyable; nearly 500 of them shared their experience during in-depth interviews

The survey received 1,563 responses from startup founders from all around the world and 1,447 were qualified. I added a special question to avoid blind responses: "If you read this carefully, please mark the answer with *we have it*." So, only validated responses were included. I also conducted nearly 500 in-depth interviews and case studies with startups that fell under the category of buyable or scalable startups. According to data gathered by *InnMind* (2016), approximately 100 million startups are opened each year and 1.35 million of them are tech startups. Taking into account that the total population of the research is close to infinity (1.35 million or 100 million startups around the world), the statistical results of this survey are accurate at the 95% confidence level plus or minus 3% percentage points.

Figure 2. Survey responses by startup type

Startup type

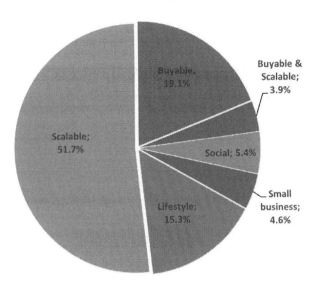

According to our definition of startups, not every new business is a startup. Therefore, my analysis was focused on startups that fell under the category of scalable or buyable startups (1,081 qualified responses or 74.7%). Many startups chose several statements describing their situation. If the scalable or buyable category was among them, their response was included in further analysis. I was not seeking to do research to precisely represent the startup community structure worldwide, but was focused on collecting responses from early stage startups in different regions (Figure 3. Survey responses by startup location) and different industries (Figure 4) which allowed me to compare their specifics and possible interdependencies.

Figure 3. Survey responses by startup location

Main location

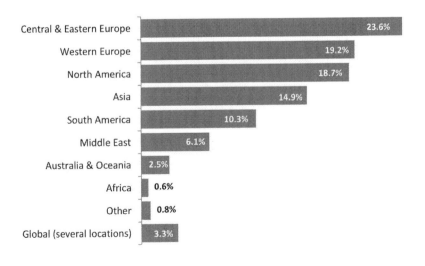

11

Figure 4. Survey responses by startup industry

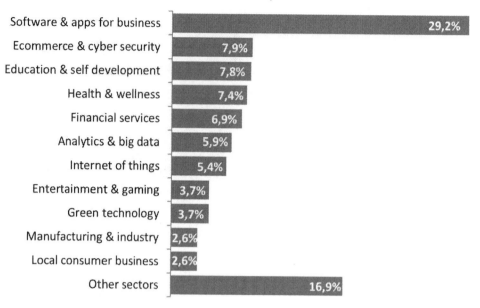

Startup funding was another important criterion used in the research (Figure 5). While it is not yet statistically confirmed, startups that were at least partly funded by founders showed greater progress in the product launch stage (when the product or service was already on the market), but startups that were mainly funded by investors had much better and deeper feasibility studies done and demonstrated more sophisticated approaches to experiments and hypotheses verification. It probably shouldn't be surprising, because investors usually are less passionate about the project than founders and require more information for decision making. Maybe it's just a coincidence, but most of the startups that indicated they were looking for investors (and were not funded by the founders), showed a very strong focus on fundraising, but a relatively weak focus on feasibility studies and very little effort on hypotheses verification.

By the way, it's interesting to note that 1.8% of surveyed startups had already managed to acquire financing from government grants or EU structural funds, by winning cash prizes in contests, or by getting funded from third parties (neither founders nor investors).

Figure 5. Survey responses by startup funding sources

Startup funding

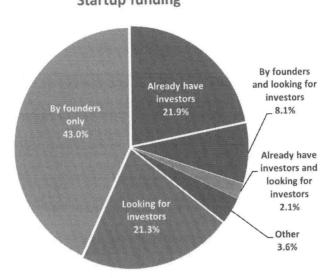

I suppose we could calculate the correlation between different variables and check to see if there is a dependency of applying one or more methodologies based on startup location, type, industry, and funding. But this is a practical startup marketing manual, not a tedious report of scientific research. So, take a look at Figures 6 - 10 to get acquainted with the type of startups that fell into the scope of the research, then let's move on to how to transform your innovative ideas into a profitable and scalable business.

Figure 6. Survey responses by progress of feasibility study

Have you already done the feasibility study?

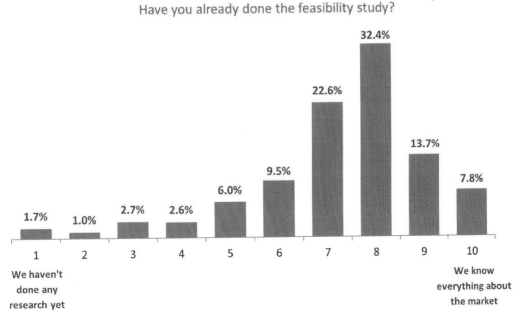

Figure 7. Survey responses by progress of prototyping and hypotheses verification

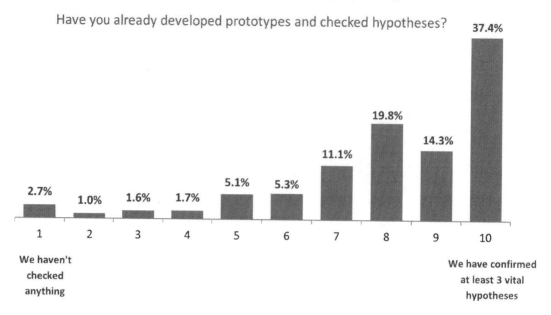

Have you already developed prototypes and checked hypotheses?

We haven't checked anything

We have confirmed at least 3 vital hypotheses

Figure 8. Survey responses by progress of startup funding

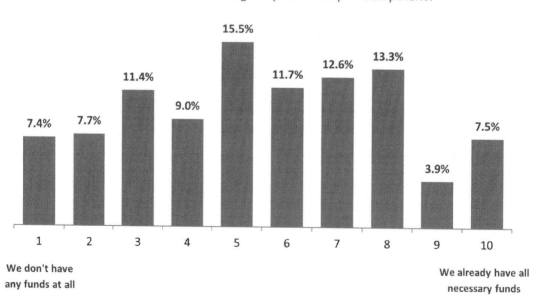

Do you have sufficient funding for your startup development?

We don't have any funds at all

We already have all necessary funds

Figure 9. Survey responses by progress of product launch (market entry)

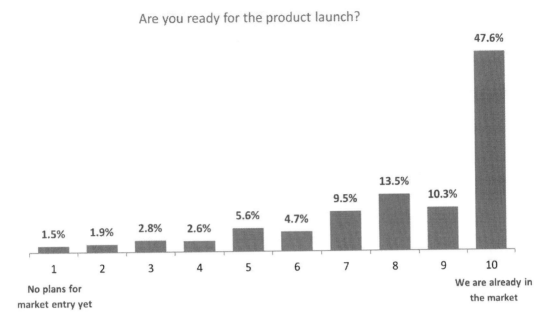

Are you ready for the product launch?

Figure 10. Survey responses by progress of business growth

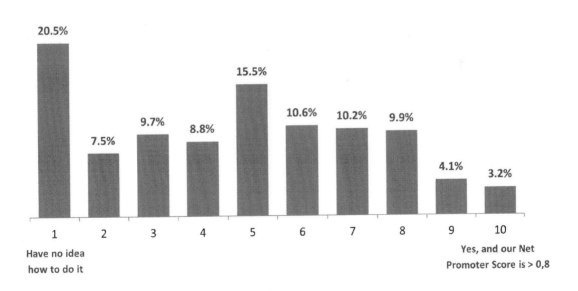

Have you addopted any business growth engine?

The founders of thousands of scalable and buyable startups have shared their experience and contributed to hundreds of in-depth interviews in order to create this marketing manual for early stage startups. It seems like it has taken a long time, but finally, you hold this book in your hands! It doesn't represent just a single point of view of an author or expert, but the experience and advice of more than 1,000 startup founders from all around the world! I hope you will read it and take from it what seems the most valuable to you.

Most dangerous mistakes in startup marketing

A quick search on Google will tell you that around 90% of startups fail. They simply never become a profitable or scalable business. Why is this failure rate so high? What critical mistakes are these failing businesses making in their strategic marketing?

I've been in strategic and practical marketing for more than 10 years and have observed some common mistakes that most early stage startups make. But, observations are not as conclusive as data. Therefore, in my global research on startups, I was looking for success factors and valuable lessons to be learned. But, unexpectedly, I've also found some common mistakes made by one after another in startup marketing. Following are the most common and most costly.

1. *Creating the product first, thinking about marketing later*

This is one of the most common and expensive mistakes a startup can make. Who would create a product that nobody wants to buy? It seems so logical, but there are many, many startups that have invested their time, money, and effort in developing products without having a clue as to whether customers will buy it. Many startups, especially in the tech industry, think that the hardest part is to create an innovative product, to "make things better." The notion that the main success factor of a business is to create a product is a business mindset that was popular and very effective in the 1960s. It is certainly not a valid business premise in the 21st century and even less so for startups.

It's great to have a strong focus on product innovation, but you have to create products that will be loved and used by customers, not you!

2. *Offering "nice to have," but not essential value*

Many startup founders focus on creating products that solve a particular problem that is important for them, but not necessarily for their potential customers. If the problem you are trying to solve is not really painful for customers or the value you try to create is not essential—but just "nice to have"—the chance of success for your startup is very low. First of all, it will be much harder to sell non-essential products. If your customer's financial situation worsens, your "nice to have" product won't be on your customer's priority list. Secondly, the price and your profit margin strongly depend on perceived value. The more valuable your product seems to be for the customer, the higher the price he is ready to pay. So, you definitely want to focus on creating essential value and solving painful problems.

3. *Lack of market verification; saying is not the same as paying!*

This is closely related to the "nice to have" mistake. The fact is that 42.6% of startups that are trying to address really serious problems and create tremendous value don't *test it in the market* or they do it in the wrong way. It would be hard to find a startup founder who hasn't heard about market verification, the process of validating their business idea in the real market. But most of them either don't take the time to do it thoroughly or do it incorrectly.

For example, you can't just ask your customers to answer a survey to get market verification. Instead, ask them to buy or at least pre-order your product. If customers say your product is great and that it solves a meaningful problem for them and gives great value, that's great! But, if they still don't buy it, guess what? Saying is not the same as paying! You'll never have real market verification until customers give you their money for your product.

4. *Anything to please investors instead of customers*

Pleasing investors instead of customers must be some kind of disease. I don't know what else to call it. Startups too often focus on the show while pitching a business idea to investors instead of proving their business concept and growth potential. Sadly, some investors foster such behaviors by raving about exciting pitches—those without a solid foundation and marketing background—just because the startup founder was so charismatic and put on a great performance during the pitch. Other startups notice this trend and the next time focus more on the pitch and the performance rather than verifying their business model and proving the business's potential durability and scalability.

Trying to please potential investors has a reasonable justification: investors can bring money, their network, and quick solutions to some of the challenges of a startup. Yes, it's true, but only if you have a valuable and verified solution. Customers, not investors, should be at the center of your startup's radar. If the customer is happy and satisfied, many things follow automatically, including the investors standing at your door to provide you needed funds.

5. *Thinking that "we have no competitors"*

I don't know why startups believe in such a fairy tale. In my global research on startups, I didn't find a single case where there were no competitors. Anyone who knows at least the basics of marketing knows that there is always direct and/or indirect competition. If your startup is developing some kind of innovation, it's possible that you won't have direct competitors for some time until you are copied. But if you are solving a real problem (which should nearly always be the case), there's already a way that people handle this problem. This is your indirect competitor! The customer's decision to ignore the problem is your indirect competitor as well! Why? Because there is an alternative for the customer: not to buy your product!

My in-depth interviews with startup founders showed that most of them did only a very sketchy feasibility study into the market competition. Only 33.9% of startups have evaluated their micro and macro business environment, while others hadn't even thought about it and were focusing mainly on market fit verification in the best case. It's better to ask yourself "how can we find out with whom we are competing" instead of thinking that "we have no competitors."

6. *We have brilliant idea and it will go viral by itself*

Really? Are you sure? Why should anyone recommend your service or product? What's in it for them to do so? I don't say people won't recommend you to their friends if your product or service is great. But it's very dangerous to rely on that. That is called "hope marketing," which basically means we do nothing in essence but hope for the best. Is it wise to make bets on such a strategy?

There are at least three types of growth engines clarified by Eric Ries years ago: viral, sticky, and paid. The sooner you take action to implement at least one of those engines, the faster your business start growing with the help of other people.

7. *A good growth hacker is all we need!*

About two-thirds of startups I interviewed said they would like to get help on business growth by so-called growth hacking. Growth hacking is a strategy whereby every decision made by the business is focused solely on growth. Of those, only half had already found their problem-market fit. Incredibly, this revealed that nearly one of five startups is willing to waste their energy and resources on growth hacking without having validated their value proposition.

Another surprising statistic is that only about 20% of startups have developed their up-sell and cross-sell strategies. It means that the other 80% of startups have no idea what they will do with potential customers even if growth hacking succeeds. They are not yet prepared to sell more and will basically leave money on the table.

The majority of startups strive for growth, but only a few of them have a well-prepared foundation to handle what growth hacking could bring to them. Don't waste energy on growth hacking until you've laid the foundation for growth.

8. *Marketing needs a huge budget, therefore we'll take care of it after fundraising*

If you are targeting a large-scale market, you'll probably need a big budget for communicating your unique value proposition. But it's simply not true that you can't start efficient marketing without significant funds. Not all marketing measures and tools need big money. If you want to see this can be achieved, take some time to read some books and articles about guerrilla marketing.

As my research showed, 47.9% of startups were already on the market, but only 17.4% had a consistent marketing plan and only 39.4% had developed their brand and positioning. Crafting positioning statements and creating marketing plans requires effort, not money!

Before putting money in a startup, any rational investor will check to see if there is traction. Investors need proof that the business model is viable and durable. How are you going to show it without doing any marketing? You are on the right track if you don't want to spend a huge amount of money on marketing in the early stage. But, you can still plan and run marketing experiments to find a problem-solution-market fit, validate your communication and distribution channels, and get some ideas about possible growth engines. Once you have that, you can prepare a comprehensive marketing plan with potential profit estimations and then seek out investors to ask for the budget you will need to implement your brilliant marketing plan.

9. *We'll enter the market with "big boom" launch*

Wrong! That's not efficient anymore! Big launches might be a strategy for the well-established, traditional business, but for startups, it usually just causes failure in the form of wasted money and insufficient sales. Startups typically introduce innovative products and services, thus they have to do things that don't scale at first: verify the market fit, acquire their first clients (early adopters), create user evangelists, test communication channels, and search for an efficient growth engine. Sometimes, a big launch might be a good marketing strategy for a startup, but only if you have done the aforementioned tasks and much more. It's much better to get some traction in advance before considering a big launch.

10. *Burning money instead of investing*

Sounds crazy? Who would do such an idiotic thing? You would be shocked at how many startups burn their investor's money by spending it on things that don't add value to the startup. Yes, it might feel comfortable and safe paying yourself a salary from the investor's money. And, it might be cool to work in a nice office and attend the greatest startup conferences and other events. But, what's in it for your startup? How does it help your business? One thing is definite: it increases your cash burn rate. The higher the cash burn rate, the less time you have to create a profitable and scalable business.

Startup founders with an entrepreneurial mindset achieve more because they see the difference between fundraised and earned money. They don't spend on shiny things but instead, they invest in what builds value for the startup.

The Concept of Startup Evolution Curve

Steve Blank (2010) cites Sean Ellis, a well-known expert on startup development, who stated that, "the cost of a consultant's time can never be justified working with startups pre-product market fit because the failure rate is just too high." And I have to admit it's true. In my global research on startups, I found only a few exceptions to this observation. Most of the 1,447 startups I surveyed couldn't bear the costs of a marketing or business development consultant before they'd found their product-market fit and got on track to earn revenue. There were few exceptions, but those were startup founders who were serial entrepreneurs with solid personal and financial backgrounds who could afford to hire consultants at any time. But for startups that are bootstrapped from zero, with no connections and financial capital (as are most startups), hiring consultants can be extremely beneficial. Why? As I delved deeper into the research, I became more confident that a solid and hard-to-copy value proposition is essential for a startup to be successful. Sean Ellis believes that hired consultants can improve the growth trajectory *after the first business model is developed.* This means that startups are on their own to build a great value proposition by finding their problem-solution-market fit and the initial traction. Once you have that, you can attract investors and hire consultants to help scale your business, but at the very beginning—at the hardest period—startup founders are alone and have to find their way based on their own efforts.

The good news is that the results of my research are included here in the *Startup Evolution Curve*, the book you are holding, to help you with this issue.

Startups, unlike traditional businesses, can measure their success not only by revenue but also by the knowledge they gain on the way to confirming the problem-solution-market fit and building a profitable and scalable business. *Startup Evolution Curve* covers five stages of startup development with different objectives in each.

It doesn't much matter if you develop a buyable startup or any other kind of startup, this methodology keeps you focused on creating a profitable and scalable business. The concept can be applied to different kinds of businesses: whether it's an online or offline business, a service or a product, business-to-customer, or business-to-business. There are few exceptions (for example, medicine and biotechnologies) where this methodology would be hard to apply in whole, but different aspects could be adopted.

Figure 11.   Main goals of each stage of Startup Evolution Curve

Feasibility Study
- Create value proposition
- Analyze potential market
- Define business model

Hypotheses and Experiments
- Test 3 main hypothesis
- Adjust business plan
- Develop marketing strategy

Fundraising
- Set fundraising milestones
- Create fundraising material
- Become visible for investors

Product Launch
- Craft an irresistible offer
- Plan how to communicate it
- Execute—Measure—Learn

Growth Hacking
- Create a viral loop
- Choose the right growth engine
- Use leverage everywhere

If you run an ordinary business, it's possible for you to learn from the experience of others, to check what works and what doesn't, what your competitors do, and how you could do something better. But this book is designed for business pioneers; for those who are taking their business journey to where no one else has gone before. Therefore, the *Startup Evolution Curve* goes up with each stage, even if there is some turbulence in building a solid base of knowledge or verified business model with an actual revenue stream.

Some tasks might look like they are being repeated in different stages in this book. This is intentional because many aspects of a startup business must be reviewed and updated at least a few times with deeper understanding and precision each time. Percentages in conceptual startup evolution curve (Figure 12) indicate the progress and how many tasks are completed in particular development stage. It's quite possible that due to iteration process startups will have those percentages changing up and down.

You can read this manual as an ordinary book—from the first page to the last one. But *Startup Evolution Curve* is designed to be convenient for people without much time

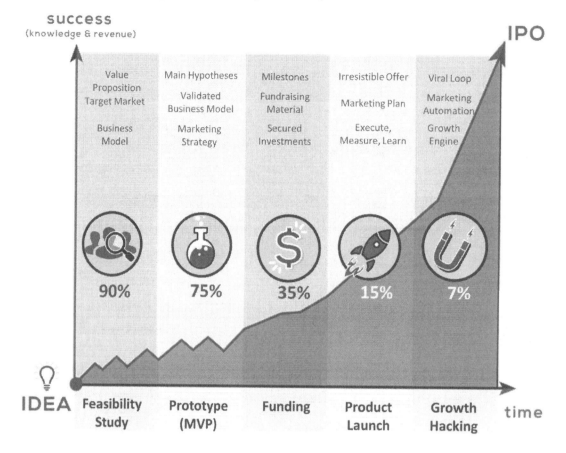

Figure 12. Concept of Startup Evolution Curve

and who want to take action right now. If this describes you, here is how you should use this book:

1. Choose one of the five stages you are currently most interested in
2. Review the topics to get an overview of what should be done in that stage
3. Review the "how to do it" infographic at the beginning of the topic and follow the instructions

If you are not sure which stage of the *Startup Evolution Curve* you should focus on first, take the online self-assessment test (www.evolutioncurve.com/test). It will help you to find out where to focus your attention to get the most value from this book in your particular situation. Plus, by answering the questions, you'll better understand the whole methodology and get some insight into how you could improve your startup business.

Icons mark the tasks to be done in each lesson

Each stage of the *Startup Evolution Curve* has the same number of lessons to be learned, but each lesson includes a different number of tasks. There are 164 tasks in total. You can quickly run through these tasks highlighted by the icons to review the whole concept. Read those tasks that are most relevant to your situation and follow the instructions. If any questions arise, you are welcome to join the Startup Evolution Curve group on Linkedin where members of the startup community and I share our experience and answer questions.

Key thoughts before you start:

1. The founder of a startup never feels relaxed until he sells all his shares of a venture and takes a well-deserved break before creating a new startup. You should not relax after successful fundraising. On the contrary, now it's time to prove the trust that investors put in you.

2. A one-man band will never sound as good as an orchestra. It's highly beneficial to have an advisory board of experts in different fields meaningful to your business. This can yield not only great insights, but valuable connections, investments, and even your first clients. Don't be too self-contained. It's better to seek out potential advisors.

3. Testing, testing, testing! Never stop testing, but do it reasonably. Get used to the fact that you'll have to run many tests and most of them will end up in failure. During my research, I didn't meet a single startup that became successful without raising weighted hypotheses and wisely testing them one by one. To build a successful startup without testing is something like winning a jackpot in a lottery, but the failure price in the startup is much higher.

4. Use wise metrics and measure only what really matters. It's good to see growing numbers and justify your decisions. But only wise metrics show your real progress towards a profitable and scalable business. Don't become obsessed with useless vanity metrics.

5. Get used to planning and change your plans quickly. In today's economy, not the largest but the fastest wins. Use any online or offline planning tools that are convenient for you, check templates at Evolutioncurve.com, or at least plan on a whiteboard in your office or at home. If you want to keep progressing, you must keep track where you are now, where you are going, and what tasks you should do next.

I sincerely hope this book not only will give you some insights, but will also help you to gain additional knowledge, mindset, and needed skills.

Stage 1: Feasibility Study

Generally speaking, a market feasibility study is a way to minimize a startup's risk. Why should you develop products or services that customers won't buy? Why should you risk creating a non-profitable business? My global research on startups that I conducted in 2016 showed that 1 hour spent on a qualified feasibility study saves 2.7 work days (or 21.6 hours) on average in product development and market entry stages. That's amazing return on investment (ROI) of your time. So don't ever assume that a correctly performed feasibility study is a waste of time. I've personally conveyed a number of feasibility studies in recent years and can tell you that it can save huge amounts of money as well. I remember a $59 million case where the startup founders already had investments from Switzerland, but the feasibility study showed that their project as it was planned has no chance to become a profitable business. Even if everything went according to the most optimistic scenario, they could expect only about 80% of the revenue needed to reach the break-even point. It was sad and disappointing that such huge business project was never launched, but the feasibility study helped avoid burning out $59 million!

The correct attitude to market feasibility study should be to find out what customers need and want, check whether it's a profitable opportunity, then create and give it to them. Following this, the market feasibility study:

- reduces the amount of time, money, and energy it takes to create profitable products and services
- aligns your solutions and possible offers with customers' needs and wants
- helps to increase targeted traffic and bring you more potential customers
- increases the likelihood that customers will like and trust your product or brand more
- allows you to achieve higher sales conversion and retention (get new customers and sell more to existing ones).

Usually, the preliminary feasibility study is performed based on secondary data (information which is already collected by somebody else). It's much cheaper or sometimes even totally free, allows you to approximately evaluate the potential of your idea, provides insights how it could be adjusted, and identifies what you should test in practice. In the empirical part of the feasibility study you have to collect data by yourself: run surveys, interviews, and experiments. The goal here is to test assumptions about your business idea and get as solid as possible facts how this business idea might work out in the best way.

Main goals of this stage:

✓ create a value proposition
✓ evaluate the potential market size
✓ define a possible business model

1. The Essence: Define the Value Proposition

WHY IT IS NEEDED

The very first step of what you should do is to define what value you will deliver to your customers. I mean this seriously! If you can't describe what real value you provide to your customers, you shouldn't plan anything else and you shouldn't build any products. This is a vital and most important step. The essence of a successful startup is not about the modern technologies, fancy innovations, venture capital investments, or large media coverage. The value proposition is the critical element for startup success. If you can create real value to potential customers, it will be much easier for you to:

- attract investments (which might be necessary for creating and delivering the value proposition)
- earn consistent revenue and profit
- get viral word of mouth recommendations to help grow your business fast.

The outcomes of creating your value proposition and using it in your sales strategy can be significant. The following are real examples of startups that created very efficient value propositions:

- *Classloom* is a social platform dedicated to helping parents and teachers have better and more qualified communication. Without any promotion, they have acquired users from 37 different countries including Malaysia, Brazil, Egypt, United Kingdom, France, India, and Saudi Arabia.

- *Share2Style* collected more than 1,000 pre-registered users in one week. Within a few days after their launch, they received proposals from a few investors without putting any effort towards fundraising.

WHAT'S IMPORTANT TO KNOW

According to Osterwalder and Pigneur (2004), a company's value proposition is what distinguishes it from its competitors. It is the collection of products and services a company offers to meet the needs of its customers. The value proposition provides value through various elements such as newness, performance, customization, design, brand, status, price, cost reduction, risk reduction, accessibility, and convenience, etc. In other words, a value proposition is a promise of what a customer will get from your business. Generally, it is the main reason why a customer would choose to engage with your company instead of your competitors. It is a concise statement that highlights the relevance of a product offering by explaining how it solves a problem or improves the customer's situation.

The value proposition should be seen from a wider perspective than just a listing of what benefits the company can offer the customer. Usually, there are three levels of value emphasized in value proposition (Table 2):

1. *List of features.* Though it's not very effective, a list of features is the easiest way to construct a customer value proposition. You simply list all the features the offering might deliver to target customers. Some people mistakenly think that the more features can be listed the better, but that is not always the case. This approach requires the least knowledge about customers and competitors and, thus, it is the least effective.

2. *Points of difference.* Regardless of the product or solution, customers always have the option to buy a similar product at a competitor or solve the need in another way. Therefore, companies should focus on how to differentiate one product or service from another in the market by citing their points of difference. Listing the points of difference is a more efficient method to create a value proposition rather than a list of benefits. However, there can be a problem when a product or service has several points of difference from the rest of the market: it becomes difficult for a customer to understand which ones deliver the greatest value. Therefore without knowing the customers' preferences and what it is worth to fulfill them, companies (especially startups) may stress points of differentiation that deliver relatively little value to the target customer.

3. *Customer-oriented value.* This approach is well suited to the B2B (business-to-business) market but could be adopted in most B2C (business-to-customer) market cases as well. Customers are more likely to buy from those providers who fully grasp critical issues and deliver a simple but powerful value proposition

that is most appealing to customers' current needs. The company can create a customer-oriented value proposition by making the offering superior on the few attributes that are most important to target customers. They must also demonstrate the value of this superior offering and communicate it in a way that resonates with their customers' priorities. In other words, the company must show the exact value this offer can deliver to the customer.

Table 2. Types of value proposition

	List of benefits	Points of difference	Customer-oriented value
Consists of:	All the benefits customers receive from an offer	All favorable points of difference compared to competitors	The key points of difference which deliver the greatest value to the customer
Answers the customer question	Why should I buy it?	Why should I buy from you instead of your competitors?	What true value will I really get? Why is this offer so beneficial for me?
Requirements	Knowledge of own offers	Knowledge of own offers and closest best alternatives	Knowledge of how own offer delivers superior value to customers, compared with closest best alternative
Potential pitfall	Benefit assertion	Value presumption	Requires customer value research and should not be built just on assumption

For a long time, traditional companies using classical marketing techniques built value propositions on one of three main strategies:

1. *Operational excellence*—customers just want a good product at the lowest possible price. In this case, companies are not trying to come up with new or better products, just trying to produce more volume at a lower cost. This strategy works when there is a possibility of achieving economy of scale.

2. *Product leadership*—customers care most about the product and want to get the best. Companies are dedicated to innovation and quality and are constantly working on improvements that can be brought to the market. Keeping an eye on competitors and trying to stay one step ahead is a requirement for this strategy to work.

3. *Customer intimacy*—the market is full of similar products and services at various quality and price points. But, customers are not always satisfied with just a standard product. They want customized solutions. Companies are trying to learn as

much as possible about customers' needs and put their efforts into building successful relationships so they can deliver the most compelling products, services, and solutions.

The customer-oriented value proposition and the customer intimacy strategy allow companies to achieve the greatest results in a free market economy. Therefore, any innovative business should first take the customers' perspective and define what value can be delivered.

When you create your startups' offer to a customer (regardless if it is a B2C or a B2B market), you should always evaluate how the customer perceives your total value proposition. It's important to understand that most customers will consider the sum total of all your offerings and experiences during their interactions with your company. The offerings are usually the WHAT you sell and deliver, and the experience is the HOW you do it. So it's not enough to just write down a great commercial offer or give an appealing promise to the client. You must deliver it in a manner that brings the best experience for your customer. Sometimes you shouldn't even inform the customer, you should just do it. As an example, there is no point in telling your customer that you are very helpful and provide outstanding customer support. Customers will feel and see how helpful you are from the very first interaction, whether they are visiting the website, downloading your app, or meeting with your sales executive. To succeed with your innovative business idea, you must fully understand the rational, emotional, social and sometimes even political elements of the value you deliver.

There are many theories explaining *perceived value*, the method by which customers evaluate offerings and make a decision to purchase. But the classic concept of perceived value is probably the simplest, yet easily applied in practice. Every offer provides both benefits and costs to the customer, as shown in the diagram below:

Looking at Figure 13, where you could create additional benefits for your target customers? Where can you help them cut costs? If the benefits outweigh the customers' costs, the perceived value is positive, therefore your value proposition is logically acceptable. But don't fall in love with your value proposition just yet! Even if the customer's perceived value is positive, it doesn't mean that the customer will buy from you. Why? Because your offer is probably not the only one in the market! If you want to check if your offer is truly good, you should evaluate at least your main competitors' offers (more about this in next chapter).

The best way to understand the value you deliver is to put yourself in your customer's shoes and to involve the customer in the creation of your value proposition. As Steve Blank and Bob Dorf (2014) noted: *"in a startup, the founders define the product vision and then use customer discovery to find customers and a market for that vision."* Authors in their

Figure 13. Structure of customer perceived value

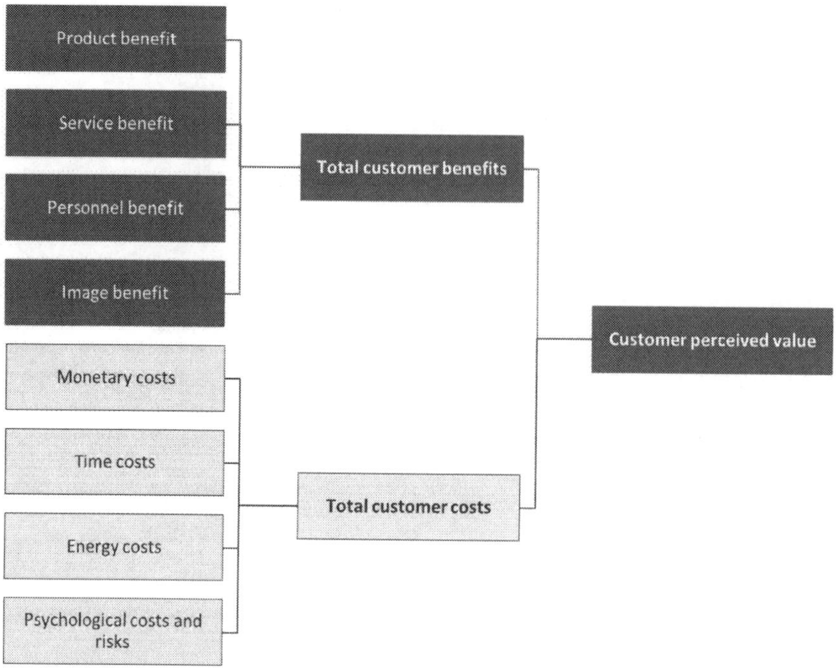

Startup owners manual also suggested four startup development stages which are very important in crafting the value proposition:

1. *Customer discovery* captures the founders' vision and turns it into a series of business model hypotheses, which have to be tested and turned into facts

2. *Customer validation* tests whether the defined business model is repeatable and scalable (if not, you should get back and repeat customer discovery)

3. *Customer creation* is the start of execution, which builds end-user demand and drives sales to scale the business

4. *Company-building* transforms an early stage startup into a company focused on executing a validated business model.

You should craft your value proposition in the very first stage and then test if it is meaningful and appealing for your customers. If it's confirmed, you can build your business model around it. If not, you should go one step back and redo your value proposition. To make the process easier, I would recommend using the value proposition canvas introduced by Alex Osterwalder, Eves Pigneur and Greg Bernarda in *Value Proposition Design* (2014). This tool helps startup founders design, build, test, and manage their customer value propositions. Some of the steps in "how to do it" section are based on tasks arising from this canvas. For a better understanding of this concept, I highly recommend you to spend few hours reading the book *Value Proposition Design*.

You are free to choose any methodology for creating your value proposition, but if you want it to be effective, the value that you intend to deliver must be:

- important to the customer
- unique and hard to copy
- strong enough to initiate word of mouth

Your customer should be able to read and understand your value proposition in about five seconds. It has to communicate the concrete results a customer will get from purchasing and using your products or services and it must differentiate your product from your competitors. Creating your value proposition means that you have one vision of what you are providing for your customers. This is like the master blueprint from which all sales stories, marketing messages, and individual offers are developed. This saves huge amounts of effort, time, and resources on the part of the sales and marketing staff, internal communications, and product development people, who otherwise might have totally different perspectives on the value they are creating.

HOW TO DO IT

01 — **Indicate Business Idea and Customer**
Define what you intend to create and to whom it might be most useful

02 — **Identify Problems, Jobs, and Gains**
List all customer's problems, current jobs, and desired gains

03 — **Prioritize the Puzzle**
Arrange problems, jobs, and gains according to known importance to the customer

04 — **Bundle the Solution**
Design how to help your customer with his most important problems, jobs, and gains

05 — **Propose the Value**
Describe your main value proposition in one simple and clear sentence

Indicate your business idea and target customer

Start by writing one sentence that describes your business. Don't worry too much about how nice and precise it sounds. It's just a starting point that will help to focus your attention. The main objective here is to answer what general or specific value your business intends to create for other people. Here are some examples:

- *Pixpie* is platform which optimizes content loading on mobile devices
- *Share2Style* allows you to earn affiliate commissions from global fashion brands
- *SlideModel* professionally designed and easy to use PowerPoint templates

Identifying your target customer is the next step. Describe the customer for whom you are developing a solution. What kind of customer (person or company) would benefit most of your proposed solution and how? You can check for ideas how to do it in chapter 3 Segmentation and potential market size. Here are some examples:

- *Pixpie* helps content publishers to serve their readers faster and allows media agencies to show more ads at the same time.
- *Share2Style* offers fashion bloggers over 1,000 global brands with hundreds of thousands of products that can be easily used for creating collages to publish onto their blogs instantly. Bloggers earn money once their visitors purchase any of the items from the collages.
- *SlideModel* - helps to save hours of valuable time for individuals and businesses creating professional presentation decks with little effort and without the need for design skills.

 Identify all possible customer problems, jobs, and gains.

1. Start by identifying and documenting your customers' real problems in precise terms

Evaluating your customers' real problems and needs is an important step if you want to create a really great value proposition. Write down all the challenging issues your target customer has to face, including risks and obstacles. It might be helpful to have in mind that Steve Blank and Bob Dorf distinguished four types of problems customers can have:

Figure 14. Problem perception levels

Latent problem - they have a problem but aren't aware of it yet and don't think about it

- *Passive problem* - they know of the problem but aren't motivated to look for opportunities to solve it

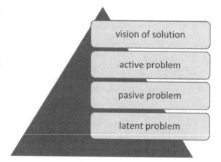

- *Active problem* - they recognize a problem or passion and are searching for a solution but haven't done any serious work to solve it
- *The vision of solution* - they have a problem, they want to solve it, and may even have a workaround, but are prepared to pay for a better solution.

It is important to describe the customer's problems as precisely as possible. For example, when a customer says *"I hate to wait for videos and photos to be uploaded on a mobile device,"* you should also ask about their tolerance for an upload time. A more precise description of the problem would be, *"Customer doesn't want to wait more than x seconds for the video and photo content to upload on their mobile devices."* When you can precisely measure the target customers' problems, you can create better products and services to solve those problems.

List as many problems as you can, but keep in mind, those problems must be real and important to your target customer, not just to you. As an example, *Tech4Freedom* has developed a device for spatial recognition and audio description for the blind people. This project generated a great deal of excitement at *The Telecommunications Night* event in Barcelona, has received awards for social commitment, and has attracted interest from associations of blind people in 14 countries. The prototype testing process created an echo in the media outlets, which led to Jaume Cunill, CEO of *Tech4Freedom*, to contact different target customer and partnership groups in Europe. That once again confirms how important it is to focus on solving a serious problem, instead of just creating a nice-to-have benefit.

You can use sticky notes for each problem during the discussion, but later it is best to list them as shown in Table 3. The table also shows some example questions you can use during your interviews and discussions (an Excel template is available for download).

2. Identify all possible jobs and tasks that customer is trying to complete

Jobs describe the tasks your customers are trying to get done in their business, at home, or even during their leisure time. A job could be a simple, routine task they are doing every day (downloading media, for example) or something more challenging and complex they are trying to implement and complete (selecting and implementing a new CRM, for example). Jobs sometimes depend on the specific context in which they are performed, therefore you may also have to make note of the specific context in which the job is performed (for example, only during non-production hours or on weekends).

Just like customer problems, not all jobs will have the same priority and importance to your customer. Some may have a higher priority because failing to get them done could cause other major problems. Others can seem totally insignificant in the current mindset

Table 3.   Discovery of customers' problems

No.	PROBLEMS	Importance 1 - 10	QUESTIONS
SEGMENT:			
			What makes customers feel frustrated and annoyed?
			What requires too much time, efforts, or nerves?
			What costs too much? And how much is too much?
			What risks do customers fear most?
			What are they afraid to lose or not to achieve?
			What keep customers awake at night?
			What's lacking in current value propositions on the market? What features and benefits are missing?
			What common mistakes do customers make?
			What are barriers that might keep customers from adopting a new value proposition? Are there any investments of money, time, and effort needed?

of the customer. Alex Osterwalder, Eves Pigneur and Greg Bernarda in *Value proposition design* (2014) summarized all possible customer jobs into four main categories:

- *Functional jobs* - customers try to perform or complete a specific task or solve a specific problem (e.g., brush their teeth in the morning, prepare breakfast, wash the car).

- *Social jobs* - customers want to look good or gain power or status, to be perceived by others in a specific way (e.g., to look fashionable, to be popular at school).

- *Personal/emotional jobs* - customers seek a specific emotional state (e.g., feel more secure, get rid of the feeling of regret, confirm a decision they made).

- *Supporting jobs* - the customer has different roles (buyer, co-creators, the transferor of value) therefore additional supportive jobs arise. These jobs can be related to buying value (e.g., comparing offers, deciding which products to buy, bringing products at home), to co-creating value (e.g., posting product reviews, participating in focus group during the design of a product or service), and to the end of a value proposition's life cycle (e.g., canceling a subscription, disposing of or reselling used product).

List as many jobs as you can, but keep in mind, those jobs must be real and important to your target customer, not just to you. You can use sticky notes for each problem during the discussion, but later it is best to list them in a table such as an example shown below. Table 4 also shows some example questions you can use during your interviews and discussions (an Excel template is available for download).

Table 4. Discovery of customers' jobs

SEGMENT:			
No.	JOBS	Importance 1 - 10	QUESTIONS
			What do customers have to do to every day in a job or at home in the context of my product or service?
			What do customers dream about? What do they have to accomplish to achieve their main goal?
			What do customers have to do for other people or together with them? What's so important about that?
			Which tasks and activities are unpleasant for the customer?
			What would customer like to avoid doing?
			How do customers want to feel? What tasks do they have to do for that?
			How would it be possible to make use of current products easier or more pleasant?

3. Identify all possible gains the customer would appreciate

Think about as many as possible gains, outcomes, and benefits your customer would be happy to receive. Be as specific as possible. For example instead of "Customers would like to spend less on upgrades" consider "Customers would like to reduce the cost of upgrades by 20% on cash outlay and 25% of labor costs."

List as many gains as you can, but keep in mind, those gains must be real and important to your target customer, not just to you. You can use sticky notes for each problem during the discussion, but later it is best to list them in a table such as an example shown below. The table also shows some example questions you can use during your interviews and discussions (an Excel template is available for download).

For illustration purposes, I'd like share with you the experience of Patricia O'Sullivan, the founder of AutoPixie. AutoPixie is a mobile app for auto mechanics that saves time by explaining car faults to car owners and automating all the paperwork. There are three main benefits for auto mechanics in this app:

1. AutoPixie explains faults to car owners in a way they understand, resulting in rapid decisions.

2. Using a little psychology, AutoPixie enhances trust, builds respect, and secures on-going loyalty.

3. The app automatically builds estimates, parts orders, and invoices, eliminating this annoying part of the car repair process for both the mechanic and the customer.

Table 5. Discovery of customers' gains

No.	GAINS	Importance 1 - 10	QUESTIONS
SEGMENT:			
			What do customers dream about? What they desire most, even if it seems not realistic at the moment?
			Which savings (money, time, efforts) would make customer most happy?
			What quality do customers want? How should it be modified?
			What would make the customer's life easier?
			What makes customers look good and feel great?
			What would eliminate customers' risks and their possible problems in the future?
			How would customer like to feel in a particular situation?
			What would encourage customers to try and adopt this value proposition?

Here is how Patricia came up with her value proposition: "*I interviewed 106 auto repair shops in 5 countries about their frustrations and pains. Some I interviewed 5 or 6 times to dig deeper and deeper into pain points. I never once mentioned software. Just said I had been a small local business owner and my business had failed in the recession and I was starting again and hoping that something that was a problem for them might be an opportunity for me. This prevented them thinking about software they knew and freed their minds to think of pain points. I documented everything and the top three all sounded like they were things software could not fix. Then one day while at the dentist, I had a sudden insight into how software could pretty much eliminate the three top pain points. If I had focused myself and others on things we thought software could do we would have talked about 'me too' solutions, instead we were free to think creatively and laterally.*"

 Prioritize the puzzle: arrange all problems, jobs, and gains by the importance to the customer

Next, you want to sort the problems, jobs, and gain by the importance or priority to the customers. Pay particular attention to the method you use to rate the importance. You can do it in one of two ways:

1. *Based on assumptions*—the evaluation is based on your assumptions, guesses, or one of the potential customers' subjective understanding. It is far better to

have in mind your customers' assumptions instead of yours, but in either case, they are just assumptions that might be far from the truth.

2. *Based on real facts*—this means that the particular statement is proven by statistics, technical specifications, or some other kind of facts. Sometimes you can find secondary data proving one or more statement, but for startups, it's typical for the initial concept of the product (or the entire business model, for that matter) to be based on assumptions which have yet to be validated (more about this in Stage 2: Hypotheses and Experiments).

It is helpful to arrange the problems, jobs, and gains in three separate columns with the most important problems, jobs, and essential gains at the top, and with the less painful problems, least important jobs, and nice-to-have gains at the bottom. Using this Excel template (Table 6) will make it much easier to arrange and to see the whole picture.

Table 6. Prioritizing customers' problems, jobs, and gains

PROBLEMS	Importance	JOBS	Importance	GAINS	Importance

SEGMENT:_____

 Bundle the solution - which customer problems and gains will your value proposition address?

Now, review the most important problems and gains you listed in the previous task and think how you could help your customers to:

- achieve their goals and deal with challenges
- save time, money, or effort
- avoid mistakes, failures, and risks
- reduce their pain points
- feel better and look good in other people's eyes
- make their work or personal life easier
- get better quality and higher performance for their current solutions
- get something specific that they are looking for but can't find

Now that you have a clear picture of the customers' problems, jobs, and gains, it time to describe which of their problems you intend to solve and what extra gains you plan to create. Once you are absolutely clear on what you are going to address, try to cross-references those *pain relievers* and *gain creators* with your ideas for your products and services. It might just be that one product or service will solve multiple problems and provide multiple gains. Don't forget to evaluate the importance of each pain reliever and gain creator for the customer. A best practice to focus your products and services based only on those pain relievers and gain creators which rate at least an 8 out of 10 in importance to the customer.

Table 7. Prioritizing customers' problems, jobs, and gains

CORE OFFER:				
(what exactly we will offer to the target customer)				
PRODUCTS	PAIN RELIEVERS	Importance	GAIN CREATORS	Importance

You will end up with a list of all the products and services your value proposition is or could be built around. You can read more about tactics to create profitable product bundles in Chapter 31: Profit hacking: leads, conversion, and economics.

 Define your main value proposition in one simple and clear sentence.

Now that you have identified what solutions and gains your products or services will offer to your customer, it's time to define your main value proposition. There are more than few different recommendations for how to write a value proposition, but at the very least, it has to address three main questions:

1. What exact value you will create?
2. For whom will it be delivered?
3. How will you do this or how is it different from other alternatives available to your target customers?

Explain your value proposition in one simple sentence that even your grandmother could understand. Don't use jargon, slang, or acronyms. It might be helpful to just start writing the sentence and work iteratively until you are satisfied. Or, work collaboratively with some other members of your team until you all agree that you have captured the essence of your value proposition.

After successfully finishing the tasks in this chapter you should have completed the following:

✓ have defined the target customer for whom your value proposition is designed

✓ brainstormed about product or service addressing at least one main problem or desired benefit of your target customer

✓ explained how your product or service solves your customer's problems and creates gains for them

✓ have proposed a solution that is unique or very different from current offers in the market

✓ written a simple, one sentence value proposition that clearly and concisely communicates what value your proposed product or service will provide your customers.

 Recommended reading

1. Alexander Osterwalder, Yves Pigneur, Gregory Bernarda, Alan Smith. *Value Proposition Design: How to Create Products and Services Customers Want (Strategyzer)*

2. Eric Ries. *The Lean Startup: How Today's Entrepreneurs Use Continuous Innovation to Create Radically Successful Businesses*

3. Steve Blank, Bob Dorf. *The Startup Owner's Manual: The Step-by-Step Guide for Building a Great Company*

4. Cindy Barnes, Helen Blake, David Pinder. *Creating and Delivering Your Value Proposition: Managing Customer Experience for Profit*

5. Peter Thiel, Blake Masters. *Zero to One: Notes on Startups, or How to Build the Future*

2. Alternative solutions & competitive analysis

WHY IT'S NEEDED

No matter what kind of product or service you are planning to offer, you should research what's already on the market and ways your customers are already solving the problem. For example, if there is a real, existing problem looking for a solution, your customers are probably already using some variation of your solution or some workaround. For example, when automobiles were first manufactured, horses and carriages were the main competitors. People already had a solution to their transportation needs, but the automobile created innovative and superior gains and benefits for the customers. So, even if you think you have an absolutely brilliant solution, your need to spend some time to research how people are currently dealing with the particular problem.

The goal of a competitive analysis is to help you avoid being blind to the validity of your own ideas when compared to the direct or indirect competition. You will undoubtedly spend a lot more time on competitive analysis, but at this early stage, you should at least check to see how your value proposition looks in the context of your competitor's solutions and the alternative ways customers are already solving the problem. By conducting even a simple competitive analysis, it will help you avoid being too passionate about your idea and perhaps even blind to the fact that it might not be as unique or innovative as you want to believe. Furthermore, it will also help you to save money on creating prototypes and testing them. By analyzing current solutions and what better options can be proposed, you can gain valuable knowledge for improving your value proposition even without any major experimentation.

Once you finish this simple analysis, you'll be able to show your target customers and potential investors how your solution is better and what unique value you deliver that can't be provided by any other means. You'll have the answer to the most important question: why customers should buy from you instead of your competitors or keep using their solutions. You'll be able to show that you see the whole picture of the market situation and that you have something unique and valuable for your target customers and your potential investors.

Google for Solution
Check to see if there are easy-to-find
solutions to the problem you intend to solve

Talk to People
Discuss your ideas with experts in the field
and people who might need your solution

Compare Offerings
Check for direct and indirect competitors,
and what and how they offer

Find Blue Ocean
Based on facts, prioritize the problems, jobs,
and gains of the target customers

Indicate Five Forces
If you are an emerging competitor, how
might the situation in the market change?

Google for the solution of the problem you intend to solve.

Keep in mind that your competitors aren't who *you* think they are. Your competitors are who *your customers* think they are. It's a good idea to start the competitive analysis as if you were a potential customer and look for solutions to the particular problem. The Internet makes conducting a competitive analysis easier than it has ever been, even for those products and services which are not sold via the Internet.

Begin by running few of searches with the most appropriate keywords that could be used by potential customers or using keywords that search engines recommend. Look through the list of results in both paid and natural search results. You won't get all of your possible competitors (especially if your product is truly unique or innovative), but you will get those that are working hard to get traffic to their websites. A few other ways to search include:

- *Google Adwords keyword tool*—allows checking how many searches per month are performed with select keywords. If you see that people are looking for some kind of solution, problem, or benefit, that might be a good indicator that you are on the right track with your value proposition.

- *Google Trends*—basically show what the trendiest keywords are and how their popularity changes over time. If you see specific keyword related to your value proposition, check the trend. Is it increasing, decreasing, has seasonality, or isn't visible at all?

- *Google Alerts* - once you know how your closest competitors, you might want to be updated once they are mentioned somewhere online. Google Alerts does exactly that—lets you know when it notices new content with a specific keyword. (You can set up an alert on your startup or brand name to see if anyone else is talking about you.)

In addition to Google and other search engines, you can also use social media, product reviews, and app marketplace sites to see what customers think of your competitors, as well as get some indicators on how many followers and fans they have. Furthermore, it's quite possible that you'll find free-of-charge solutions to the problem in the form of advice, how-to articles, free downloadable tools, apps, and all kinds of other resources. And, don't be mistaken—these are your competitors, too!

Use a table such as the one below to document how your competitors and customers are dealing with the problem for which you are proposing a new solution.

Table 8. Problems and their best solutions today

Problem	Today's solutions	New solution

A word of advice: the challenge with conducting a competitive analysis in this manner for really innovative products is that they are unknown for most potential clients, therefore clients don't search for such products and your search results may yield little useful information.

Talk to at least 10 people who encounter the problem you are proposing to solve

The main goal here is to get insights into how this particular problem is being solved today. What options are currently available? What types of customers choose one particular solution over another? What factors influence their decision? Based on experience, the most valuable insights are usually extracted from interviewing three main groups:

1. *Ordinary users and expert users of today's solutions* are your potential clients, so take some time to get to know them better. Find out how you can provide them the best solution to the problem or an extremely valuable benefit or gain, which they may have never dreamed possible.

2. *Experts in particular markets* can tell what is selling the best, where the highest profit margins are, how customers are making decisions, and what motivates them the most.

3. *Experts in production and technology* will often tell you how it is difficult or even impossible to do one or another thing, but these are exactly the people who will help you to find the way to build an innovative solution, once you gain insight as to what exactly needs to be developed.

You can use recommended form (Table 9) in order to conduct more structured interviews and get meaningful insights during the interviews with experts. You don't have to exactly follow the same guidelines, but experience has shown that in most cases these aspects trigger valuable findings.

Table 9.   Customer interview findings card

Respondent's name: _____	Date: _____
Aspect to discuss	FINDINGS
Is it a painful problem?	
Is it a meaningful gain?	
Situation walkthrough	
Current solutions and what's missing in them?	
Important criteria?	
Ways of searching for solutions?	
Feedback about the new proposed solution?	

Once you have gathered some initial insights from qualitative research (for example, individual interviews with a few clients and market experts), you can run an online survey.

This allows you to have a quantitative evaluation and better understanding of how each aspect is important to your target customers or even the whole market, instead of just having initial insights from few persons.

Check the offerings of both direct competitors and indirect competition

After spending some time searching for particular solutions and conducting interviews with users and experts, you will start to have a rough picture what's available in the market for your ideas. A competitive analysis will have little practical use if you don't look at your own value proposition. Therefore, place your findings aligning your value proposition side by side with your competitors' offerings and see how you match up. If there are many competitors in the market, you should group them by similar value propositions and define how many competitors are offering each type of value. You should analyze as many competitor groups as seems reasonable.

Ventafun, a startup from Spain, is a social network focused on influencers. It connects brands with influencers and influencers with their followers. Brands upload their products to the platform and influencers add those products to their profiles. Influencers promote both their profiles and the products they curate and get a commission on every sale. Ventafun was not the only one who provided the influential people with the possibility of earning extra revenue by promoting some products. Founders of Ventafun have analyzed over 90 competitors, whom they considered as key players in the market, and found two key issues:

1. Affiliate marketing platforms were really difficult to use and had a very high churn rate.
2. Influencer marketing platforms were usually focused on a single platform, paid attention only to influencers and brands, and didn't think about the consumer (product buyer).

Ventafun knew they needed something different, including a more special connection between all types of users (product providers, influencers, and product buyers). Once they understood that they must provide users with more than just money in the form of discounts and commissions and that they needed to create a better user experience, that was their *Eureka!* moment. After conducting the initial competitive analysis and in-depth interviews with early adopters, Ventafun decided that the platform should help to build a community around the influencers and the products. That community would give confidence to consumers to buy and convenience for the influencers. Carlos Tíscar, co-founder of Ventafun, summarized: "*We need more engagement with our users, we need products on the platform, and we need to provide customers a better online shopping experience throughout their favorite influencers and an educated buying experience complemented with good quality content on the products they search.*" Well, I would say that's quite a detailed picture of how you plan to deal with your competition!

Table 10 will be useful for gathering and systemizing the data for the competitive analysis:

Table 10. Comparing main offers in the market

	Our offer	Competitor group #1	Competitor group #2
Main value proposition: What exactly is included in the main offer? How is the problem being solved?			
Additional value: What extra benefits are offered? Are there any special conditions which make this offer more attractive?			
Technical and other details: Provide more specifics about technical (if applicable) and other details of product or service.			
Customer's cost: How much money, time, and effort does it cost for a customer to obtain this solution to a problem or realize a gain?			
Pros and Cons: Brief summary how this offer is better and what are the reasons this offer might be rejected by the customer.			

Once you have identified the main competitors and made a brief summary of their offers, it's time to identify indirect competitors. It is worth noting that my global research on startups showed that more than 42% of early stage startups didn't analyze their indirect competitors, which was a huge mistake for most of them because their value proposition was built on the wrong assumptions without analyzing the full picture.

For the indirect competitive analysis, you need to think a bit outside the box. How else can this same problem be solved or the gain realized? Look at the big picture of the situation. Maybe there are solutions that cost no money at all, but customers must put more effort and time? Maybe there are alternatives that make the particular problem unimportant? Maybe there are some circumstances where the customer won't be willing to solve the problem at all? Add some more columns to the competitor offer summary table (above) describing the indirect competition.

Draw your value curve according to Blue Ocean strategy and find gaps where you could fit in

The concept of Blue Ocean Strategy developed by W. Chan Kim and Renee Mauborgne (2005) is very intriguing for startups. It aims to create value innovation not to compete, but to make the competition irrelevant by changing the strategic playing field. It assumes that market boundaries and industry structures are not as fixed as they seem to be, and can be changed by the actions and beliefs of industry players. In order to achieve that, it requires focusing on innovative value—the creation which can unlock the new demand. This is usually achieved via the simultaneous pursuit of differentiation and low-cost. As the market structure is changed by breaking the value and cost tradeoff, so, too, are the rules in the market changed.

The Blue Ocean Strategy suggests that you draw the proposed value curves for your products and competitors' products and determine how innovative value can be created. It might sound complicated, but, actually, it's not, especially if you use the template from www.evolutioncurve.com and follow the steps below:

1. *Define criteria for how value can be perceived and measured in your situation.* A few years ago, I was working on an idea and invested my personal savings to build an online platform that helps patients choose clinics and doctors for various medical services (from a simple blood test to heart operations and plastic surgery at the most prestigious clinics). So how would the value of such an online platform be perceived by users? What's important to them? To figure this out, I ran five focus groups with different target customers in my country and abroad as we were targeting to the medical tourism niche as well. I only asked two questions for potential customers: 1) how do they choose a new clinic or doctor and 2) what would they expect from an online platform to help them to do that? Results from all five focus groups were quite similar in terms of what creates value for them:

   - a wide range of clinics and doctors to choose from
   - easy to compare prices
   - easy registration online (no need to call to book an appointment)
   - ability to see doctor's available times online
   - honest patient testimonials about doctors
   - honest patient testimonials about clinics
   - a detailed description of medical service
   - detailed records about doctor's qualification

- to see which clinics are in the closest location
- to see which clinics apply for government compensation programs
- to have personal medical history saved online
- to get individually customized offers online (without traveling to the clinic first)
- to send one request to all selected clinics at once

2. *Find out how important each of those criteria is for your customers.* You can do this by running a survey with Likert's or percentage scale questions. Ask the potential user to rate the importance of each criterion on a scale of 1 to 10 (1—totally unimportant, 10—absolutely necessary). I did the same for the online medical platform. By surveying 527 target customers (patients of private clinics), it allowed me to find out the importance of each of those criteria (Figure 15) and where to focus my main attention.

Figure 15. Importance of different value criteria for target customers

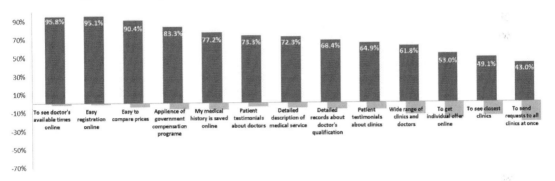

3. *Evaluate your offer and your competitors' offers to see how well they deliver value according to your criteria.* I recommend evaluating on a scale of 1 to 10 (with one being low and 10 being high) how each offering delivers value on each criterion. If the evaluation is 10, it means this is the best proposition in the market according to particular criterion and the customer doesn't even dream about anything better. Accordingly, a rating of 5 means that this is an average proposition in the market. It is not bad, but it is also not outstanding. There is an example in Table 11 that shows how value is delivered by the current options in the market: private clinics that work as standalone (one website - one clinic), state medical platform (unites only some of the public and none of the private clinics), private medical platform (the only online platform that unites many private clinics). A new medical service platform will have to compete with all those options, but the private medical platform will be the main competitor. To succeed in the market, the new platform must provide some kind of value innovation by offering something that is different and significantly better. The last column in Table 11 shows the strategic decision on how the value for customers will be created).

Table 11. Data for creating value curve

Value criteria	Private clinics (stand alone)	State medical platform	Private medical platform	NEW medical platform
To see doctor's available times online	1	8	9	10
Easy registration online	1	7	8	10
Easy to compare prices	1	4	2	10
Government compensation program	5	10	2	8
Wide range of clinics and doctors	1	3	7	7
Detailed description of medical service	6	2	7	7
Detailed records about doctor's qualification	8	6	8	6
Patient testimonials about clinics	3	5	7	6
Patient testimonials about doctors	3	5	7	5
Personal medical history is saved online	1	1	1	5
To get individual offer online	1	1	1	5
To send requests to all clinics at once	1	1	1	5
To see the closest clinics	1	1	3	1

4. *Draw the chart with your value curve and your competitors' value curves* and then brainstorm how you could find the blue ocean, which would include a value proposition combination that is unique and highly desired by your target customers. The authors of the Blue Ocean Concept suggest making four possible changes in your value curve if it is not yet surpassing your competitors:

- *eliminate* the proposed value which is not perceived as highly important by your target customers, which might help you to save significant costs
- *reduce* the value which is non-essential and you'll save even more costs
- *raise the* value which is most desired and appreciated by your target customers
- *create* new aspects of value by providing something that is important to your target customers, but yet not offered by any of the competitors. When running a startup, this change has the biggest chance to make your offer unique and appealing.

Continuing with our example, we could draw all four value curves and make sure that our strategic decision will allow us to create a unique and innovative value proposition based on what is most important for target customers. But for the sake of illustration, let's take only the main competitor's value curve and compare it to ours (Figure 16).

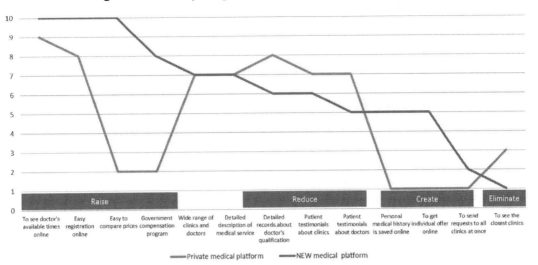

Figure 16. Comparing value curves to find value innovation

Based on the three highest criterion (most potential customers would like to see the doctor's available times online, compare prices in different clinics, and easily book an appointment in chosen clinic), it was decided to *raise* the value created based on these criteria. Government compensation program was also included in this bundle because it is directly related to medical service prices. It also provides a discount in certain private clinics. Those criteria that were not the highest priority for surveyed customers (detailed records about doctor's qualification and patient testimonials) were *reduced* in new medical platform's value curve or even *eliminated* (to see the closest clinics). In addition, new value was *created* by finding a solution to simply and safely to store the patient's personal information online, so it would be easy and convenient for customers to share their medical history with clinics while sending a request or booking an appointment.

The comparison of value curves shown in Figure 16 illustrates how the new project will be different and more beneficial for target customers. Value is also a good guideline for product or service development because it shows you where to focus your main attention and resources. So if you plan to create a new product or service, draw your value curve first and compare it to your competitors. Can you see how your offer is better than your competitors and any other solutions for the same problem? If you can't see a major difference between your offer (value curve) and your competitors, don't expect the average customer to be able to figure it out either!

Changes implemented in the value curve on the chart should be transformed into your real value proposition. It is quite possible that you have already developed a unique value proposition from the previous chapter, but if that's not the case, take time to experiment with the value curve and crafting your value innovation.

Use Porter's five forces field to summarize competitive situation

Porter's five forces field assumes that there are five important forces that determine competitive power in a business situation, as shown in the diagram below:

Figure 17. Porter's five forces field

Bargaining power of suppliers

Threat from new entrants (competitors)

Potential New Entry

Suppliers

Competitive Rivalry

Buyers

Threat from substitution of products or services

Substitutes

Bargaining power of customers (buyers)

1. *Competitive Rivalry*—this is the number and power of your competitors. If you have many competitors who offer equally attractive products and services, then you'll most likely have little power in the situation, because suppliers and buyers will go elsewhere if they don't get a good deal from you. That's why it is important to find your Blue Ocean Strategy based on value innovation. If no one else can provide what you can and it is important to customers, then you can expect to have strong position in the market.

Competitive Rivalry

✔ Advantage through innovation
✔ Powerful marketing strategy
✔ Economy of scale
✔ Level of advertising spending
✔ Concentration ratio
✔ Transparency & regulation

2. *Supplier Power*—this concerns how easy it is for suppliers to drive up prices. The fewer the supplier choices you have and the more you need their help, the more powerful your suppliers are. Defining and securing key resources and suppliers in the early stage might be one of the essential conditions of your startup's success.

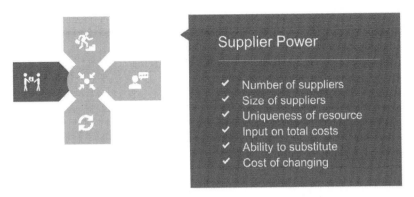

3. *Buyer Power*—this concerns how easy it is for clients to drive prices down. If you deal with just a few, powerful buyers, then they are often able to establish pricing conditions for you.

4. *Threat of Substitution* this includes the ability of your target customers to find a different way of solving the same problem or getting the same gain as you offer. If substitution is easy and viable, then this will weaken your power and your chances of success in general. As we discussed in the previous chapter, you must

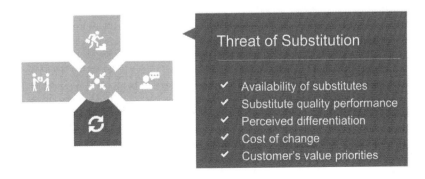

address serious problems and gains, not just the "nice to have" benefits. Otherwise, you'll have plenty of substitutes!

5. *Threat of New Entry*—this is the ability of new competitors to enter your market. If you have strong and durable barriers for new competitors to enter your market, then you can preserve a favorable position and take fair advantage of it. But if the cost of entry requires little time and money, doesn't require any patent-protected technology or know-how, and there is not yet any economy of scale in the market, you are certain to face new competitors in the near future.

There are a number of ways to effectively use Porter's five forces analysis in early stage startup feasibility study. The main goal is to define how strong your position in the market can be and what obstacles you'll need to overcome. It is fairly simple to use this analysis method as a checklist to review the reality of the market and to make insights about your future decisions for your startup.

Note: using Porter's five forces analysis is not a required step at the moment because Chapter 4 addresses competition as one of the key elements in the business environment. But, to be successful, each startup must have a clear vision of the competitive landscape and even more—to understand which players in the market have the most influence. When you start to create your Business Model Canvas in Chapter 5, you'll have to identify key resources and key activities vital for your business. Therefore, Porter's five forces field will come in handy.

 Recommended reading

1. Michael E. Porter. *Competitive Strategy: Techniques for Analyzing Industries and Competitors*
2. Philip Kotler, Gary Armstrong. *Principles of Marketing*

3. David Goldsmith. *Paid to Think: A Leader's Toolkit for Redefining Your Future*

4. W. Chan Kim, Renée A. Mauborgne. *Blue Ocean Strategy, Expanded Edition: How to Create Uncontested Market Space and Make the Competition Irrelevant*

3. Segmentation and potential market size

WHY IT IS NEEDED

The easiest way to go out of business is to attempt to be all things to all people. It is impossible to be the best choice for everybody. If you try to do this, in the best case you will end up being a mediocre, average provider of average products or services. Instead, you should choose a targeted group of customers to whom you can be the best provider. If this group is large enough and you are able to create a value the customers will pay for, your business will have a strong foundation for success.

Segmentation generally means identifying which consumers will best fit your business. In other words, you will divide the whole market into smaller segments in order to identify the group of target customers you want to attract the most. If you clearly define and choose to serve a particular segment of target customers, you will be able to:

- make more effective marketing decisions
- create more appealing and more effective marketing materials
- choose more effective communication and advertising channels, thus saving money.

Defining target segment is one of core aspects of creating a marketing strategy. If you can't identify the segment you are targeting, all of your other marketing decisions and tactics might not make sense. If you see that the size of the target segment is too small and there is not much money to be earned, you still have time to redefine your business model. For example, you could choose additional or absolutely different target segments, adjust your value proposition, pick other communication and distribution channels, and so on.

Define the market type you plan to address.

Defined the market type impacts everything. Different market structures require different marketing strategies. Considering the perspective of the economy or classical marketing, there are four main market structures:

✓ *Monopoly* - if you are attempting to enter a monopoly market (where one company is the sole supplier), a guerilla marketing strategy would most likely give you the best chances of success. You should choose a very small segment (niche) that is so small that the main competitor wouldn't bother much about this tiny segment, but yet is large enough for your business to be sustainable.

✓ *Oligopoly* - when a market or an industry is dominated by a small number of sellers, a guerrilla marketing strategy (or flank attack strategy) should also work well. The main task in this situation is to find underserved segments and develop for them special your value proposition, which is much better that any competitor can offer. Usually, it is enough to find at least one main feature or benefit that is not delivered very well with competitors' generic value propositions but would be highly appreciated by particular target segment or niche.

✓ *Competitive monopoly* - when companies offer products or services that are similar (but not perfect substitutes), the most important task is to find the differentiating benefit that is important to a significantly large group of target customers and find a way to communicate it. Targeting multiple segments with different value propositions can also be an effective strategy.

✓ *Perfect competition* - this market structure is nearly impossible because it requires following five criteria to be met: 1) all companies sell an identical product 2) all companies are price takers - they cannot control the market price of their product 3) each company has a relatively small market share 4) buyers have complete information about the product being sold and the prices charged by each company and 5) the industry is characterized by freedom of entry and exit. But if you are trying to enter a market with perfect competition, there are two general strategies: cost leader strategy (if you have lowest costs in the industry and customers care only about the lowest price) and added value strategy (adding some kind of value to the standard product to make it stand out from others in the market).

The market can be single-sided or multi-sided. A single-sided market means that you are selling something to customers. That's quite standard and the typical business model. In a multi-sided market, the focus is on two or more distinct groups of customers who rely on each's participation in the market. Crowdium is a great example of a successful startup in a multi-sided market (Figure 18).

Figure 18. Multi-sided market addressed by Crowdium platform

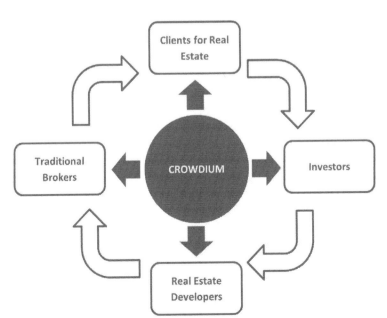

Real estate crowdfunding started in 2013 and has been one of the hottest sectors ever since. This market has reached around $3.5 billion in transactions in 2016 alone (Waleed Esbaitah, 2016). There were more than 250 companies worldwide, but there has never been a real estate crowdfunding company in Latin America until Damian Lopo and Manuel Estruga from Argentina launched *Crowdium* in May 2016. Real estate crowdfunding involves the collective buying of real estate projects, where clients can invest from $1,500 through safe legal structures managed by the Securities Exchange Commission (Argentina) controlled Trustee. The launch of Crowdium benefited the whole value chain as it offered financing alternatives to real estate developers, new clients to traditional brokers, more accessible products within the clients' reach, simplicity, safety, and property management services for those investors who do not have enough time or knowledge to manage their own investments. Successfully addressing the needs of different segments of this multi-sided market helped *Crowdium* to win Redinnova 1ˢᵗ Prize as best Argentinean fin-tech startup in 2016. Crowdium has also been selected as a top 100 Startups Worldwide in the South Summit contest, competing for best worldwide startup among more than 3,000 companies.

More and more startup businesses are building solutions for this multi-sided, shared economy. It means that you are working in two or even more different markets and must provide a great value proposition to all of them.

Steve Blank and Bob Dorf (2014) noted that not all startups are alike from the point of view of entering new markets. For startups related to innovations and new products, there might be several different situations:

- a new product is brought into an existing market
- a new product is brought into a new market
- a new product is brought into an existing market by offering a low-cost or niche value solution
- a product is brought about by cloning a successful business model to another geographic market.

When a **new product** is brought to an **existing market**, the following aspects should be considered:

1. What are the existing markets that customers might come from? Who are those customers?
2. What unmet needs do those customers have? What value will you offer them to entice them to abandon their current suppliers?
3. Why don't existing companies already offer the value that you plan to offer? What is the risk that your offer will be copied? Do you have any points of differentiation that are meaningful to your target customers?

4. How much time will you need to introduce your new product and educate customers? Do you have a plan for how you will do this most efficiently?

5. How long will it take to reach your break-even point of sales? What are the realistic sales forecasts and what they are based on? Can you test that?

When planning to **create a new market**, be ready for the long haul. You'll have to spend a lot of energy, time, and money on educating your target customers. It's different from introducing a new product to existing market. If you are an early stage startup, it will be a huge and costly challenge to create a new market. It's not realistic to think you can be successful if you don't have answers at least to these key questions:

1. What is so unique and extremely valuable in your offer that customers will use it and pay for it? Why should they buy your products instead of satisfying their needs in the old way? What proof do you have?

2. What markets are related to the new one that you intend to create? Will you have customers coming to you from these markets? How can you use them?

3. How much time will you need to introduce your new product and create a new market by educating customers? Do you have a plan on how to do this efficiently? What viral effect does your business model have built into it?

4. How long will it take to reach your break-even point of sales? What are realistic sales forecasts and what they are based on? What if you don't reach the break-even point in time? How long will you be able to survive with your assets and what do you plan to do when they are depleted?

5. What will stop competitors from taking over your newly created market? Once you educate the target customers and create market demand for your product or service, how you will secure it from being taken over by competitors who might have better finances, networks, and so on?

 Identify most important criteria for segmentation.

Not all segmentation criteria are equally important in every situation so don't waste your time on activities that won't help you to develop your startup faster. Decide which criteria you want to define your segments and which of them best fit your business model. You can characterize segments by any combination of these groups of criteria:

- *geographic* criteria include either your location or the location of your target customers, where your product or service will be used

- *demographic* criteria are the statistical characteristics of your target market, such as age, gender, education, household size, socio-demographical group (e.g., student, pensioner, disabled)

- *psychographic* criteria describe target customers by psychological or emotional traits, (e.g., risk-taker versus risk-averse early adopters versus late-stage buyers introverts versus extroverts)
- *behavior-based* criteria focus on the activities of target customer in any environment and situation (e.g., what the customer is doing at work and at home, what hobbies and vacations they choose, and when, how, and for why they use the product).

Segmentation based on demographic and psychographic criteria is sometimes called pre-existing segmentation and it is the most basic way of creating market segments. In pre-existing segmentation, the market is split according to pre-existing demographic or geographic criteria such as age, sex, social economic status, location, and type of living place. Demographic and psychographic criteria combined can describe the life stage that groups have in common: for example, college and career, young families, empty nesters, etc.

Pre-existing segments are easy to define and easy to target with advertising and media in classical marketing. But it doesn't tell much about how these different target customers will perceive the value your startup wants to deliver and how they will respond to your marketing message. The world is changing: today we often see the same product being used by different age groups, e-commerce has made the location of the customer nearly meaningless, and digital products can be instantly delivered to nearly any place in the world with an Internet connection.

It's a bit more difficult to do segmentation based on psychographic and behavior-based criteria. It requires some additional effort to measure the size of segments if they are not directly related to existing statistics. But customer needs and behavior-based segments are typically the most actionable forms of segments because you already know what drives your customers and how they're currently solving their problems. That allows you to create the most appealing value proposition and most effective marketing communication.

Let's look at a couple of examples that show how important it is to define the right segmentation criteria. Share2Style (based in the UK) offers fashion bloggers over 1,000 global fashion brands with hundreds of thousands of products. Bloggers can consequently browse through those products and filter them according to their needs (price, brand, color, keywords, and categories). All of the products in the system are affiliated and have unique affiliated links. Consequently, bloggers can create collages with the products and publish them onto their blogs instantly. As a result, bloggers earn money once their blog visitors purchase any of the items from the collages. However, there are different types of fashion bloggers and that was the main segmentation criterion for *Share2Style*:

- those who recently started out blogging
- mid-tier bloggers (with some experience and getting temporary income)
- bloggers who are major influencers and make millions in blog earnings

The most important thing for *Share2Style* was to admit that their product couldn't target all the groups at the same time. First, they identified all the target groups in terms of their pain points and then looked at the product. Founders of *Share2Style* wanted to build the product with minimal resources that would solve the pain of a particular type of blogger.

Another startup faced serious issues because they missed one important segmentation criterion. *VahanCheck,* a vehicle inspection system for insurance companies and inspection agents, is already used across more than 28 states in India. But results could have been better or achieved faster if they had considered cultural aspects during segmentation. India has more than 50 local languages, but localization of the app was not foreseen during the launch (starting with an English version only). Therefore, end-users of *VahanCheck* faced a training and interface language barrier. Even though initially it wasn't perceived as a serious problem, it actually slowed down the market entry and growth of *VahanCheck*. So, be careful when defining your target customers; the more you know about them, the better your chances of success.

 Divide the market into measurable segments that might be interesting for your business.

Once you have chosen segmentation criteria, it's time to identify key segments. To be successful, implementing a segmentation strategy involves alignment of your value proposition to each target segment you choose. But be cautious: the more segments you choose, the more difficult it will be to align your marketing strategy because each segment will require investment if it is to be properly addressed.

Once you divide the market into segments, check if all your segments meet the requirements (Table 12). If at least one of those requirements is not met, it means you haven't correctly performed segmentation and you should revise your plan.

Table 12.   Requirements for effective segmentation

Homogeneous	Customers in the same segment should be somehow similar
Heterogeneous	Segments should be different at least by one criterion
Measurable	It is possible to measure the size of segment
Substantial	Segments are large enough be individually substantial
Accessible	It is possible to promote to and reach each of these segments
Practical	You have enough capabilities to market to any segment
Responsive	Each market segment should respond to your targeted marketing efforts better than to a generic communication

Draw a segmentation scheme and create your target customer profile

This is not a required task, but it will make your life easier when you go to talk to potential investors or when you start launching your product into the market. A segmentation scheme shows visually how you came up with your target segment, what criteria you were considering, and what options you have chosen. Having a segmentation scheme makes it easy to explain your decisions and to revise them if needed (for example, if you discover that your target segment is too small, you can look through the segmentation scheme for possible secondary segments).

A target customer profile defines your customer. Some literature suggests creating an avatar or persona of your target customer with as many details as possible. The more details you can define for the target customer profile, the easier it will be for you and your marketing partners (online marketing agency, media agency, PR company and etc.) to create and deliver the most appealing and effective message to your customer. Even putting a photo of a person who best represents your target customer is helpful. If you wish, you can put few smaller photos of different people representing the same target segment.

The details of the target customer profile should include the following:

- Are they male/female?
- How old are they?
- Are they married/single?
- Where do they live?
- What do they do for work?
- What do they do for fun?
- What do they read?
- What do they watch?
- Where do they hang out on the Internet?
- What do they desire most?

Let's take *Mod Garden* from Canada, for example. It is a smart and stylish modular system that allows the growing of vegetables and herbs in the living room all year round. A standard unit is the size of a coffee table and they can be stacked one on top of another to ensure the needed capacity. Each unit has sensors inside that not only takes care of the irrigation but also sends data to a mobile app where the user can track the whole process, from planting seeds to taking harvest. Basically, *Modgarden* is built for the busy urban dweller who maybe even doesn't know how to garden.

Aamar Khwaja, the founder of Modgarden, has defined his early adopters segment and set his go-to-market campaign goal as shown in Table 13.

Table 13. Modgarden segmentation breakdown

Location	124.5 million households in USA
Food gardening	31% of all US households (estimated at 36 million) did food gardening in 2008 (2015 data is available under paid subscription at National Gardening Association)
Climate zone	22% of the 36 million households (or 7.92 million) are cold climate gardeners
Gardening purpose	Vegetable gardeners are 23% of 7.92 or 1.7 million households Herb gardeners are 12% of 7.92 or 0.95 million households
Target market size	1.7 + 0.95 = **2.6 million households**
Campaign goal	2,000 households, which is less than **0.08%** of the estimated target market size

To estimate the market potential, Modgarden found statistics that there are 47 million North American organic eaters, which makes a $38 billion organic food market size. To make segmentation even more precise and effective, I would suggest additional criteria such as:

- Living in a condo/apartment/townhouse/flat in town or in the suburbs. The assumption is that if you have a house, you'll probably have a garden and this product might not be as interesting, except for during the winter season.
- Healthy lifestyle could be defined by various criteria (for example, practices yoga or meditation, goes to the gym two or three times a week, cares about nutrition, is interested in organic food).
- Household monthly income could help to narrow the early adopters segment by defining which households would be financially capable of making a purchase.

While a customer segmentation scheme is mostly used to clearly and exactly define who your target customer is and to define the size of your chosen segment, creating target customer profile helps you be more creative with your marketing. Once you have your typical customer profile (for Modgarden, it could look like Figure 19), it becomes more personal, and you can better understand what is important for your target customer, where and how you could reach them, what fears and concerns they might have about purchasing your product, and what arguments would the most effective for your sales pitch and advertising.

Figure 19. Modgarden target customer profile

Name: Anna	**Gender:** Female	**Age:** 30
Occupation: accountant, secretary	**Education:** college degree	
Work location: business center in city	**Living location:** condo in suburb	
Monthly income: $ 1,500	**Family status:** married, 2 children	

Other details:
Family monthly income $ 2,000 – 3,500
Have one or two family cars, but uses public transport as well

Number of similar customers:	42,500	Potential revenue in segment:	$ 1,000,000

Description:

- cares about healthy lifestyle of the family
- goes to the gym at least 2-3 times a week
- loves gardening, but has no garden at home
- loves cooking on weekends
- reads professional and lifestyle magazines, romantic novels

Motivates	Demotivates
- natural source of vitamins and minerals - fresh vegetables and herbs for weekend cooking - aesthetics and modern look of furniture - being proud about home-grown	- Doubts about durability and maintenance - New furniture needs additional space - Price

 Choose one to three segments you want to serve most.

Once you have selected a target market from your list of potential market segments, you need to evaluate how attractive that segment is for your business. Evaluate your target segment size, growth potential, profitability, competitive advantage, and accessibility. Below is a table that will help you determine which segments you should target. The table includes five aspects you can use to measure the attractiveness of each segment. While there may be more aspects you can use for evaluation, I've included the most important aspects from a marketing perspective. If you rate each segment according to all five aspects on a scale of 1 to 5 (with 1 being the lowest and 5 being the highest), you'll easily come up with a logically calculated decision about which segment is most attractive. In addition, I recommend checking to see how each of those top-rated segments aligns with your business strategy and model.

Table 14. Target segment evaluation

Segment	Size	Growth potential	Profit margin	Competitive advantage	Accessibility	Total
A						
B						
C						

Try to complete this table as accurately as possible. Based on this table, you'll make one of the most important decisions of your business. Therefore it will require some analysis and you should consider the following questions as you rate each segment

- How large is the segment now? Is it large enough to support your startup business and its growth?
- Will the segment grow or expand in the future? How far into the future can it grow?
- Does it have a natural and organic demand or is it being driven by active sales and marketing activities?
- Can this segment create a viral effect? If you reach this segment, could it initiate demand for your products or services in other segments?
- Can you have high gross margins in the segment?
- Can you apply a predictable pricing model for this segment (for example, subscription or regular, repeat purchases)? Can you somehow lock in the customer or create an exit barrier with a high cost to switch to a competitor?
- How much better is your value proposition than the current alternatives in the market? Do you have a sustainable competitive advantage or it will be easily copied?
- How easy or difficult will it be to reach the segment?
- Does this segment really fit with your business model? Can you immediately meet their needs or will it take a significant change in direction to meet their demand?

 Recommended reading

1. Philip Kotler, Gary Armstrong. *Principles of Marketing*
2. Dan Olsen. *The Lean Product Playbook*: *How to Innovate with Minimum Viable Products and Rapid Customer Feedback*

4. Business model and fatal flaws

WHY IT IS NEEDED

It's great to be passionate about the innovative idea you have. There are many inspiring stories about startups who encountered difficult challenges but persevered because of their passion. No matter what circumstances and obstacles you might encounter, your passion is what will keep you going through the hard times. Unfortunately, while passion great, it's not enough to help you reach your goals. You need to have a plan! But, I'm not talking about a standard business plan with hundreds of pages full of mundane ideas. If your business idea is innovative, the standard approach hardly is the best choice. In this chapter, I'll introduce you to a method of developing a simple business plan that is much faster and cheaper to develop than the standard approach. It allows you to draft your business plan on one page and review, improve, or even abandon the idea if you see no chances of success and profit.

During my global research on startups, I met many startup founders who spent from just a few minutes up to many hours just to outline and review their business idea. It's much more effective and fun to use your passion for implementing your business idea and seeking funding for your goals when you have a clear plan on how to do it!

The Business Model Canvas (2009) was initially proposed by Alexander Osterwalder and Yves Pigneur based on Osterwalder's earlier work on Business Model Ontology (2004). The concept of the Business Model Canvas is simple, easily applicable, and can be very effective during the startup phase when the whole business model is regularly reviewed, updated, and sometimes reworked from scratch. The popularity of the Business Model Canvas speaks for itself:

- more than one million copies were sold by 2014
- it has been translated into 30 languages
- the Business Model Canvas is included in numerous university study programs
- new canvases for specific niches have appeared, such as the Lean Canvas, which is quite often used for a startup business.

You can use the Business Model Canvas as a dynamic business plan. If you are a true startup, you are faced with much uncertainty. What could you do to make your life easier and increase your chance of success? One option is to build your product or service, launch it to the market, and just hope everything will work out. But that's not a very wise approach. Another option is to use the *Lean Startup* methodology, which helps you can clear out uncertainty by raising and checking hypotheses (you will learn more about this in Chapter 8: Get ready for hypothesis verification). Once you have checked your hypothesis, you can review and update your Business Model Canvas, if necessary. If you can view the updated canvases as a series of snapshots over time (for example, in a PowerPoint presentation), you'll be able to track all the progress of your startup business development. Or, you can use one of many online tools to create and track the progress of your Business Model Canvas (for example, see the tools at https://canvanizer.com).

How will you know if your business model is great or not?

- *profitable*—the business must be self-sustainable and generate positive cash flow over time
- *repeatable*—it should be a continuous activity, not just a one-time endeavor
- *scalable*—you should be able to grow your business fast and at large scale
- *predictable*—it's hard to foresee the future unless you create it if you do your homework during the feasibility study while creating your business model, you should see main issues and trends in your industry and can prepare for possible changes
- *valuable*—it should increase your startup valuation, which means that the startup as a company becomes worth more.

HOW TO DO IT

01 — **Answer Key Questions**
Go through the list of essential questions of your business and find the answers

02 — **Draft Business Model Canvas**
Prepare your one-page business plan on paper or online canvas

03 — **Review and Clarify**
Look through each element of the business model canvas and clarify your assumptions

04 — **Foresee Fatal Flaws**
Identify the main risks of your business idea and how you plan to deal with them

☑ Briefly, answer key questions about your business model

You can start filling out the Business Model Canvas right away, but it's usually more effective to think through the key questions about the business model and then write it down on the canvas. Following are some questions you should consider:

- How do you plan to get customers? What value will you offer to them? Which channels will you use to communicate your offer?

- How will you be better than your competitors currently on the market or new ones that will emerge and try to copy your idea?

- After you land a new customer, what kind of relationship do you plan to have with them? How do you plan to get their feedback? How will you encourage the client's involvement with your business or brand?

- What is your revenue model? What will customers pay you for and how much will they pay you? Can you calculate your forecasted revenues for the month, quarter, and year? Are these calculations based on solid facts or just your assumptions?

- What assets are available to you to run this business? What capabilities do you lack at the moment and how do you plan to make up for the gap?

- Who are your key partners? Do you need to get any additional partners in order to make the business run as well as it should?

- What key activities do you need to do in order to deliver your value proposition to your customers? Will you be able to do all of them? If not, then what kind of resources or partners will you need?

- What fixed costs you will have to bear independently of your sales volume? Which of your variable costs will depend on your production or service provision volume? Can you calculate your total costs for the next month, quarter, and year?

- Does your revenue forecast demonstrate increased profitability towards the end of the forecast period?

Don't worry if you don't have all the answers right away. Just start from something and you'll update your business model over time. Quite often, even established and revenue earning startups change their business model significantly. For instance, *Pony Zero* was launched in 2013 as a bicycle delivery service, but made two major pivots before 2016: they switched from Pony Express to post delivery and then to massive delivery for international shippers. *Pony Zero* started in Italy and reached €20,000 in revenues during 2013. But they understood they were proposing their service to the wrong market (small companies and consumers). At the end of 2014, they had started to deal with international shippers, but their bikes and dispatching model did not fit the shippers' requirements.

Therefore, the founders made just a small test and raised €100,000 in revenues. They developed a convoy box (a large, bike-mounted box for carrying cargo) for their bikes in 2015 and started working with few international shippers at once. At the end of 2015, *Pony Zero* developed another convoy box and software in order to automate the dispatching routing process. That year the company made €523,000 in revenues. *Pony Zero* expanded by acquiring new clients in food delivery (Just Eat) in 2016 and developed new software to fit this kind of market. The year was finished by earning close to €2.5 million and they are estimating €5 million forecasts for 2017. So, don't worry – pivots are inevitable in almost any business.

 Create your Business Model Canvas

I recommend using the free online tool canvanizer.com because I find it to be very useful when working virtually with startup founders. One great feature that saves a lot of time and helps with collaboration is that you can share a Business Model Canvas with anyone. You can give them review-only or full editing rights. If you prefer to use a paper format or if all of your team wants to sit around the table and work together, you can download an MS Word template from www.evolutioncurve.com

There are several different approaches for working with the Business Model Canvas as well as a few variations of the canvas itself. For most startups, I recommend the following sequence which starts from the essential part, the value proposition.

1. Value proposition: What will you exclusively offer to your customers? How is this offer unique, interesting, and attractive for the customer?
2. Customer segments: Who is your target customer? To whom is your offer most beneficial and most appealing?
3. Channels: How will your reach your clients? Through what channels will your communicate and deliver your offer to them?
4. Customer relationships: How will you receive feedback from your clients? What relationship will you have with them?
5. Revenue streams: How will you make money? Who will pay you and what will they pay you for?
6. Key resources: What resources are necessary to create and deliver the value proposition to target customers?
7. Key partners: What partners are necessary to make this business model work?
8. Key activities: What activities and tasks will you have to handle to create and deliver your value proposition?
9. Cost structure: What fixed and variable costs will you have to bear?

Ash Maurya presents an updated Business Model Canvas in his book *Running Lean* (2012) and calls it the *Lean Canvas*. Actually, this canvas is better adapted for scalable startups because it replaces key partners, key activities, key resources, and customer relationship with four new aspects: problem, solution, key metrics, and unfair advantage. Though these new aspects better address some of the major risks in a scalable startup, my global research on startups showed that Ostervald's and Pigneur's Business Model Canvas can be as effective as a Lean Canvas for the same type of scalable startups as long as it's implemented in the right way. If you'd like to try sketching a Lean Canvas for your business idea, I'd suggest you do this in the following order:

1. Problem: What is the real problem you are solving for your target customers? Is this problem worth solving?

2. Customer segments

3. Value propositions

4. Solution: How exactly will you solve the problem? How will the solution be delivered? Keep in mind, that in the Lean Canvas, this field can sometimes contain all of the aspects related to key partners, resources, and activities as they are directly related to delivering the solution.

5. Channels

6. Revenue streams

7. Cost structure

8. Key metrics: What is your goal and how it can be measured? Which metrics will show your real progress?

9. Unfair advantage: What's your competitive advantage? How will you secure your business from competitors copying it?

Once you have created your Business Model Canvas, I recommend you take a short break. Have a cup of coffee or tea, go for a walk in the fresh air, or just chill out for few minutes before your proceed to the next task. A break will help you clear out and prepare your mind for a critical review of your business model.

 Review your business model and clarify assumptions

Review your business model from the perspective of a potential investor. You are skeptically looking at this business idea and have to decide whether to invest in this opportunity, skip it, or somehow to improve it before you invest. Ask yourself the following questions:

- Will it really work? Do the revenues outweigh the cost? If you want to dig a bit deeper, you can download a business model checklist from www.evolutioncurve.com for additional questions.

- What can be changed to strengthen the business model or reduce its risk?

- How do you know if what is written in each Business Model Canvas block is true? Is it based just on the founders' assumption or are there documented facts or other solid evidence?

- If you have documented facts, I suggest using green labels on those particular blocks of the Business Model Canvas and making a note of your evidence.

- If you have made assumptions, I suggest using yellow labels on those particular blocks of the Business Model Canvas. This will help you in the future to see unverified parts of your business model and take actions to clarify them.

- List your assumptions about the business model into the table below. Use this table as a task—you have to find facts and solid evidence for each statement that is currently just an assumption. Once you have the facts, update your Business Model Canvas by replacing the yellow label with a green one, which indicates that you have solid evidence. Once it is complete, review your Business Model Canvas once again—maybe something has essentially changed and you might need to adjust your business model.

Table 15.   List of assumption and facts

No.	Question	Fact with evidence	Assumption
1.			
2.			
3.			

 Foresee the possible fatal flaws of your business model and manage risks

Seeing the fatal flaws of a business model was the second most common mistake I found during my research. Not foreseeing risks might suddenly close the door, not only to your potential investors but your business as well. If you want your startup to achieve success, you must foresee possible risk factors and make decisions in advance about how you will deal with them. Can you list the major risks of your business model? What parts of your business model are most risk-sensitive? What could kill your business?

In order to identify risks and figure out how best to deal with them, you can use a simple yet very effective framework for classifying risks. All risks have two dimensions: the likelihood of occurrence and strength of the impact. These two dimensions form four quadrants, which in turn suggest how you should attempt to manage those risks.

Figure 20. Risk management matrix

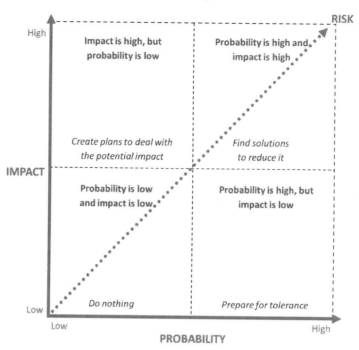

There are many different risk classification methods, but for most startups, the simpler the better. Analyze each of the following risk groups and brainstorm what risks your startup might face. A simple way to do this is to use post-it notes. Use one note for each risk and place it in the most appropriate quadrant according to the likelihood of the risk and consequences of the risk.

- *Market risks* refer to whether or not there is sufficient demand for what you have to offer at the price you set. Startups usually don't sell common products, therefore there is no easy way to know how the market will react to any new product. One of the most cost- and time-effective ways to clear out this uncertainty is to run experiments to validate or reject the market-related hypothesis. Because market risks are one of major failure or success factors of startups, we'll be talking about hypothesis and experiments in the next stage of *Startup Evolution Curve*.

- *Competitive risks* are related to what others might do to try to take a share of your business. It's naive to believe you don't have competitors. As we discussed in Chapter 2, even if you have an innovative product or service, there might be plenty of alternatives as to how to solve the same problem or achieve a similar gain. Competitive risks include such factors as copying your business model, trying to out-innovate you, out-spending you on marketing, starting price wars, initiating rumors about your product, trying to steal your commercial secrets, and overcoming your patents, to name a few. Just think what might happen in the worst case and be prepared for that.

- *Technology and operational risks* generally cover all aspects of execution. For instance, can your team develop and create the product on a limited budget? Will your suppliers be reliable? Can you optimize manufacturing of the product? Will you have an effective support network and infrastructure? Do you have a backup plan if someone hacks into your servers?

- *Financial risks* can be described as simply running out of money. Many startups fail because they risk their financial success on the help of outside financing. One of the biggest financial risks is not having a Plan B in case you don't succeed in attracting investors as quickly as you want. Running out of cash is one of the most common problems, which can usually be managed by reducing cash burn rate and preparing a plan for bootstrapping. During my research, I found startups who chose to take the control of their financial situation instead of putting all their efforts into additional fundraising.

- *People risks* are hardly predictable, but it is clear that people risks are the most crucial and sometimes least predictable element of a startup. Failure to recruit, motivate, and retain key employees can be just as lethal as running out of funds, having technical issues, or mistaking the market needs. Therefore, most successful startups determine the key activities they must perform and don't hire employees to manage these until the appropriate stage. In the early stages, the founders of the startup will take responsibility for each key activity.

- *Legal and regulatory risks* can include various limitations on your business activity, tax complications due to your choice of legal entity or state of incorporation, industry regulations (for example, in fields like medicine, alcohol, tobacco, insurance, and financial services), and possible disputes arising from gaps or misunderstandings in agreements. If you are an early stage startup and don't have enough money to pay for a consultation with a business attorney, check for fostering programs for entrepreneurs and online mentors. There are a number of ways to get initial legal consulting for free, but it varies in each country.

- *Systemic risks* threaten the viability of entire markets, not just your startup or any other company in the market (for example, an economic downturn or breakthrough technology that renders your ideas obsolete).

Once you think you have thought of all the major risks, explain your business idea to your most pessimistic friends and ask them to find more problems. Although it might be unpleasant to hear criticism, let it be a learning experience. Listen and note if there are any possible reasons for failure you haven't foreseen. Put them in your plan and address them accordingly.

Creating a list of risks is not enough. You must also develop a plan to manage those risks. Don't become obsessed with it, but identifying the risks you might face and how you will deal with them could save your startup from failure. Complete the Table 16 to provide you, your partners, and your investors a comprehensive understanding of the potential risks and how your startup is prepared to meet them.

Table 16. Summary of risk management solutions

Risk factor	Type	Likelihood	Consequences	Tactics	Costs

1. *Risk factor* - list any potential risks.

2. *Type* - assign the risk to one of the categories described above (market, competitive, technology and operational, financial, people, legal and regulatory risks, systemic). This might suggest who would be best qualified to manage that particular risk (for example, the CMO might be responsible for dealing with market and competitor risks).

3. *Likelihood* - think of the relative likelihood of manifesting this particular risk factor. Simply state if you have a high, medium, or low possibility of facing this risk factor in reality.

4. *Consequences* - describe what would happen to your startup if this risk factor becomes reality.

5. *Tactics* - list the things you can do to either reduce the likelihood or minimize the impact of the consequences if this risk factor manifests itself. Even if there is a tactic available, it doesn't mean you should employ it. Think about the most appropriate, cost- and risk-effective solution.

6. *Costs* - think about the implementation costs of each risk management tactic.

 Recommended reading

1. Alexander Osterwalder, Pigneur Yves. *Business Model Generation: A handbook for Visionaries, Game Changers, and Challengers*

2. Peter Thiel, Blake Masters. *Zero to One: Notes on Startups, or How to Build the Future*

3. Patrick Van Der Pijl, Justin Lokitz, Lisa Kay Solomon. *Design a Better Business: New Tools, Skills, and Mindset for Strategy and Innovation*

5. Business environment and breakthrough innovations

WHY DO YOU NEED THIS

You need to evaluate your business environment in the feasibility stage because you are not launching your business in a vacuum. Independently of what you want and imagine, your business will be influenced by various factors. Most of those factors you won't be able to control you will only be able to react and adjust your startup development accordingly. So, if you like surprises, especially bad ones, you can skip this chapter. Otherwise, spend some time to get acquainted with the environment into which you will launch your business. This will help you avoid most of the bad surprises and reduce the risk in advance!

HOW TO DO IT

01 Plan the Research
Create a brief plan of your market research to save time and reduce the chance of failure

02 Evaluate Macro Environment
Identify the factors that you can't influence that might impact your business

03 Evaluate Micro Environment
Identify the factors you can partly influence that might impact your business.

04 Estimate Market Size and Growth
Define the size and growth potential of your target market

05 Check for Breakthrough Innovation
Foresee the possibilities of breakthrough innovations in your target market

06 Update Value Proposition
Arrange problems, jobs, and gains according to the importance to customer

Create a brief plan of your market research

List out the information about the market that would be useful to have, what decisions you need to make as to how you will use it, and how you expect to get it. Take a look at your Business Model Canvas. What assumptions have you made? What information do you need to find to replace your initial assumptions with solid facts?

Depending on your data sources, you can do both secondary and primary research. Secondary research, or desk research, is based on data that already exists in one or another form. In most cases, secondary research is faster and cheaper but does not always provide you with the exact information you need. In any case, it's wise to start your research from reviewing the information about the market that is already available. Sometimes this information is even free. Following is a partial list of free, secondary research sources:

- trade associations and their reports
- national and local press, industry magazines
- professional institutes and organizations
- national and international government reports
- national and international statistics databases provided by governments and agencies
- trade and company directories
- published company accounts, announcements, and press releases
- *websites* (competitors, suppliers, news portals, etc.)
- *business and scientific libraries* (these are especially useful for conducting research in the context of innovation)
- reports of omnibus surveys

Primary research is based on data collected for the first time. It is original and is collected for your specific purpose. Usually, it is more expensive and time-consuming, but it can provide details and insights that you can't get through secondary research sources. Following is a partial list of methods for primary research:

- *Telephone interviews* tend to be very structured but often lack depth. Telephone interviews are convenient for collecting data from a geographically dispersed sample and are cheaper to conduct than face-to-face interviews.
- *A mail survey* is an older type of research that is still used by some companies. I don't recommend conducting a startup feasibility study by mail survey.
- *An Internet survey* is probably one the fastest and cheapest ways to get direct feedback from your target group. There are many free online tools to do that.

I used Google forms for my global research on startups. Although it had some issues (for example, Google was blocked in China, the survey form didn't have a responsive design, and it was hard to read on mobile devices), this tool cost nothing and helped to collect a huge amount of responses. You can find a more sophisticated solution with a nice design and mobile-friendly approach, but most of them are fee-based or have limited free plans. If you need to run a short survey with up to 100 responses, you can find plenty of free online tools like Survey Monkey, Typeforms, Zoho Surveys, Survey Planet.

- *An Omnibus study* is a large-scale interview (usually of at least 500 or 1000 respondents) where a company can purchase either a single or several questions in the interview. The company will be one of many that simply wants a straightforward answer to a simple question. This type of research is much cheaper and less time-consuming than conducting your own large-scale interview.

- *Mystery shoppers* act like customers and make real purchases. They collect data on customer service and the customer experience. This type of research could be used not only to check up your competitors, but also to evaluate your own team's performance (the main point here is to keep this research in secret—if you tell your sales team that you are running a mystery shopper research, their behavior might not be fully natural).

- *Focus groups* are made up of a number of selected respondents based together in the same room. Experienced researchers moderate the discussion in focus group and gather in-depth qualitative feedback.

- *Product tests* can be of different types and purposes, but probably the most important are product usability tests. It's a wise decision to have some beta users of your product before planning a market launch. Give the product to customers and ask them to use it and then collect feedback from them.

- *Experiments* are the main form of primary research for most successful startups. Instead of wasting a huge amount of money on creating a product that nobody wants, you can run a series of experiments that show your value proposition, advertising, landing page, product prototype, improved product modifications, and other aspects of your business. We'll talk much more about experiments in Stage 2: Prototyping.

- *Observations* are somewhat different than experiments. With observations, you just observe people using your product without interacting with them or influencing any of their decisions. This research method is very useful for startups who are trying to identify their customers' problems, jobs, and desired gains. By observing your target customers, you will come to understand their situation better and will be able to create better products and services for them. Observation can be used for other purposes as well (for example, to measure the traffic of potential clients, to find out how competitors serve clients, etc.).

- *Diaries* are used by a number of specially recruited consumers who are asked to complete a diary and track their purchasing behavior or use of a product for a period of time. This form of research is quite rare because it demands a substantial commitment on the part of the respondents and accuracy is not fully ensured.

Use the Table 17 to create a brief plan of your market research. This will save you time by helping you to avoid procrastinating and spending too much time on details that are not essential.

Table 17. Briefing for market research

What information is needed?	What decisions will it be used for?	Where and how can we get it?

 Evaluate business environment factors that you can't control or influence

In this step, you will identify the most important factors of the marketing macro environment and their possible influence on your business. According to PEST analysis, macro environmental factors include *political, economic, social* and *technological* forces. The extended approach to macro environment factors is called PESTEL analysis, which adds *environmental* and *legal* forces. You can't control these forces, you can only prepare for changes. Look through each group of macro environmental factors in Table 18 and draw some conclusions about what influence they might have on your startup.

BizON started in Canada 2014 and is now approaching 4,000 active members; connecting close to 500 buyers with sellers in Canada, USA and Australia; and is on track to redefine how people buy, sell, and grow businesses or franchises in the digital world. A properly done analysis was one of the key factors of their successful start. Nunzio Presta, the founder of BizON, identified the problem as 10.5 million baby boomers are planning to retire and sell their business in North America over the next decade, and most do not have a succession plan. This inspired him to look deeper into the issue in order to ensure BizON can service this market. They quickly uncovered that most brokers were uninterested in helping small businesses sell (typically with asking prices of $330,000 and under). Brokers would rather help multi-million dollar businesses sell since the commissions are higher. BizON also discovered that most small businesses would simply resort to shutting down instead of recovering some money for retirement and allowing their legacy to be carried on. Nunzio Presta decided to address both of

Table 18. Factors of PESTEL analysis

Political	Economic
• regulatory bodies and processes	• target market economy situation and trends
• government term and change	• secondary market economies and trends
• government policies	• general taxation issues
• international legislation	• taxation specific to product and services
• ecological and environmental regulation	• seasonality and weather issues
• future legislation	• market and trade cycles
• current legislation in the target market	• any specific industry factors
• funding, grants, and initiatives	• market routes and distribution trends
• target market lobbying groups	• customer drivers and motivators
• international pressure groups	• interest and exchange rates
• wars and conflicts	• international trade issues

Social	Technological
• lifestyle, fashion and role models	• research funding
• demographics	• competing for technology development
• customer attitudes and opinions	• associated and dependent technologies
• brand, company, technology image	• technology maturity and replacement
• customer buying patterns	• manufacturing maturity and capacity
• major events and influences	• information and communications
• ethnic and religious factors	• consumer buying technologies
• advertising and publicity	• innovation potential
• ethical issues	• breakthrough innovations

Environmental	Legal
• solving environmental problems	• technology access, licensing, patents
• requirements regarding pollution	• technology related legislation
• carbon footprint targets	• intellectual property issues
• the scarcity of raw materials	• advertising standards and regulation
• corporate social responsibility	• law changes affecting social factors
• poverty reduction	• product labeling and product safety
• global sustainability	• health and safety at work regulation

these concerns and that opened the door to additional findings. For example, the interest in helping baby boomers sell their business allowed BizON to uncover other opportunities, such as understanding that millennials see value in buying establish businesses - something that provides them with a blueprint to success. Therefore, BizON was able to accurately target segments that would be interested in entrepreneurship through acquisitions (that is, buying an existing independent business) and individuals who would want to become franchisees.

Evaluate the business microenvironment factors

Microenvironment factors are closely related to a business and have a direct impact on business operations and success. These factors include the company and its current employees, suppliers, marketing intermediaries, competitors, customers and public groups. These forces can sometimes be controlled or influenced.

- *Company.* Although classical marketing suggests that analyzing the company itself is one of the microenvironment factors, there are two main takeaways for startups. First of all, don't be in a hurry to officially establish the company and increase your cash burn rate with unnecessary extra costs. You should officially establish the company only when it is absolutely necessary to allow further development of your startup. When establishing your company, be sure to check which type of company and which country of registration would be most beneficial for you. The second point here is that in startups, everybody must work in integrity with the marketing plan. After all, the core of a startup is to create a solution for a customer's particular problem and monetize it. Trying to do that without marketing, is like taking a shot in the dark and trying to hit a small target.

Figure 21. Factors of business microenvironment

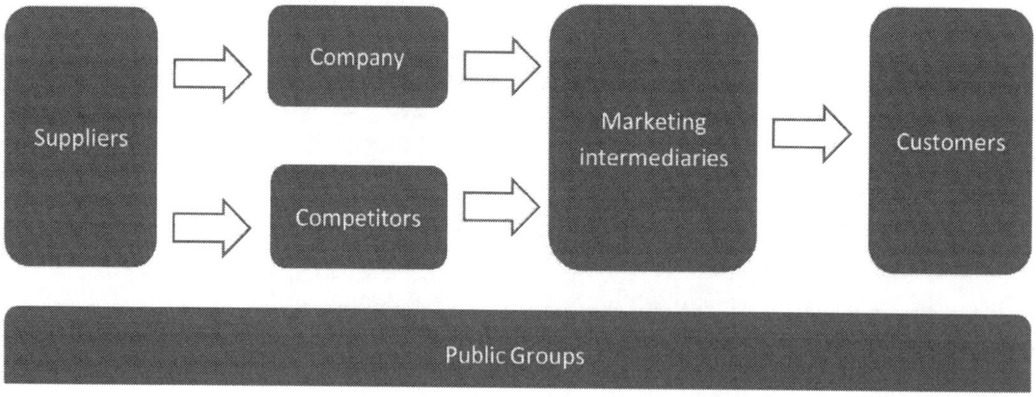

- *Employees.* Employing staff with relevant skills and experience is essential. This process begins at the recruitment stage and continues via ongoing training and promotion opportunities throughout an employee's employment. Training and development are critically important to achieving a competitive edge. If a company employs staff without motivation, skills, or experience, it will affect both customer service and sales in a negative manner. What's even more important for startups is that you have to decide what functions should be handled by the founders themselves, what can be delegated to employees, and what should be outsourced. If the startup faces hard times (for example, low cash) employees might simply leave their job and suppliers might stop providing services until you pay your debt, but the founders will be the warriors who will fight until the end, even if they don't get payment for their work right away.

- *Marketing intermediaries* include the network of distributors of your product, your advertising channels, mass media, influencers, and any organization or person who might help you to bring your product or service to your target customers. Startups shouldn't believe in the false hope that once they get on media, all their problems will be solved and customers will stand in a line to buy their product. Startups need to manage and work with media as well as with other marketing intermediaries. During this analysis, you should identify your key intermediaries and think about how you will get their support.

- *Suppliers.* Suppliers provide businesses with the materials they need to carry out their business activities. A supplier's behavior will directly impact the business it supplies. Do you need any special materials or services? Who has the most power to influence the price of materials and services you need? Quite often, close supplier relationships are an effective way to remain competitive and secure quality products. Will you be able to do that with the current suppliers in the market? Maybe you'll want to secure some level of exclusivity via suppliers so that none of the current or new competitors will be able to provide the same product or service as you do?

- Competitors. Can you offer better gains and benefits than those offered by your competitors or than those available from other alternatives in the market? We have talked about the importance of having a unique value proposition from the very beginning and you should already have clear answers about this. If you are unaware of your competitor's activities and efforts, it will be very difficult to win market share against them.

- *Shareholders.* Because startups require investment to scale up their operations, they usually decide to raise money by attracting outside investors (we'll talk more about that in Stage 3: Fundraising). Bringing in new shareholders brings new pressure because shareholders want a return on the money they have invested in the startup. The main goal here is to decide what kind of outside investors you'll need and when to bring them in.

- *Customers.* How many potential customers there are to be served? What is their concentration? Who are they and how easily they could be reached?

Are they locked in with a competitor with some sort of monthly or annual contract? Do they prefer to buy online or only from salespeople? Which of their needs are under satisfied in the current market? What are they generally willing to pay for other similar services or products? How is the market growing?

- *Public groups* are any groups of people that may have a real or potential interest or impact on your startup. These groups may help or hinder your ability to achieve your objectives, whatever they may be. Public groups include:

  ✓ *Financial publics* typically include banks, investment houses, and stockholders. How these groups perceive you will directly affect your ability to get loans, favorable payment terms, and even whether or not other people choose to do business with you.

  ✓ *Media public groups* can be extremely valuable or a real nuisance. Media public groups usually include news, press release distribution, and features and editorial opinions in newspapers, blogs, magazines (print and digital), radio (broadcast and the Internet) and television (broadcast and digital channels like Youtube).

  ✓ *Government public groups* involve keeping an eye on the current state of laws and regulations that affect your business (for example, regulation of manufacturing or the methods you can use to sell your products and services). You might need to consult with government officials, their lawyers, and sometimes even lobbyists.

  ✓ *Local and action public groups* in classical marketing include neighborhood residents and community organizations. But startups should think broader than classical marketing guidelines. Thanks to the Internet, you can reach various groups around the world (for example, single moms in the USA, disabled person organizations in the EU, or starting entrepreneurs in India). Think about what socio-demographic groups your startup might concern. Maybe they are not your clients, but you can be engaged under some circumstances.

  ✓ *General public groups* influence the perception of your business, especially your startup brand, products, or services. They might even affect the buying habits of your target consumers. The good news is that until you are an early stage and unknown startup, it's not vital for you to care about general public groups.

It's not realistic for a startup to pay attention to all of these public groups at the same time. Therefore, you have to decide where to spend your time and resources. It's most likely that, sooner or later, you'll have to deal with all of these public groups in some capacity. So it's better to identify the most important groups and take the initiative to interact with them once you know who your target customers are and you have a value proposition to share with them.

📊 Calculate the size of your potential market and estimate its growth

You should have already evaluated the size and growth potential of your target segment (we've talked about that in Segmentation and potential market size). Now it's time to check the product or service life cycle stage in your chosen target market. Classical marketing theory defines four lifecycle stages for product or service, but startups should also include the development stage if you are creating an absolutely new product or some kind of innovation.

1. *Development stage*—the product is being created and tested and it's not yet available on the market, but there is a solid proof that product will solve a serious problem or deliver extreme gain for customers.

2. *Introduction stage* - the size of the market for the product is small and sales are low, but there is proof that they will be increasing (that is, the product-market fit is confirmed).

3. *Growth stage* - characterized by a strong growth in sales and profits. The company can start to benefit from economies of scale in production and the profit margin, as well as the overall amount of profit, increases.

4. *Maturity stage* –the product is established and the aim for the company is to maintain the market share they already have. This is a very competitive time for most products, therefore businesses need to invest wisely in any marketing activity they undertake.

5. *Decline stage*—the market for a product starts to shrink. It could be due to the market becoming saturated (for example, all the customers who will buy the product have already purchased it), or because the consumers are switching to a different type of product (another innovation emerged into the market) or perhaps the problem itself has disappeared.

Try to identify the lifecycle stage of your product category at this point in time. Try to look not only at your product but the general situation in the market. If you can't find proof that the market is growing, it might be a serious indicator that you should revise your business idea or the target market. Otherwise, you might be targeting a mature or even a declining market.

Estimate the factor of breakthrough innovation and how it may influence your business model

Usually, innovation related questions should be analyzed in a marketing macro environment as one of the technology factors. But breakthrough innovations are very important for startups, therefore I recommend paying attention to it separately.

By definition, breakthrough innovation involves pushing the boundaries of science and technology, with all the uncertainty and risk. Such innovations can change the fundamental conditions of competition and maybe even make it absolutely irrelevant for a period of time until new competitors emerge into the market to deliver their value proposition based on the same breakthrough innovation. It's difficult to analyze the market potential of breakthrough innovations and evaluate whether there is a real market pull for a new solution or not. You can quite easily check whether target customers are willing to use an innovative solution to the problem, but it's highly complicated to find out whether any of your competitors are working on innovations which might change the rules in the market. But, in any case, that should not stop you from the initial research based on two main aspects:

1. If you are planning to bring a breakthrough innovation to the market, how it will shape the market? How will you secure your innovation and business model? What will you do when competitors try to copy or imitate your innovation?

2. If your startup is not based on a breakthrough innovation, what are the chances that somebody else will introduce the breakthrough innovation in your market? How would this influence your business? Is it possible to predict how much time you have until such breakthrough innovation will take place in the market? Would this be enough time for you to create your business and earn desired profits?

UNLOQ Systems was founded in the UK in 2015 with an initial focus to provide better authentication through a distributed authentication system. The main focus was to offer organizations the possibility of increasing their cyber-security by eliminating passwords (the weakest link), through some sort of breakthrough innovation. The demand for a strong authentication solution was increasing, so the founders of *UNLOQ Systems* decided to go ahead with product development after their initial analysis was complete.

The following trends contributed to their decision and are expected to massively affect the development of the phone-based multifactor authentication market in the years to come:

- Massive adoption of smartphones
- Fingerprint technology embedded into all major smartphones
- The increase in the number and complexity of hosted, cloud applications or enterprise applications that are available from outside the organization
- The increase in the sensitivity of the data hosted in cloud applications or enterprise applications that are available from outside the organization
- Rapidly growing identity theft
- Bring your own device trends (BYOD) in workplaces
- Wars on crime and terror
- The increasing importance of user convenience

UNLOQ Systems found that the personal encryption key market is in its very early stages but is expected to increase, mostly driven by the same factors as the multifactor authentication market. Classical solutions would help to some extent, but without full encryption of data at rest, they still remain vulnerable. The multifactor authentication market size worldwide is expected to be $9.6 billion by 2020, of which *UNLOQ Systems* aims to capture $100 million.

 Check if your value proposition still remains the best option for your target market

Now it's time to summarize all the findings from the analysis of your business environment. You don't have to prepare a multiple page business environment report, but it's very helpful to see all your findings summarized in one page. There is not much value in having a pile of facts and data if you can't see what's in it for you. Therefore, I always encourage startup founders to ask the question, "So what?" once they have finished their research. Now, it's time for you to make your own insights from your facts!

Fill in the Business Environment Insight Card below (Table 19). It summarizes all your main findings from the micro and macro environment and will help you gain some insights about the decisions you need to make for implementation of your plan.

Once you have completed the Business Environment Insight Card, it's time to check and update, if necessary, your value proposition and the whole Business Model Canvas (or Lean Canvas if you prefer it). Initially, your business model might have been based on some assumptions that you should have validated during the business environment analysis. Review your Business Model Canvas and replace assumption-based statements with facts. If you see that there are some doubts about business viability, market size, or any other factor, take some time to revise your business model.

Table 19. Business Environment Insight Card

	MACRO environment	MICRO environment	
Technological	Is there a chance of any breakthrough innovation in the industry? How will it shape the market? What has to be done to avoid negative consequences and to use these technological changes to boost your business?	What are your target segments? What are the most efficient ways to reach them? What are customer needs and motives to buy from you? Are there any important behavior patterns?	**Clients**
Economic	What is your target market size? What economic factors influence the purchasing power of target customers and what are the tendencies of these factors? Which stage of economic development cycle is your market currently in?	What is the current state of your startup? Is it an established company or not? How many employees do you have now and how many will you need in the future? How do you plan to control your cash burn rate? How will you ensure that everyone in the company works efficiently?	**Company**
Social	Which are the most important social environment factors that drive the demand for your product or service? Is it related to fashion, lifestyle, religion, ethics? Who are the key influencers for your target groups? How are demographics changing?	How many direct and indirect competitors do you have? What do they offer to your target customers and how will your offer be better? How are your competitors doing financially? What are their revenues and profits? What marketing strategies and tools are they using effectively?	**Competitors**
Political	What are the most important and specific regulations in your industry? Are there any opportunities to get support (grants, subsidies, tax exemptions, etc.) from government or international organizations? Is the political environment stable and predictable?	Do any specific suppliers need to be secured? Do you have key suppliers already or at least know how to secure contracts with them? Will it provide you a competitive advantage?	**Suppliers**
Legal	Are there any issues or tasks to be done related to any licenses, patents, technology, or intellectual property access? Are there legal requirements for your products and services?	Are there any public organizations that could have a meaningful impact on your business (either support or interfere)? Consider financial organizations, media, government and public organizations, and local and general public groups.	**Publics**
Environmental	Is your business involved in any environmental issues, either causing problems or solving them? Do any of the environmental factors and trends have an influence on your business?	What key marketing intermediaries (for example, distributors, advertising channels, mass media, influencers, etc.) do you need to succeed in the business? Have you secured partnerships with them?	**Intermediaries**

CONCLUSIONS and DECISIONS	
Conclusions and Insights:	**Decisions and Actions:**
Summarize all your research just in up to 3-5 sentences including key insights: 1. ... 2. ... 3. ... 4. ... 5. ...	List your decisions and tasks to be done to take advantage of conclusions and insights you've just made: 1. ... 2. ... 3. ... 4. ... 5. ...

 Recommended reading

1. Philip Kotler, Gary Armstrong. *Principles of Marketing*

2. David Goldsmith. *Paid to Think*: *A Leader's Toolkit for Redefining Your Future*

3. W. Chan Kim, Renée A. Mauborgne. *Blue Ocean Strategy, Expanded Edition*: *How to Create Uncontested Market Space and Make the Competition Irrelevant*

6. Customer Journey Map

WHY IT IS NEEDED

It's well-known that profitable products can hardly do without services. Whether it's an extended warranty, convenient delivery, or something totally outstanding (like renting a product instead of buying, giving a product for complimentary use, and earning revenue from delivered services), products are bound to services. Furthermore, customer support is a service even if the customer doesn't pay directly for that. So, now you have to think about service design. Service design is a form of conceptual design that involves the activity of planning and organizing people, infrastructure, communication, and material components of a service in order to improve its quality and the interaction between the service provider and its customers.

In 2016, my global research on startups showed that 71.9% of startups have already applied or were working on the methodology of service design to create better customer experience and deliver higher value. Most of the startups who did so received significant benefits which, in some cases, became one of core elements of their success. Generally, these benefits can be created in two ways:

1. finding ways to serve the customer better in order to improve the core value proposition through increased customer retention, loyalty, repeat purchases, and referrals

2. seeing the whole process on a table allowed startup founders to gain insights into how to increase sales: attract new potential clients, propose additional offers (implement up-sell strategy), increase conversion rates, and increase customer lifetime value.

Service design may function as a way to inform changes to an existing service or create a new service entirely, including services complimentary to products. The purpose of service design methodologies is to achieve better results according to both the needs of customers and the goals of the company. If a successful method of service design is employed, the service will be useful, usable, desirable, efficient, and effective, while providing a competitive advantage for the company. It is a customer-centered approach that focuses on experience and the quality of services as the key value for success.

If you want to stay competitive, you must offer your customer a comprehensive solution that includes additional services (for example, delivery, delayed payment, warranty, regular maintenance, consulting, and training). Therefore, it is wise to model all possible processes and interactions on paper first and make decisions in advance before any negative situations emerge. Service design is a systematic and iterative process with long learning curves. In this regard, it's quite similar to the concept of the startup learning curve: startups should never stop learning and improving their customer experience.

HOW TO DO IT?

01 **List Customer's Activities**
Create the sequence of actions your target customer is usually doing

02 **List Actions That Deliver Value**
Create the sequence of actions to build value for customer and your business

03 **Draw Customer's Journey Map**
Combine the customer's actions with yours into one scheme covering the whole process

04 **Identify Risks and Weaknesses**
Check what might go wrong and where the customer might be underserved

05 **Discover Extra Possibilities**
Take a break and check what additional possibilities you can find for your business

List all the activities your customer has to do to get and use your value proposition

List all those activities in the sequence that best represents the customer journey from when they first acknowledge the problem and start looking for a solution until acquiring your value proposition and sharing their experience. You can do this initially by simply writing down a list of customer actions, or write each action on a separate post-it note and then arrange them according to the sequence of the whole process.

 List all the activities you need to do to get the customer and deliver your value proposition

It would best if you could take a different colored post-it note and write down your actions on them. Think what you need to do in order to:

- acquire the customer
- create and deliver your value proposition
- get feedback from the customer and keep a relationship
- encourage repeat purchases
- initiate word-of-mouth advertising or referrals

Align those activities according to if they are visible or invisible for the customer. Examples of visible activities include greeting a client, sending a confirmation email, SMS reminders, and delivering a package. Visible activities will directly influence the customer's overall experience. But there are always activities that are important for your business, but the customer will never see. Examples of invisible activities include storing customer contracts and order details, adopting marketing automation tools, and keeping track of time spent on each order. Startups frequently enter the market with only the minimal viable product (MVP) to test how it will be accepted by target customers. In order not to waste money, many activities at this stage are done manually instead of by automated solutions (which will be developed later, if the hypothesis is verified). Customers usually don't see and don't care about the invisible activities or how they are accomplished, but such tasks should be done anyway. It is, therefore, very common for early stage startups to have many activities that are invisible to the customer.

 Draw the customers' journey map

Service design scheme is another name for the customers' journey map. You can call it either, but the essence remains the same. It is a visual representation of how a customer or user experiences a service over time. The customer journey map can be used not only for designing a service but also to check up on the overall customer experience.

The customer journey map shows time along an X-axis (as shown in the template in Figure 22), including three periods:

1. Pre-service time period (when the service is not yet being provided)
2. A service time period
3. Post-service time period (once the service is provided to a customer).

Figure 22. Customers' journey map template

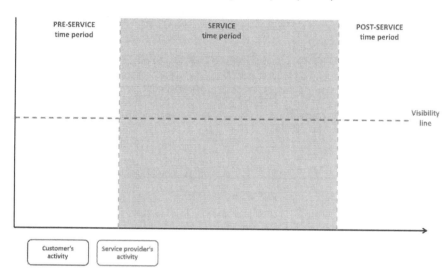

The Y-axis indicates the different activities and interactions (or touch points) at particular times. The most important element is the visibility line which is drawn in parallel to the X-axis. This line indicates what activities and interactions are seen by the customer and which are not. Probably the easiest and most convenient way to create your customer journey map takes just three steps:

1. Write up post-it notes with customer activities and put them in a time sequence.
2. Place the visible and invisible activities for both you and your partners (be careful about which side of visibility line you place them)
3. Draw the connections and add missing touch points for the what if... scenarios. For example, what if the customer downloads your app but doesn't use it for a week or more? What if a customer leaves your website without purchasing your product or service? What if the customer cancels his order in the checkout page? What if a customer is unsatisfied with the product?

The final result of your efforts should look like a logical sequence of actions showing all of the ways you acquire a new customer, how you serve them, and what actions are taken after the service is provided or the product delivered.

Identify most risky and weakest areas

Usually, customer journey maps are created as early as possible in a project and are used to check a variety of scenarios in order to improve the overall customer experience, exploit additional business possibilities (up-sell, cross–sell strategies), and avoid any failures during the process. Once you have created your customer journey map, look at it from different points of view:

- Does it represent the typical behavior of your target customer? Would it be the same or should it be modified for other target segments?
- Have you taken into account the experiences and feedback from your current customers or beta users? Is there anything to be improved?
- Does this journey map represent the first-time experience? Is there anything unclear for the first time user? Should you improve something?
- Does this represent the repeated use of your product or service? Is there anything that might get annoying to the customer?
- Is the process easy and smooth if everything goes right? Are there any activities wasting time, energy, or money on the part of you or the customer?
- What might go wrong and how you will solve it?
- When could the customer be lost? How could it be avoided?

Canadian startup BizON allows people to buy, sell, and grow a business or franchise. They target users that fall under different segments, for example, business buyers and sellers, baby boomers and millennials, etc. Because the main activity takes place on the website, the visitor's experience is vitally important. So, BizON analyzed not just a paper customer journey map, but an already working website where different customer segments had different experiences. After proper analysis, BizON version 2.0 was launched in order to provide members with a more engaging and positive experience. After evaluating user needs and the actions they needed to take on the website, the new version simplified the search function and improved the ability of users to discover business and franchise opportunities they might be interested in. That helped to achieve an annual user growth rate of 192% and a connection growth rate of 713%.

 What extra should we do to achieve better results?

Okay, it's time for a coffee break, going for a walk in the fresh air, or taking any other kind of refreshment break. Just take some kind of break to clear your mind before you go back and review your customer journey map. With a fresh mind, ask yourself these questions:

- How can we get more new customers?
- How can we create loyal customers and encourage their repeated purchase?
- What and how can we up-sell? What additional products or services could we offer at the moment when a customer decides to buy from you?
- What could we do to increase the chance of initiating word-of-mouth referrals about our products and services?

Let me share with you the story of *InnMind*, a platform that connects startup founders with investors, corporate customers, mentors, and experts on the international startup scene. It was launched at the end of February 2016 and, after six months, it already had around 1,000 active users. But the beginning of this project was sabotaged by major mistakes related to the customer journey map and overall user experience.

InnMind was a very ambitious digital project. The founders had absolutely no knowledge of coding and IT nuances, but they were convinced that the best possible way to execute the plan would be to hire the external team and outsource the development tasks to experienced professionals. Instead of making a simple MVP on one of the free or low-cost websites, the developers made a decision to create a high-quality back-end, able to handle all the features *InnMind* founders wanted to implement from the very beginning as well as in the future. The main argument was that it just wouldn't work otherwise. The founders paid for developers for several months without having even a demo, and then, after the launch, they realized that the demo was nothing close to what they imagined it to be. *InnMind* lost six months and tens of thousands of euros for nothing.

This could have been avoided if *InnMind* would have created and tested their MVP first and only then invested funds in developing a real platform. The issue is that if you want to create and test your MVP, you must understand your customers quite well and to know exactly what you are offering to them. That's where the customer journey map come into play. Nelli Orlova, co-founder of *InnMind*, shared their painful lesson: regardless of the size, experience, or competence of the IT outsourcing company, they never have enough knowledge and skills in user experience, and they never know your customers better than you. This means that you need to do your homework researching your target customers and to have the UX (user experience) expert at your side while developing a web-based project.

 **Recommended reading**

- Marc Stickdorn, Jakob Schneider. *This is Service Design Thinking*: *Basics, Tools, Cases*
- Ben Reason, Lavrans Løvlie, Melvin Brand Flu. *Service Design for Business*: *A Practical Guide to Optimizing the Customer Experience*
- Marc Stickdorn, Markus Edgar Hormess, Adam Lawrence, Jakob Schneider. *This Is Service Design Doing*: *Applying Service Design and Design Thinking in the Real World*

7. Financial assessments

WHY IT IS NEEDED

By now, you should have already developed your startup business model and have an idea what you will sell and to whom. After evaluating the business environment, you should have found a market where your product is actually capable of generating some sort of value. The next step is to understand your startup's expenses. A standard business model would at this in a straightforward manner: when and what amount of profit will this business model be capable of generating? Startups, especially based on innovative products and services, are a bit different. They have to figure out how to spend money wisely to match customer growth and, finally, earn a profit.

You have to calculate your cash burn rate (how much money you lose each month) and how much time you have until your funds get totally depleted and your venture will be closed. Cash burn rate defines the time frame until you have to reach a break-even point and start earning a profit. Startups have much work to do before they achieve positive cash flow. Obviously, the types and amounts of expenses vary from startup to startup, but what matters here is how they align with what you are trying to do and whether it is realistic.

If you find out that there is not enough time to achieve any particular results, it's better to not even start yet or reduce your costs dramatically. Revise your business model and find ways to ensure reasonable time to achieve success in product development, customer validation, and creating some traction. If you have those achieved, it's possible to attract investments and use the funds wisely for your business growth.

01 Choose Revenue Model
Choose the strategy how exactly you'll earn money, who and for what will pay you

02 Calculate Fixed Costs
Evaluate costs that you will have to cover independently of your sales volume

03 Calculate Variable Costs
Evaluate costs that are directly related to your sales volume

04 Know Your Cash Burn Rate
Estimate your cash burn rate, break-even point, and how much time you have to reach it

05 Evaluate Need for Investment
Calculate the amount of needed investments and how exactly they will be used

06 Check Viability and Update Canvas
Check financial numbers before you proceed to prototyping and make changes if necessary

 Decide what revenue model you will use

You should consider various revenue models and choose the one that allows you to grow your startup fast and earn a solid profit. Yes, I know, sometimes it might seem like two opposite objectives (grow a number of clients/users and earn a profit), but actually they both are needed for your strategy. Here are the 16 most common revenue models:

1. *Freemium*—an offering that is free of charge, but a premium is charged for advanced features, functionality, virtual goods and so on

2. *Premium*—a high-end offering with an upfront price, usually applied for prestigious, luxury, niche or limited product editions

3. *Price leadership*—lowest cost of operation to exploit the economy of scale (that is, the more you produce, the lower the costs per production unit)

4. *Predictive pricing*—future-priced offerings based on past data, performance, or customer profile (for example, insurance companies set higher prices for clients with a negative history)

5. *Pay-per-use*—customers have access to potentially unlimited features, goods or services, but pay only for what they actually use

6. *Core offering slim margin*—slim margins or even loss on the core product in order to profit from additional products or features with high demand; usually applied to products that are used with complementary products (for example, a printer is sold with low marge, but a nice profit is earned by selling ink or toner)

7. *Subscription and membership*—are quite often confused, therefore I've added them both. Membership means belonging to some kind of group and shows the relation. Membership can be free or paid. Subscription means charging customers upfront for periodic use or access to the offering. So, if the membership gives access to the product, service, or advanced benefits and it is charged for, it is a paid membership or simply a subscription revenue model.

8. *Micropayments*—very small payments on impulse or addictive purchases

9. *Bundle price*—placing several offerings together in a single package and selling for a lower price than would be charged if the offerings were sold separately

10. *Licensing*—to give permission to use your offering in a specific way

11. *Advertising revenue*—the offering is absolutely free, but backed by ads; usually, it's quite a popular solution when a customer has a high possibility of purchasing what is being advertised

12. *Franchise*—allowing a customer to use your company's successful business model for a fee (usually there is a starting fixed fee and commissions from income)

13. *Auction*—selling the offer to the highest bidding (eBay is a popular example of a place where sellers and buyers meet to carry out auctions)

14. *Switchboard or double-sided market*—a platform which brings together buyers and sellers; the operator of the platform usually takes a commission fee from confirmed deals, offer postings, or promotions

15. *Float*—the customer pays before the offering is produced according to customer needs

16. *Real-time pricing*—the price of the offering changes accordingly to the level of demand, the customer, or the state of other conditions (for example, hotels change their pricing according to the season, room occupancy rate, planned massive events, and festivals in the area).

Look broader and try to see how various revenue models would influence your business. For example, the *Share2Style* founders would have loved to have a subscription model because it is convenient for business and looks good for investors. But, many of their target customers are bloggers who are just starting out and would not be willing to pay a subscription price. So, even if the product was good, *Share2Style* would not have had any users due to their revenue model. Therefore, they chose to share affiliate commissions with bloggers (*Share2Style* earns only if bloggers earn). They also decided to implement an advertising revenue model once the platform scales up.

IIII Calculate your fixed costs and evaluate how they can change over time

This is one of the easiest tasks, even though emotionally it might be difficult to make the decision to cut some expenditures. First of all, calculate what monthly expenses (such as rent, advertising, insurance, and office supplies) you have independent of your sales volume. The concept of lean startup suggests avoiding fixed costs in early stage startups, especially if you have negative cash flow. Always stay lean on expenses. If it's not necessary, don't spend money on it. If someone makes a negative comment that if you can't afford this or that, you can't afford to run your business, don't pay attention to them or any other naysayers. You are creating a business and you will enjoy it benefits once the profit shows up or when the valuation of the company significantly grows up!

During my global research on startups, I met Mark Tuttle, the co-founder of Web Associates which was established in 1995. He shared a great story about being able to cut unnecessary costs and achieve great results. They stayed lean on expenses from the very beginning. It was web technical development and interface design company, which even didn't have an office until Hewlett-Packard decided to visit them! The company had only five employees during the first two years and most of them were publishers and assistants for online content management (they were employed only at the point when orders from clients and workload increased). How did they fare operating so frugally?

The attitude of putting the customer first allowed Web Associates to became the first external web technical development and interface design agency in both Hewlett-Packard (1996) and Apple, Inc. (1997) resulting in a multi-year relationship with both companies. In 1996, Lucent Technologies (spun out of AT&T) had Web Associates do their first corporate website and an online CMS (1997) for all domestic and international sales offices. Not a bad client portfolio, eh? In 2008, as part of a repositioning strategy to better communicate the company's status as an independent, full-service digital agency, Web Associates rebranded as LEVEL Studios. In 2010, the company was acquired by Rosetta at price of $140 million. So, do early stage startups really need a big office, large team, huge marketing budget and other fancy stuff in order to solve customers' problems in the best possible way? I think not!

Calculate your variable costs and prepare your budget draft

Variable costs are those costs that vary depending on your production or sales volume; they rise as production increases and fall as production decreases. Variable costs can include direct material costs, direct labor costs necessary to complete a certain task related to the product or service, and third party costs (for example, the more potential customers you have, the higher the price you pay for marketing automation tools and the more product you sell, the more you pay for product delivery). Customer acquisition and servicing costs are probably the largest variable costs at the moment. Calculate how much you have to spend to acquire a new customer and how much you also need to service this customer. A thorough bookkeeper would also take into account some portion of the fixed costs for acquiring and servicing a new customer. But, to be practical at this stage, it is enough to compare customer acquisition and servicing costs with the customer lifetime value for your company. In other words, you want to compare how much you spend to acquire a new customer and how much you earn from the new customer throughout the time they remain your customer (for example, when they make repeated purchases and buy additional products or services). If your costs are higher than earnings, you are in trouble! The more products or services you sell, the more losses you take. That's a terrible situation for standard business, but for startups, it might be an exception in some cases if you are still in the product or customer development process.

Once you have your fixed and variable costs on paper, you can prepare your monthly and yearly budget. You can download a startup budget Excel template with examples from www.evolutioncurve.com. Have in mind that you are creating just a budget draft to get an idea about your possible financial situation in the near future. Don't spend too much of your precious time on preparing the most detailed and accurate set of financial documents.

 Calculate your cash burn rate, break-even point, and time remaining to reach it

Startups should act on the survival instinct: build products, attract paying customers, deal with competition, be lean on expenses, and have in mind that future funding may not be available. Make a plan for how to reduce your cash burn rate. If your startup is a pre-revenue company running on investment, you should think about how to stretch your funds out as long as possible, because you don't know if you will receive any additional investment.

- Focus your attention on increasing revenue so that you become profitable. This will solve the cash burn rate problem and make your startup much more attractive for investors.

- Check for multiple income streams. Look through your business model and see if you have created any additional value that could generate you at least some income. As for instance, I have nothing against advertising income, but in most cases, it is hard to increase until you achieve large scale distribution. Therefore, when any startup says they will earn their desired profits on advertising, I became a little skeptical.

- Look for barter partnerships instead of purchasing services and products you need. Don't hurry to pay cash; offer something in exchange. Think if you have something valuable and who would appreciate getting this value.

- Consider using remote teams or even freelancers, who might be more skilled and less expensive. Maybe you don't yet need a full-time employee and the particular task could be done by outsourced specialists?

- Control your marketing budget. Instead of burning money on communication channels, it is better to focus on crafting an effective marketing strategy, positioning statement, and content. Prepare and run channel tests, measure results, and continue with the most effective channels.

- Offer equity instead of salary for your employees. If you already need employees, hire those who believe in your success and want to be in the same boat. Offer them a lower salary but with the option to acquire some share of your startup when the right time comes. Those who are passionate about your startup idea will agree to a lower salary because, with your success, their option rights will grant them much more value than any salary they ever dreamed. In the meantime, you'll reduce your cash burn rate by paying lower salaries.

- Watch your reserves. Anything less than six months of reserves signals danger. Take actions to cut your expenses or increase your revenue. Only in the worst case should you think about an additional investment source.

⑤ Calculate needed investments and how exactly those investments will be used?

Prepare a plan for how much funds you will need and how they will be used. Be ready to show the benefits to investors if you are planning to attract outside funding. Usually, investors expect to see not only immediate profit but also reduced cash burn rate, growing the customer base, and achieving a competitive advantage. Ask yourself the following questions:

- How much investment do you need and for what purpose will the investment be used?

- When are these investments needed? They might not be needed all at once but only after reaching particular milestones. For example, you'll need to allocate the actual marketing budget only when you have a product-market fit.

- What is the expected payback period? What is the projected return on investment? Nobody wants to invest money and then forget about it. You must have clear answers about when your startup will start generating profit.

- What if you won't get any investment? What is your plan B?

Echoz is an affiliate marketing platform based in Romania that, instead of products, promotes jobs in the IT sector. Basically, it's a multi-sided platform where IT companies, affiliates, and candidates interact. Nicolae Andronic, the founder of *Echoz*, identified that IT companies need to hire IT professionals in a cost-efficient manner. He also considered using affiliates as a viral growth engine. Creating and promoting the platform based on this strategy helped save a lot of money and reduced the required amount of investment. The total cost of creating this startup (except for the web development part, where Nicolae did the job himself) was under €1,000. Although *Echoz* is still in the early stage, they already serve about 40 IT companies in Romania, have more than 100 affiliates (bloggers, online publications, Facebook, and LinkedIn influencers) that together have an estimated reach of 50,000 – 60,000 IT professionals. Not a bad achievement with such a small investment!

 Check the numbers before proceeding to prototype

Review your financial estimations. Will your business model be profitable? If you barely can see the positive cash flow perspective, there is not much sense going any further and creating prototypes and checking hypothesis. But if you see great revenue potential, you should have already prepared financial estimates about the conditions under which you will achieve the revenue (for example, the price of the product or service, sales volume, fixed and variable costs). If so, it's time to go to the next chapter and check the most important hypothesis about your business model and replace your initial assumptions with facts.

If you are building a scalable or buyable startup, you might want to estimate how much your startup will be worth if you succeed in achieving your goals? Forget about the unicorns, those startups that eventually become valued at $ 1 billion or more. Those cases are as rare as creatures from fairy tales. Instead, estimate what could be a realistic evaluation of your startup and whether there would investors or corporations willing to acquire your company at such a price? If not, you should revise your financial estimations or even the whole business model if your financial assessments are very, very lean.

 Recommended reading

1. Philip Kotler, Gary Armstrong. *Principles of Marketing*
2. Cynthia Kocialski. *Perfect Pricing in One Simple Lesson: Find Your Pricing Edge, Attract More Customers, and Earn More Profit*

There are many possible ways to make your feasibility study more in-depth, but the speed of decision making and actions for startups is also essential. I don't know who was the first to say, "done is better than perfect," but I totally agree with it in this startup development stage. You did your homework well if the following statements are true:

- You came to an idea about a possible product-market fit. The problem you intend to solve for your customers is a real headache with significant demand for solving it.
- You have assumptions or even confirmed facts about who your customers are and how you can reach them.
- You see the potential to make money and grow the company. The only unknown might be if you grow predictably and large enough.

In the next chapter, we'll talk about why hypotheses are essential for your startup business, how to rise and check them, what tools can be used, and what to do with your findings. If it happens that hypothesis verification leads you to results different from your expectations, you should come back to a feasibility study and recheck your financial assessments, and whether your business model is viable and sustainable under such conditions.

Stage 2. Hypotheses and Experiments

You should have already prepared a value proposition based on facts you researched. It's obvious that you shouldn't waste your time and money to build products that nobody wants to buy or use unless you like playing a high-stakes lottery. But what do you do when you only have assumptions and educated guesses instead of solidly based facts? How do you minimize the risk of failure when you intend to sell something new which has never been sold before? How do you know that customers will buy it? Are you sure you have established the optimal price and that you are not leaving money on the table by selling at lower price than you actually could?

These are ordinary issues for any innovative startup business. Experiments and primary data from the market are the best cure in this situation. Startups formulate a hypothesis and validate or reject them in actual conditions. Usually, it's more expensive than checking already available data. Therefore, it's highly recommended that you do your homework with an initial feasibility study before you go to hypothesis and prototyping.

This stage helps to make decisions based on facts related to how well your product will be accepted in the market, what should be changed or adjusted, who is your target customer who is willing to buy your product as soon as it is available in the market, what distribution and communication channels might be the most effective, is there enough profit to be earned and market potential for your business growth, and so on.

This stage of *Startup Evolution Curve* answers the main question: what insights do you need to check and what are the most appropriate ways to do that? This chapter is a step-by-step action plan that will lead you to a much clearer vision of your business plan.

The main goals of this stage:

- Test hypothesis
- Adjust business plan
- Develop marketing strategy

8. Get ready for hypotheses verification

WHY IT IS NEEDED

Anybody who knows anything about Lean startup knows that in order to create a successful startup, you should rise and check your hypothesis. Yes, you can take a chance and build a business without any hypothesis verification, but the chance of success for an innovative business is rather low. During my global research on startups, I found that majority of startups don't pay enough attention to hypothesis verification because they don't know how to do it efficiently and effectively. Most of the frustrated startups acknowledged that they knew the concept of Lean startup, but were not sure how to apply it. Then I remembered a similar trend that was noted by Steve Blank and Bob Dorf (2014). They indicated that most startups lack a structured process for testing their business model hypothesis, therefore, the authors offered a solution in their book *The Startup Owner's Manual*, which I highly recommend reading!

This chapter introduces you to how to rise and prepare to check your hypothesis step by step. These action steps were found to be time efficient and easy to implement during the empirical research phase in most startup cases. So, I sincerely hope that almost any startup hoping to create some innovative business will be able to achieve that dream faster and with less investment if they follow these steps.

HOW TO DO IT

01 List all the Assumptions
Get clear on what assumptions need to be checked in at least three main areas

02 Complete Experiment Cards
Prepare a task card for each experiment and don't forget to capture the results

03 Find Potential Customers
Use real potential customers in your experiments in order to get realistic results

04 Choose the Type of Engagement
Decide what type of engagement and how much data you need to check your hypotheses

05 Prepare to Note New Insights
Prepare one file where you will store all of additional insights and ideas

Get clear on what assumptions need to be checked

Finding the problem-solution-market fit is the most popular approach and it's hard to argue with that. Basically, it means that you must find and confirm a problem which is worth solving. Once you have a confirmation from potential customers that this particular problem is a real headache for them, you must create an acceptable solution. Once you have a general approval from customers that the solution is suitable for them, then you ask them to pay for it. If you get paid the price acceptable for you, congratulations! You have found the problem-solution-market fit. But there might be much more important hypotheses which could help in developing your startup. Consider the following:

1. Value proposition hypotheses
   - Problems, jobs and wants hypothesis (is a problem or desired benefit strong enough?)
   - Problem-solution fit hypothesis (does the solution fit the customer expectations?)
   - Value proposition-market fit hypothesis (is the customer ready to pay a certain price?)
   - Segment hypothesis (do we know who our early evangelists are?)
2. Business model hypotheses
   - Distribution and communication channels
   - Costs and revenue
   - Unfair competitive advantage
   - Others
3. Business growth hypotheses
   - Business evolvement potential (how large could the new market be?)
   - The probability of initiating a viral effect (what are the chances of initiating a viral effect so that current customers bring new customers?)

My research of nearly 1,500 startups worldwide showed the broader scope of possible hypotheses to be checked. Generally, there are three groups of essential hypotheses. The first one, the value proposition hypotheses group, refers to the above-mentioned approach but is extended with additional segment hypothesis. This additional hypothesis aims to find the "hottest" target segment, or so-called early evangelists. Classical marketing defines that early adopters are a small portion of customers from the target segment who are generally open to innovations and constantly willing to try new products. Customers who are willingly promoting the product and initiating word-of-mouth advertising are called evangelists. Obviously, it would be very beneficial to know which customers belong to the early adopters and evangelist category at the same time. Such customers are quite often are called "early evangelists." So if you are a startup preparing to launch an innovative product, starting with early evangelists might be a very effective and cost-saving strategy. Thus, you should try to identify those customers.

The second group of hypotheses is called business model hypotheses and refers to checking any uncertainties arising from the Business Model Canvas or Lean Canvas. If you remember correctly, you completed the canvases based on assumptions and facts. It is normal to build your business model on at least one assumption that couldn't be replaced with fact during the feasibility study (you couldn't find enough statistical or other data to prove the assumption). I recommend that you check such assumptions by rising and checking hypotheses. My in-depth interviews with the global startups showed that most startups have already checked or were preparing to check hypotheses related to distribution and communication channels (46.2%), cost and revenue model (41.3%), and competitive advantage (39.6%). Undoubtedly, you could have additional hypotheses related to any other aspects of your business model, but the current ones were most often met in early stage startups.

The third group of hypotheses is called business growth hypotheses. These are more important for more developed startups. Early stage startups should validate their business model first (check the value proposition and business model hypotheses) and only then should look for business growth. It doesn't make sense to try to grow your business and implement any growth hacking techniques if your value proposition is not good enough or if your business model has serious gaps. The only thing you will achieve from your growth hacking is wasting your resources. But, if you have already validated your business model and started generating revenue, maybe it's time to think about how to boost the growth of your business.

You can use this simple template (Table 20) to track hypotheses that you've already validated, are currently working on, and those that have yet to be checked. Use the Comments section for notes about the progress of each hypothesis. Don't hesitate to include your custom hypotheses that need to be checked in order to prove the viability of your business model.

The *Izzui* platform was initially launched just in Brazil, even though co-founder Alfredo Leone had greater plans. He wanted to build an interactive visual content sharing platform and target the global market of English-speaking countries. They did two major pivots (not minor changes like logo or colors) and only the third version of the product found a problem-solution-market fit. They had checked their different assumptions for each product version. But, it wasn't until they ran real life experiments that they realized the prospective business opportunity and how the value for multiple client segments could be created and delivered. The third version of *Izzui* platform combined content owners (to monetize, contextualize, and empower their content), users (to have fun, learn, and win prizes), and brands (to engage, sell, and increase loyalty). The platform was designed to be used for different goals like e-learning, e-commerce, marketing, loyalty, etc. Drag and drop functionality empowered users to easily create campaigns without having any technical or coding skills, while detailed analytics helped to improve the efficiency of campaigns.

Table 20. Main hypotheses to be checked

Hypothesis	Validation			Comments
	not started	working on	validated	
Problem	☐	☐	☐	
Solution	☐	☐	☐	
Segment	☐	☐	☐	
Price	☐	☐	☐	
Channels	☐	☐	☐	
Other hypotheses related to business plan				
...	☐	☐	☐	
...	☐	☐	☐	

Izzui onboarded their first B2B clients manually and launched six content sharing campaigns. Each of those campaigns brought 100,000 visitors just in two to four weeks. That provided a couple of proof points: the platform was functional and generated great traction. The fact that approximately 80% of visitors were new showed a strong potential for viral growth. Now the founders of Izzui had a valuable and realistic business for scaling to larger markets.

 Complete an experiment card for each hypothesis

Not all startups use experiment cards as recommended by Eric Ries (2014). But those who do so (98.6%) agree that this simple tool made startup development much more structured, saved money, reduced risk, and helped to show additional possibilities. Based on my interviews with startup founders from different industries, I've updated the experiment task and result card. It's a two-part table which fits on one page. The experiment task explains which hypothesis you want to check, how exactly you plan to do it, and the next step if the hypothesis is confirmed. The same sheet contains the experiment result card which describes your findings based on facts from the experiment and obligates you to make a decision about what you will do next.

I would recommend having an experiment folder (whether it's a folder on your computer or a real physical folder) where you can save printed experiment cards. Because there are many different types of hypotheses, testing a hypothesis only once won't be sufficient unless you get extremely strong results to support your initial hypothesis. Usually, the same type of hypothesis must be checked a few times to evaluate different alternatives or pivot scenarios. For example, you may want to test if your proposed solution is accepted by target customers by checking which one of several different solutions fits the customers' expectations best, which customer segment appreciates a particular solution the most, and so on. Therefore, you'll have plenty of experiment cards! It is called a learning curve; the more experiments you run, the more you learn about your market and business and the more chances your startup has to succeed. If you store all those experiment cards (tasks and results filed correctly) in one place, it will be much easier for you and your colleagues to follow up. You'll have an archive of your own fact database. This is your knowledge base, your asset!

Table 21. Experiment task and result card

EXPERIMENT TASK		
Experiment: _____	Responsible: _____	
	Starting date: _____	
We believe that... (Describe the hypothesis you want to test.)		
In order to check that, we will... (Describe methods and tools you will use to check the hypothesis.) *Note: this is the topic of next chapter*		
We will measure these results by... (What are key metrics which allow you to measure the fact.)		
The hypothesis will be confirmed if... (What is the validation rule? Be as precise as possible.)		
If the hypothesis is confirmed this will allow us to... (Why it is important for you? What next steps will you take if the hypothesis is confirmed?)		
EXPERIMENT RESULTS		
Hypothesis was confirmed rejected	Factual costs: _____	Result date: _____
We observed and noticed that... (Describe the parameters of the experiment.)		
We determined that... (State the clear measurable facts/results of the experiment.)		
We will take these following actions... (Decisions about how to develop your startup if your hypothesis was confirmed or what to do if the hypothesis was rejected)		

When you are pitching your idea to a potential investor and get questions about why you are not doing this or that, it's quite possible that you'll already have an answer in your experiment folder. I haven't met an investor yet who doesn't take into account important facts. The more facts you have, the more professional and valuable your startup will look in the eyes of investors and possibly new partners.

So your task is to complete the experiment card (Table 21) for each of your hypotheses. If you are just starting, you should think about the value proposition hypothesis: problem, solution, market fit, and early evangelists.

Visit www.evolutioncurve.com to download this experiment card template and more examples.

After showing your MVP (minimal viable product) to potential customers, you might not get a clear picture of how they perceived your product. After showing their MVP, startups can usually divide potential customers into four categories:

1. Customers who love your product and are ready to buy it without any changes. It is great if you have the majority of these kinds of customers. However, if you have less than 10% of the total of your tested customers falling into this category, it might mean that your product is not yet good enough for the market or you've been testing your MVP with the wrong customer segment.

2. Customers who like your product, but still want some adjustment, additional features, or other change before they will be ready to buy it. My research showed that this is the largest category for most startups: 84% of the startups in the study indicated that after showing the MVP to potential customers, the product is positively accepted, but 45—95% of customers are not ready to buy it because they want something to be changed or added. So, if you show your MVP to potential clients and a half or even more of them ask for some changes, it means you are a normal startup.

3. Customers who understand the product after a detailed explanation, but are not willing to buy it. That's a problem! There could be two reasons that a significant percentage of your customers can barely understand the essence of your product. First of all, maybe your product is not as beneficial as you think or maybe you have overestimated the customers' problem or the value you can deliver to them. The second most common issue is poor communication of value. In this case, your product might still be good and interesting for the customer, but your marketing message, your positioning idea, maybe even the whole presentation of the product doesn't reveal enough about the value customers could get by having your product. In this case, you need to determine what to fix: the product or your marketing.

4. Customers who don't see much of a need for your product or say it is like more of a "nice to have" rather than "must have" product. If more than 10% of your

potential customers fall into this category, it might indicate that your product is not solving a major problem for them. Yes, your startup business could be built under such conditions, but it's very risky because it's much harder to sell products and solutions that are not highly valued. And, it becomes even more difficult when the economy goes down and customers need to start saving money.

Find potential customers for your experiments

Once you've filled your experiment cards, it's time to start the real job: engage your potential customers and run the experiments. You will need to find a significant number of potential customers and not fall into the trap of just showing your assumptions, solutions, and prototypes to your friends, relatives, and classmates. There are two problems with this approach:

- Not all of your friends and relatives are your potential clients. Double-check how you defined your target segment in Chapter 3. Segmentation and potential market size. Does your chosen group for the experiment exactly meet the same criteria?

- Most of your friends won't be willing to hurt your feelings by saying that your idea is totally stupid, even if it's true. Answers from people who don't know you personally tend to be much more objective.

Generally, it's far better to interview only 10 potential customers rather than 100 friends who might never need your product. There are different ways to find potential clients depending on what kind of engagement you are looking for and what kind of experiment you are running. Consider such channels as:

- *Your personal network* is very good for low fidelity prototype testing, but as we have already discussed, be careful about that.

- *You can use Google Adwords* to find out if people are searching for how to solve a particular problem and then you can show them your solution and see how it is accepted.

- *Social network groups* are very convenient for segmentation because each of them unites people according to particular criteria and gives you scalability. Personally, I love LinkedIn. I did the research and a few experiments for this book mainly through Linkedin. It was quite easy to find the largest startup communities such as the "On Startups" group which had nearly 600,000 members interested in startups! It would have taken ages for me to get at least 1,000 responses to my survey if I had not used social networking.

- *Partnerships* allow you to save costs and get in front of target customers. Take a minute to think about who is already serving your potential customers but is not competing with you. What benefit could you give to such ventures or individuals and how could they deliver your message to your target customer? HolyCup is a Portuguese tea company that developed 100% natural teas in capsules compatible with Nespresso® machines. HolyCup offers a faster, convenient, and healthy alternative, combined with an appealing design for the young and irreverent consumer. They even have tea for after-parties and hangovers! HolyCup agreed on a partnership with the municipality of Lisbon: the city has a program for start-ups, and thus invited HolyCup for multiple events that allow them to get feedback from customers, earn some revenue, and promote the brand among the city's young people. That's a nice example of multiple benefits in a simple partnership.

- *Chosen advertising channels* include e-commerce portals, physical shops, news portals, blogs, and so on. It could be a direct gateway to potential customers, especially if you have a prototype and want to test the market fit of your value proposition. Actually, you even don't need to have real products; just place a description of your product and enable ordering or buying. At the end of the experiment period, you can count how many potential customers have added your product to the shopping cart, submitted an order form, or asked for a demo.

- *"Go to the street"* or, as is more commonly said, "go outside the building." This may be one of the easiest ways to test some of your hypotheses: just go to the street and ask people. But be careful here. In order to deliver reliable results, you must be sure you've talked to your target group, not just random people. If you do talk to random people, do it at higher volume and note which segmentation criteria each person meets (for example, age, education, and lifestyle).

- *Paid users* might be a solution when none of the others is available in your situation. There are different platforms that help developers test their mobile apps (UserTesting, Killerstartups, Ubertesters, PreApps), websites (UserTesting, Enroll, StartUpLift, TestingTime), software, or even a physical product (Vyprclients, UserTesting). Most of those platforms are designed to help developers to find and fix technical issues. But some of them also allow testing the app, website, software, or in some cases even a physical product, by bringing beta testers from all around the world. Most of the platforms help developers track everything beta testers submit, like screenshots, photos, bug reports and also to have individual Skype interviews. But, in most cases, it's much better to run experiments on real users, not paid ones. Why? Because you can test two different groups of your assumptions at once: any issues related to the product or prototype as well as your assumptions about your marketing techniques and communication channels.

Tatiana Arslanouk, CEO and co-founder of *Tarnish-Me-Not*, a startup based in the USA, noticed a problem that metal jewelry is highly susceptible to tarnishing and discoloration due to the inexpensive base metals that are used to manufacture it. More importantly, the base metals used in jewelry are notorious for causing contact skin allergies, such as irritation, discoloration, and rashes. Tatiana, together with the other co-founders, wanted to create the most effective, accessible, and affordable solution for consumers to preserve their jewelry and protect their skin.

On the assumption that product research and development in laboratories would require a few years, they needed to be absolutely sure they were addressing significant problems with a highly prospective business opportunity. Keeping in mind the time and investment required for product development, they couldn't take a chance on the wrong initial product offering. In order to gain the most accurate and appropriate data, the founders of *Tarnish-Me-Not* conducted a market research study to measure the addressable market, market opportunity, and the impact the product would pose on other markets. As a start-up with limited resources and budget, they conducted the study themselves in the local shopping mall. Every day over the course of six months, they surveyed 6,000 women through a systematic sampling technique, asking them three questions. The results showed that the current fashion jewelry market is comprised of about 73% of women; that 84% of women experience jewelry tarnish and/ or skin allergies caused by jewelry; and finally, 92% of women said that they would purchase a product that prevented the issues of tarnishing and skin allergies to jewelry. Today (after three years of this research) *Tarnish-Me-Not* is a well-known product that passed the Human Repeated Insult Patch Test (HRIPT) with a 100% success rate and has had great success in the market. *Tarnish-Me-Not* got accepted as a wholesale supplier to one of the largest retailers in the world within the first 30 days of operation. The company currently is selling to 12 different countries around the world and sold about 530,000 units after being in business for only 4 months.

Maybe it's not necessary for you to run a survey for six months to validate your business idea. But when stakes are high, it would be foolish not to check the viability of your business idea before investing your time and money into it.

Choose the right type of engagement

Decide what type of engagement and how much data you need to check your hypotheses. Ask yourself what insights or assumptions need to be checked to move forward. Then think about the simplest test you could use to check it. The first step is to do your homework and identify the most painful problems and most desired gains for the customer. But without testing in actual conditions, it's just an assumption which may be far from the truth. Generally, there are four main types of engagement:

1. *Talk to potential customers*—Describe the problem and solution and get their feedback. Check if you are on the right track. It is a rule of thumb that if you talk

to at least 50 potential customers and 30—40% of them say that your idea is great and they'd love to try your product or service, it's a good indicator.

2. *Show some kind of visual prototype*—It might be just a napkin sketch, design mockup, presentation, or video. Get customer feedback once they see (not only hear) what you plan to deliver.

3. *Offer to buy or preorder*—This is an essential point. Anyone can say that you offer nice products and they'd love to use them, but the moment of truth comes when you ask them to pay money for the solution.

4. *Ask to be recommended*—Check to see if those customers who showed initiative to pay for your product would recommend you to their friends and colleagues. A net promoter score (NPS) is usually used in this case. The main question to be asked is, "How likely from 1 to 10 is it that you would recommend this product to your friends?" You could even go further and ask them to name their friends to whom you could talk to and show your product. You will learn more about NPS and how it is calculated in Chapter 29: Viral loop and key metrics.

Before launching a highly specific product (multi-factor authentication, transaction authorization, and data encryption service), *UNLOQ Systems* had to check many aspects of their offering, therefore they made two prototypes. The first was released in May 2015 and the second after three months. During the prototyping phase, the company collected continuous feedback from users on Hacker News and also from the community on Reddit. This feedback was used to fix bugs in the product and to improve the overall user experience. Even when the final version was released in April 2016, the company was still developing new features and continuously improving the product.

 Prepare to make note of additional insights

Practice shows that the more hypotheses you test, the more additional insights you get from your experiments and endeavors. Don't lose them! Be ready to capture them! Prepare one file or folder where you will store all of these valuable insights and ideas. If you wish, you can go to www.evolutioncurve.com and download set of templates. There you'll find an "Insight vault," a convenient spreadsheet that will help you make notes about all of the valuable ideas and findings you discovered while developing your startup. Upload this file to Dropbox, Google drive, or any other cloud-based storage device and share it with your colleagues. That will help you capture even more ideas and use them in more efficient way.

Whenever you are engaging a potential customer, try to sell your solution. Even if your experiment is not directly related to sales (though it's hard to imagine such situation), be ready to make a list of your early adopters and evangelists, potential clients who are most eager to try your product and to share the news with their friends. Wouldn't it be great to know who those people are? Just imagine how much efficient your marketing could be if you could identify your early adopters and evangelists before you launch. In order to know your clients better and find out the most efficient ways to reach them when introducing your product, try to ask questions like these whenever you have a chance:

- What are you reading (newspapers, magazines, blogs, portals)?
- What events do you attend (conferences, trade fairs, concerts and etc.)?
- What would the ideal seller look like? How should he/she interact with clients?

 Recommended reading

1. Ash Maurya. *Running Lean: Iterate from Plan A to a Plan That Works.*
2. Eric Ries. *The Lean Startup: How Today's Entrepreneurs Use Continuous Innovation to Create Radically Successful Businesses*
3. Steve Blank, Bob Dorf. *The Startup Owner's Manual: The Step-by-Step Guide for Building a Great Company*
4. Pat Flynn. *Will It Fly?: How to Test Your Next Business Idea So You Don't Waste Your Time and Money*

9. Creating minimal viable products: purposes and types

WHY IT IS NEEDED

I'm pretty sure you don't want to waste your time and money building a product no one will use or pay for. One of the major mistakes early stage startups often make is not seeing the difference between customer talk and action. What your customers say and what they eventually do is far not always the same. Interviewing or surveying customers is not enough to verify the need for your new product in the market. Getting paid for it is a much more valid indicator. But that is the problem: how do you get paid for a product that does not yet exist? This is where the minimum viable product (MVP) comes in handy.

Minimum viable product (MVP) is a version of a new product that allows a team to collect the maximum amount of validated learning about customers with the least amount of effort (Eric Ries, 2011). Generally speaking, MVP includes perhaps just a few essential features that allow you to ship a product to early adopters and get some feedback from them to check your hypotheses. Getting paid for your MVP or product pre-order is one of the best indicators for validating your business idea.

As my global research on startups showed, most early stage startups understand the importance of validating their business model, but they still lack a structured process for testing their hypotheses. It becomes complicated because there are different types of MVPs that are used for different purposes in different cases. MVPs could be classified into different groups according to various criteria, like:

- *Coverage* is the number of customers reached. An interview is done with few people while an Ad-Words campaign can reach thousands.
- *Product fidelity* defines how similar the MVP is to the end product. A software prototype has a higher fidelity than a paper mockup.
- *Feedback time* defines how much time is needed to prepare for the experiment and get results. Conducting an A/B test of the landing page will give you results of the experiment much faster than creating two different product prototypes and showing them to potential users.
- *Reliability of results* defines the possible margin of error in the results of your experiments. If you show a hand-drawn mock-up of a product, it won't give the same impression to your potential user as a video demonstrating all of the features and benefits of the product, so there might be a significant difference in customer behavior after interacting with different MVPs.

From my research, it was noted that most startups tend to use high-fidelity and high-coverage MVPs. This results in much higher costs. Experiments take much longer, the learning is slower, and more money is spent. It's normal for many of your initial assumptions to be wrong because they are just guesses. Your main objective is to get on the right track as fast as possible. Therefore your first MVPs should be as fast as possible and as cheap as possible. Using low-fidelity, low-coverage MVPs at the very beginning might be the most reasonable way. Once you have validated some of your assumptions using low-fidelity, low-coverage MVPs, you can move further and employ higher fidelity, higher coverage, and more expensive MVPs.

 Select the type of MVP that fits best for your particular hypothesis

Selecting the right type of MVP depends upon the reason you are creating the MVP. There is still some debate about which type of MVP tends to be high fidelity and low fidelity. I don't see much sense in wasting time on this debate. I firmly believe that the fidelity of the prototype mostly depends on how much effort is needed to make the MVP look as similar as the final product. For instance, you might decide to create a landing page to test if there would be a demand without having a physical product. Normally, it would be considered a low-fidelity prototype because it's just a landing page, not the real product. But, what if you create a landing page for your experiment that looks like your actual sales page in the future when you have the real product? Even though you don't have a product yet, a potential customer will see exactly the same website as they would see when you are really are selling the product. So, should we spend time debating whether it's a low or high fidelity prototype? I don't think so. Categorizing MVP types into low versus high fidelity is always relative to the real product. It's much more important to understand when it's more practical to use low and high fidelity MPV regardless of their label.

Low fidelity prototypes usually are used to:

- Better understand the problem and related issues
- Check how important the problem is for customers
- Get confirmation if the problem is worth solving
- Understand what kind of solution would be most welcomed

High fidelity prototypes help to:

- Determine how much customers are willing to pay for the solution
- Find early adopters and evangelists (passionate and enthusiastic customers who will spread the word about the product)
- Optimize various aspects of marketing strategy (value proposition, call to action, communication channels, etc.)
- Identify most potential viral growth techniques

While choosing the type of MVP for your particular hypothesis verification, you should consider:

- What is the biggest risk you have right now and how you could check it?
- How much time do you have to build this MVP and get results from it?
- How much money do you have at this stage? What amount would be smart to use? Don't plan anything fancy for your first tests!
- What makes the most sense in your case? Which of the hypothesis validation strategies would bring your startup to the next level?

Table 22 shows examples of low fidelity and high fidelity MVPs. Each is explained in detail in the following section.

- *Customer interviews* are designed to collect information about the problem customers have and the solution to the problem you intend to provide. It is recommended that you run unscripted interviews which open the possibility of capturing uninfluenced and maybe even unexpected customer feedback, insights, and suggestions. The interviews should try to explore customer needs rather than sell your product. This can be done by listing the problems you intend to solve and then asking what customers think about them and how they would rank each problem (from the most painful down to not essential). Keep in mind that if you started developing your startup business idea based on assumptions and secondary data, customer interviews should be one of your first choices for problem verification.

Table 22. Types of MVPs

Low fidelity MVP	High fidelity MVP
• Customer interview	• Wireframe
• User story	• Single featured
• Paper prototypes (including a napkin sketch)	• Physical product prototype
• Digital prototypes	• Concierge
• Blogs and forums Explainer video	• Wizard of Oz
• Landing page and A/B testing	• Piecemeal
• Audience building	• Crowdfunding
• Micro survey	
• Ad campaigns	
• Fake doors	

- *A user story* is something more than just describing what your product is and does. It is a short story about a user, what problem he has, how he uses (or will use) your product, and how he captures (or will capture) value from it. A user story usually describes a process or steps taken by a user and captures the value of the product. Products already in the market usually have many user stories, but to create an MVP you can start from a single story and modify it according to your findings. The most important thing is that a user story must end with the value captured by the user. If it is your MVP, you should also employ a testing mechanism (for example, invite users to signup after the user story is told, do a customer interview of the user, or even offer a pre-order). Startups mostly use user stories to identify which features of the product should be built. But practice shows that a user story is a great tool even in later stages when you have to communicate your value proposition and differentiate your product in markets where competition is intense with many alternative products available.

- *Blogs and forums* are a great way for checking your ideas within the target market using minimal efforts. To set up a blog on WordPress or Joomla costs little except for the cost of hosting services. Having your own blog gives you a two-way communication with your potential customers, which might be extremely valuable in the process of creating your high fidelity MVP. Of course, you'll have to figure out how to drive traffic to your blog, but at the same, it's possible to check other hypotheses: what channels are more effective, what aspects of your message drives more attention, is there an interest in your topic at all? If you are in very early stage and wondering about the importance of the problems you intend to solve, you can search for different forums and browse them. You even don't need to create your own blog or forum. Just visit a dozen or so forums and check if there is a topic relevant to the problems you want the address. If yes, check to see what people are talking about. Maybe there are many alternative solutions and your chosen problem is not a problem anymore. In case if you can't find relevant topics, initiate your own in as many forums as possible and wait for the community to respond.

- *An explainer video* is a short video that explains what your product does and why people should buy it. Often it's a simple, 45 - 90 seconds animation. Sometimes it's extended with developer and customer interviews. You can hire a freelancer (Freelancer, UpWork, Fiverr) to create quite a decent video with voice over at price of $200 or even lower. Sometimes it's cheaper to create a video than a website! I don't think that a professional high-end video representing your product can be made for such a low price, but remember, you are just testing now! Once you are ready to launch your product version with customer confirmed features, then you can create fancier and more expensive video, if you think it's necessary. (To see some examples of explainer videos, do a Google search on explainer video.)

- *A landing page* is the main web page where visitors are directed after clicking a link from an ad, e-mail, blog post, or any other another communication channel. The main task of a landing page is to instantly communicate the value of your offering, overcome possible objections, and call visitors to action (usually to submit their contact details, place a pre-order, or even purchase a product). The landing page helps validate your value proposition (product-solution-market fit), sales arguments, pricing of the product, and even to choose most effective communication channels (if you drive traffic to a landing page from different channels, comparing the conversion rate through Google Analytics will let you know which channel brought you the most early adopters). Don't forget that there are other free tools as well. Weelytics is a site that makes it easy to track the moves that customers take on your site without the need for coding skills. If you are just starting, I would recommend OprimizerPress to create your landing page MVPs. This is an inexpensive tool (with no monthly or other recurring fees) that helps to create awesome and highly customizable websites on WordPress in minutes!

- *A/B tests* are used to measure the effect of any changes to your product or marketing. There are many analytical tools which could be used to test how visitors react to various changes on your website, whether it's design, introductory video, value proposition, call to action, pricing, guarantees, testimonials, or other elements. Generally speaking, A/B testing allows you to test two versions of a web page or marketing copy and let visitor interactions determine which one performs best. You are not asking your customer which one they like more, you just measure and make decisions based on metrics, not opinions.

- *Digital prototypes* such as mock-ups, wireframes, and actionable prototypes can be used to demonstrate the product's functionality in a way close to the actual experience and perception. These prototypes can be low-fidelity sketches as well as more complicated interactive applications that a beta user could test and feel the experience as close to using a real product (app, platform, website, etc.). Check Ninjamock—a free online tool to create your mockups, you might find it very helpful and cost effective.

- *Paper prototypes* are quite similar to digital prototypes, except these are physical. You can make a simple sketch on paper or make cut-outs to show your product and help to visualize the user experience. The main advantages are that paper prototypes can be used by almost anyone, requires little time and efforts, can be easily and quickly modified, and need very little explaining or not at all.

- *A physical 3D model* is a more impactful prototype but is also more expensive than a paper one. Usually, 3D models can be printed or molded from several types of plastic and metals. If your startup is building a technical product that has to be manufactured, you might consider creating a 3D model first. There are companies like Optimus 3D that specialize in the production of physical 3D models or even fully functional physical prototypes.

- *Ad campaigns* are a great way to run market validation surveys. Google and Facebook advertising platforms allow you to choose demographics to target your potential customers. Other advertising channels almost always allow targeting based on the interest of potential customers, be it a section in a news portal, niche blog, magazine, newspaper or other media channel. This lets you run a low-fidelity test to see which features or aspects of your product are most appealing to potential customers (if you use different aspects in your message, but on the same channel). In addition, running a survey and driving traffic from different advertising channels gives you the chance to evaluate customer acquisition through those channels and get more in-depth feedback from potential customers through their answers in the survey. As competition in Google, Facebook and some other major advertising platforms are getting fiercer, it's important to understand that these campaigns won't give you great exposure, but will allow testing your hypotheses.

- *"Wizard of Oz"* is an MVP when you put up a front that looks like a real working product, but you manually carry out product functions. This is very efficient if you want to check whether you've got a desirable product or service before you actually build it. Plus you can also identify the pain points of the product or service, possible problems of delivering them, and unexpected customer actions, among other things.

- *Concierge MVP* means that you start with a manual service instead of providing a product. The main thing here is to make the service consist of exactly the same steps people would go through with your product. Usually, the product or service is delivered as a highly customized service to selected customers. During my research, quite a number of startups told me that they didn't have time for the concierge MVP as it required too much time and effort to handle everything manually. But, actually running through the process manually reveals various aspects of the customer experience and provides highly valuable insights in many cases. So instead of using all your resources to build a real product, it might be wise to allocate some time and energy to run this kind of MVP testing to figure out if you are building the product that customers will love and be willing to pay for.

- *Piecemeal MVP* is something between the "Wizard of Oz" and the concierge MVP. You make people go through the process of using your product, but instead of delivering them manually, you create them using existing tools. Why should you invest time and money into building your own infrastructure, when the product can be built or shown using other existing platforms and services? Putting your product image and description on eBay would save you from creating your own website and driving traffic to it. Check to see how much attention (views, clicks, orders) your product gets on such e-commerce platforms and you'll have a good indicator whether it's interesting for anybody!

- *Single featured MVP* tests a single, essential feature of the product. The theory is that, if you can't find a single, super important feature that can stand on its own (at least for early adopters), adding more features won't make your product much more desirable or essential. Using this type of MVP also prevents users from being distracted by other, maybe non-essential features, and makes them pay attention to the essence of the problem or solution. This restriction allows you to test major aspects one by one, gaining a clear understanding of which one of them is most important (which would be much harder to determine if you were running a test with a multi-feature MVP).

- *Crowdfunding MVP* could be described as selling it before you build it. The idea is very simple: launch a crowdfunding campaign on platforms such as Kickstarter, IndieGoGo, RocketHub or any other, and raise money to create a product. For the best effect, you'll need to create a prototype or demo video, and then see the reaction you get. Unlike a normal crowdfunding campaign, you shouldn't do everything in order to drive the interest of backers, because this is just a test to see whether a market for your idea exists naturally. This type of MVP will, first, help you validate if customers want to buy your product or not. Secondly, if you are on the right path, you will also raise money. Thirdly, if your crowdfunding campaign is successful, you will create a passionate group of early adopters and maybe even raving fans who will spread the word about your product.

- *"Fake door"* is an easy way to measure whether your existing customers will be interested in a new product or feature. The main idea of "fake door" is to show the access to a particular feature, benefit, or product when you don't have it yet and to measure how many of your customers would try to access it. For instance, you could put a call to action button on your website, but when a visitor clicks it, they get the message "coming soon." Actually, you even don't need to have a website to employ "fake door" MVP. It also works well if you've got a large social media audience: share the news about the product or feature on your networks using customized links and track the click-through rate. You'll easily find out how many of your followers would be interested in trying, buying, or signing up. If the conversion rate is good enough, you have a clear verification to build the real product or feature. But, a word of caution about using this type of MVP: don't get your existing customers too confused or frustrated. You should always explain and be honest with them.

- *Audience building* is a simple idea. Before creating a product, build a virtual community (tied to the problem you intend to solve or even to your end product). If you can create such community using low-cost or even free methods (Facebook or Linkedin groups, newsletter, blog, etc.) it would be an indicator that there is a group of people interested in the topic and, you would already have a list of potential customers, once you create a higher fidelity MVP or even the product itself. Creating such group is not just a one-time test because you'll be able to run surveys, in-depth interviews, and experiments within the community to make your product more valuable to customers. As for instance, I've created a Startup Evolution Curve group on Linkedin while writing this book. There I share valuable advice and experience, useful articles and templates. Even though it was not a big community (a bit more than one thousand members), it helped me a lot with my global research on startups. Most of the group members were startup founders and they helped me to better understand their problems and interests related to startup development.

- *Micro-survey* is just one or two questions long, thus it has better response rate, is more reliable, and can be precisely targeted to the specific customer situation. For example, if you have a website, you can use a pop-up with a single question when the visitors performs an action (signs up for a free trial, downloads free material, or visits the pricing page). To answer a single question in the pop-up window doesn't require much effort from the visitor, especially if the answer is yes or no. Once the answer is submitted, you can ask one more question and it may be an open-ended. Always consider making your micro-survey questions specific but open-ended in case if you want to get more insights and more feedback. In addition to pop-ups, you can also deliver your micro-surveys via email.

The goal of Brazilian startup Futstat is to register the achievements of amateur and professional athletes and teams and help them to share their story with others. All athletes (professionals and amateurs alike) are proud of their accomplishments and would love to save their records, but none of them actually have their own detailed history nor a convenient way to share it. Futstat decided to offer these athletes a tool to monitor the evolution of their performances throughout their career, compare their performance with other athletes, and see their position relative to the ranking of other athletes and high-performance teams. But the value of such a product was just an assumption and the founders of Futstat needed to determine if their idea is viable, if it really is a meaningful problem, and if it is possible to build a business around it.

Because this startup was totally bootstrapped, their idea had to be checked in a fast and inexpensive way. Before the founder started to run conduct potential customer interviews about the idea behind Futstat, he spent two weeks designing a simple yet functional website to help potential customers to see what he was talking about. The example data was taken from a real professional competition in Brazil, Liga Nacional of Futsal (LNF), and in-depth interviews held with both amateur athletes and professional players and their managers. This helped Futstat to validate the idea. After the initial interviews, Futstat started to receive a lot of good feedback from professional players, and many of them started to follow Futstat posts and share the analysis in their networks. Many kept coming back to the website to check out the news and see how their teams were doing in the current competition. Futstat got their initial validation and I sincerely hope they have enough perseverance to build and develop this project to full scale.

 Decide on what features must be included in your MVP

Don't overload your MVP with unnecessary features and details. That's the main rule to follow. You are seeking validated learning. Therefore, run planned experiments with MVPs as close to the real product as possible, yet make them easy and inexpensive to build.

You shouldn't evaluate your product based on the features it has because most customers won't do that, either. You should assess if this product solves a particular problem for your targeted customers. Identify the main features necessary to solve the problem. Start your first MVPs including only most important features which are directly related to the problem and solution. Later you can add other features and benefits if you have the essential idea already confirmed. Remember, time is important! The simpler and easier your MVPs are to create, the more experiments you'll be able to run, and the more validated knowledge you'll gain. That's the main purpose at this stage of your startup.

 Create MVP or prototype on budget

Creating your MVP or prototype on a budget depends on your budget and skills. The more you can do by yourself, the less money you'll have to spend. To create your MVP on a budget, consider hiring freelancers instead of establishing an additional workplace for a new employee or even doing everything on your own. There are many platforms where you can find skilled freelancers (Freelancer, UpWork, Fiverr) to help you in creating a professional MVP very quickly and at an acceptable price range. But creating an MVP is not the only task at this stage. You should also:

- create the MVP
- foresee how potential customers will engage it
- set up analytical instruments to measure indicators important for your hypothesis verification
- set up a feedback system with customers to get additional insights and suggestions from them (live interview, online chat, survey, etc.).

Additionally, you could think about employing various online tools if you find them useful in your case. Here are just a few examples (you can find more advice on such tools by joining the Startup Evolution Curve group on Linkedin or visiting www.evolutioncurve.com):

- QuickMVP is a one-stop shop, enabling you to record and analyze your customer interviews, build and test landing pages, and calculate metrics such as market size and profit margin.
- Five Second Test helps you gather first impressions of your landing page, brochure, logo, marketing material, or home page.
- Google Forms is a free tool for online surveys. It allows you to collect a huge amount of data absolutely free of charge, unlike most other online survey platforms which limit you in one way or another.

 Plan and run the experiment to collect required data

1. *Declare expected outcomes of the experiment.* If you have completed the experiment card, this job should be already done. You should clearly know the goal of your experiment, how you'll measure results, and what criteria are being verified for each hypothesis.

2. *Clearly defined time or conditions for how long you will be running the experiment.* Decide how long you will run the experiment (for example, until you conduct 50 customer interviews, drive 500 targeted visitors to your landing page, or get the first 100 people to sign up). It's up to you to decide. In any case, it's very important to set a maximum time limit for how long you will run the experiment. It might be that you'll never get 100 people to sign up if your value proposition or call to action is terrible. So there is no sense waiting for miracles! If you don't get your expected result in a set time frame, change something and run another experiment!

3. *Seek realistic results instead of chasing precision.* You need to accept the fact that you will probably never have all needed information you really need with perfect precision. But you'll need to make a decision in any case. So it's better to seek to measure results that would reflect a realistic situation.

4. *Measure actions, not words or opinions.* As we have already discussed in the section on the Most dangerous mistakes in startup marketing, saying is not the same as paying. This rule applies to any other action you want a potential customer to make. So don't just ask "if you'd like to sign up to get product updates." Instead, create a signup form, drive traffic to it, and check to see if people are really signing up.

5. *Always have a control group.* This is probably one of the most important rules to run effective experiments. If you don't have a control group (unaffected by your experiment), you'll never be sure if your experiment results are valuable. You can only draw justified conclusions when you have a control group and their results are different from the experiment group.

Make decision: pivot or proceed

After a series of experiments (or sometimes even after a single experiment) you must make a decision: pivot or proceed. By completing the experiment card, you have you already planned in advance your next actions for both scenarios if the hypothesis is verified or rejected. Although it might look like the decision is crystal clear, it's not always so simple. Sometimes experiments can give uncertain results. If this happens, the most reasonable solution would be to run a revised experiment which could give more clear results. If you face some uncertain situations such as this, you should:

- focus on the indicators that really matter (check Viral loop and key metrics if needed)
- review all key findings and data gathered through experiments
- update your business model according to the findings and check if it is viable.

Recommended reading

1. Eric Ries. *The Lean Startup: How Today's Entrepreneurs Use Continuous Innovation to Create Radically Successful Businesses*

2. Steve Blank, Bob Dorf. *The Startup Owner's Manual: The Step-by-Step Guide for Building a Great Company*

3. Dan Olsen. *The Lean Product Playbook: How to Innovate with Minimum Viable Products and Rapid Customer Feedback*

10. Validating problem-solution-market fit

WHY IT IS NEEDED

Validating the problem-solutions-market fit is a must for each startup, unless, of course, you want to play the lottery instead of building a business. The lottery attitude means you are creating a product according to your assumptions first and then try you are going to try to sell it. You might succeed, but the chances are higher that you won't. Actually, in-depth interview in 2016 showed that 98.5% of startups currently in the market had to modify their product or service, to redefine their target customer, to find new ways of using their product, or to change the pricing strategy. This data shows the main reasons why most startups fail: they build products nobody wants to buy. This chapter shows you how to avoid such mistakes and minimize your risks.

How would you feel about creating your startup business if you already knew that customers are ready to pay a particular price for your proposed solution (product or service)? Validating three essential startup business hypotheses is all you have to do to achieve this and this chapter explains how to do it.

HOW TO DO IT

01 Validate the Problem
Confirm if the problem you are trying to solve is serious enough for your customers

02 Validate the Solution
Confirm if you intend to deliver a much better solution than current alternatives

03 Validate the Price
Confirm if customers will gladly pay the price you want to ask for your proposed solution

04 Validate the Target Segment
Know who your ideal client is and if there is a significant market worth your effort

05 Update Your Business Model
Review your business model and make needed changes according to your findings

Validate the problem you intend to solve.

You should have already created an experiment card for the problem hypothesis. If you haven't yet, now is a good time to do that before we proceed any further. The main goal here is to understand the severity of the problem you intend to solve compared to the value of your solution. The most dangerous trap the startup can fall into is creating a product nobody wants. This almost inevitably will happen if you decide to solve a problem which is not causing anyone a severe headache. You will end up delivering just "nice to have" value instead of proposing something your target customers have been dreaming about or maybe even something they didn't dare to dream!

Formulate the hypothesis about the problem you plan to solve and complete the experiment card. I would recommend that you use low fidelity MVPs which are fast and cheap, to understand how serious the customer reviews the problem. Later, if you think it is necessary, you could double check the problem hypothesis with more advanced MVPs.

Steve Blank and Bob Dorf suggested a very sophisticated scorecard including seven criteria that help to determine if your chosen problem is worth solving. As for early stage startups, I would say it's a great achievement if you can assess your chosen problem according to four main criteria (Table 23). Let your target customer rank each criterion from 1 to 5 (or 1 to 10) and explain how painful and urgent the problem is and how likely they would pay to have better/best solution. Assess if they are decision makers or at least influencers regarding purchasing the solution.

Table 23. Segment-problem validation scorecard

Customer segment	How painful is the problem?	How urgent is the need for a solution?	Would they pay for a better solution?	Are they decision makers?	Total
A	3	2	2	4	2.75
B	4	1	4	3	3.00
C	3	4	5	1	**3.25**
Average	3.33	2.33	3.66	2.66	

Always compare how many potential customers declared the problem as "very important" as opposed to those who said it is "somewhat important." You should target those to whom the problem is very important and don't expect to earn much profit from the others. Yes, you'll probably learn something from the others, but they won't become the foundation of your business.

What is the right percentage to indicate that the problem is very significant? Well, that depends on your segmentation and potential market size. You should basically reassess your market size according to the results of your experiment. For instance, if 20% of your interviewed potential customers indicated that it is a very important and urgent problem, it means you should reduce your defined target market from 100% to 20%. Let's say you did a feasibility study and estimated that the size of your target segment is 100,000 potential customers. So if the experiment showed that only 20% take this problem very seriously, your target market size is just 20,000 potential customers. Regardless of the percentage, you should answer by estimating how many of them you could sell your product to and at what price. These are your next steps.

Patricia O'Sullivan, the founder of AutoPixie, shared how she validated the problem, once she figured out three top pain points of auto mechanics: *"The process I need to automate is complex with multiple paths through the tasks, so I iterated through 26 prototypes built in PowerPoint with Keynotopia. I kept revising and going back to about a dozen of the most clued-up people in the market until they told me I'd got it right. Then I walked into three auto shops, told them the product would cost $30,000 to build (I was very wrong in that assumption) and that I would put up $15,000 and go full-time at it if three people in the market would match me with $5,000 each. The first three I asked did and I was shocked because there are very small local businesses, did not know me, and I had nothing but an idea. But that validated for me that this pain was worth solving and that people would pay for it."* Today, *AutoPixie* has already been awarded €20,000 in government grants, has signed a contract for a small government investment, got shortlisted on being accepted onto one of the world's top accelerators, and even has a Silicon Valley angel syndicate prepared to invest $500,000 at the end of the accelerator program.

 Validate the solution you intend to propose for the validated problem.

Quite often customers are solving their problems with home-made solutions. This at least shows that the particular problem is worth solving. The question is whether or not you can you deliver a much better solution. If you have validated the problem hypothesis, now it's time to see if you can deliver a solution customers will adore.

Complete the experiment card for the solution hypothesis. The type of MVPs most suitable for this hypothesis strongly depends on the specifics of your product or service. When you use higher fidelity MVPs, you can expect more reliable results. You will get more accurate data from your experiment if the customer has a positive feeling about how your product or service looks, the benefits they receive, and their overall experience. It's up to you to determine the solution validation rules, but most of the startups I surveyed used rules similar to the following:

- More than 50% of customers would like to try our product and signed up to become beta users

- More than 50% of customers who tried our product would recommend it to their friends
- At least 40% of customers consider the product or service as "must have"
- At least 40% of customers indicate that they would be "very disappointed" if they no longer have access to a particular product or service.

Artizan Fine Foods (brand name Arte&Vita) was born out of an idea to offer gluten-free, vegan, and dairy-free healthy baked snacks and bread-type products which are delicious and very scarce in the marketplace. In order to verify the concept of the product, they've created a retail packaging for each of three flavors of pita crisps along with a smaller snack size for the airline industry. The founders didn't invest in large scale manufacturing, they just prepared product samples, stuffed them in the branded packaging, and sent them to prospective food retailers, distributors, the media, and others to create interest. The solution was confirmed by sufficient inter-est by potential clients.

Validate the price of the solution you intend to deliver.

It's good to have the solution hypothesis verified, but it's still not enough. You want to earn a profit, therefore, you be absolutely certain that your product will solve a cus-tomer's problem or fill a need at a price they will gladly pay. Many traditional business owners think there are only two possible solutions:

1. Survey target customers to know how valuable the product would be for them
2. Produce a pilot batch of products and try to sell them at a different price

Startups might consider these solutions, but it's important to remember that the customer does not always know how valuable the product is until they try it. Therefore, customer surveys could be good just for the initial phase of formulating your market fit (or, simply, price) hypothesis. Survey results can only lead to some assumptions, but not to the actual facts. Producing pilot batch of products might be quite expensive, especially if you don't have any initial confirmation about the possible price level.

So what to do? Review the different types of high fidelity MVPs described in the chapter on Creating MVPs: purposes and types. Choose the most acceptable MVP type for you (evaluate the costs of the experiment and how reliable the results will be) and proceed with the experiment. Always try to sell, even if you are just doing an initial market research. This will allow you to make a list of potential clients (early adopters-evangelists) which will be very helpful once you have a product ready for sale and will need to get your first clients' testimonials.

As an example, let's take two physical products that used different ways to test the price: one of them produced a product and gave it away for free trial, while the other decided to collect funds from customers in advance and only then create a final product.

Brushee is a pocket sized disposable toothbrush that has everything: the toothpaste in the bristles, pick inside, and floss at the other end. Ian Rollin Berry, the founder of *Brushee*, decided to test the price by running a product sample give away and then sending special offers to test the price. This decision allowed Ian to collect a database of potential customers and then deliver them a real life experience with the product. The price was put to the test only when potential customers already had the real impression about the convenience using the Brushee (they received special offers to purchase a 3-pack or 36-pack at different price levels after the free give away).

Figure 23. Concept and packaging of Brushee

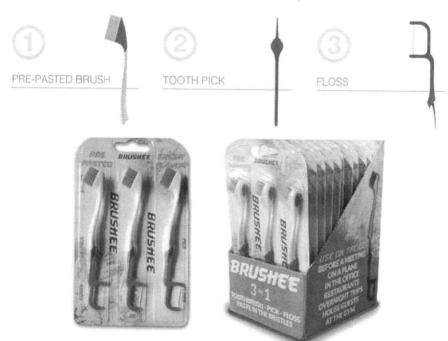

Brushee also took advantage of Amazon's Launchpad platform for startups and it proved to be one of the best decisions for the company. It allowed them to not only start receiving sales very quickly after they got the initial price validation, but also to get in front of millions of consumers without any investment, while simultaneously allowing retailers to see the proof of concept through live Amazon reviews and sales. This decision combined price testing with an effective market entry strategy. Brushee started price testing by sending initial offers to nearly 1,000 subscribed testers, and now they get more than 100,000 views on Amazon every month and are in negotiation with some major retailers overseas.

During my global research on startups, I met the Aamar Khwaja, the founder of *Modgarden*, a smart system that allows growing vegetables and herbs in the living room all year round (Figure 24). They didn't have a product yet (just visual mockups) and they were still working on a prototype. After evaluating manufacturing costs, minimal profit margin, and customer perceived value, *Modgarden* made an assumption that their standard unit should be priced around $450. But that was just an assumption that needed to be tested under real market conditions. Unlike a toothbrush, it's an advanced and expensive product, so producing even a trial batch first and expecting to sell it at the desired price would hardly be justifiable. Even a small trial batch would require hundreds of thousands of dollars to produce without any guarantee of a return. Aamar estimated that selling 2,000 units during the initial launch at a price of $450 would cover all of the manufacturing costs and would leave some funds for further development of the product. Therefore, he decided to run a market test on Kickstarter under the assumption that if he was successful there, (2,000 x $450 = $900,000), it would be a sufficient market fit validation. Knowing that crowdfunding platforms don't ensure visibility of any campaign, *Modgarden* set sub-goal of collecting at least 400,000 target customer emails before launching the crowdfunding campaign (Chapter 32: Marginal users & magnets to get them explains how to do it). If at least 0,5% of those target customers would buy a *Modgarden* unit during crowdfunding campaign, Aamar would not only validate his price but also would reach his go-to-market campaign goal. Not a bad approach to validating the price.

Figure 24. Modgarden smart growing system visual mockup

One of the cheapest and most effective experiments is to try and sell your product online even if you don't have a product yet! Create a website, upload design mockups of your product to eBay or any other platform, create a Kickstarter campaign, drive traffic to this offer, and check how many visitors will add your product to the cart. Once they click to "add to cart" or "buy now," you can politely make an excuse and explain that product is currently unavailable. You could even suggest potential customers leave their email address if they would like to be notified once the product is available. But the most important thing is that you will find out the number of people who were ready to buy your product, and these are facts, not assumptions!

These are just a few examples. You should choose the type of MVP which would be best in your individual situation. After finishing the market fit experiment, you should complete the experiment result card as usual and review your results:

- Did your MVP generate significant engagement and intentions to buy?
- Did customers who tried your offer recommended it to their friends? What was the engagement rate of those referred customers?
- What feedback did you get from customers after showing the offer and your long term product development vision? Are they willing to pre-order your product and wait for it?
- Is your business model still profitable after verifying the price and the rate of intention to buy?

It's quite easy to determine whether they are highly positive or highly negative when you get clear answers from your experiments. But what do you do if your results fall into the "gray zone." Let's say only 10% or less of your target customers confirmed that your offer is good. What should you do? Generally, there are three possible ways to proceed:

1. Find out who the 10% of your customers are. Maybe only a small portion of your real target customers participated your experiment? If so, find out what the real market potential is and determine if it would be sufficient for you.
2. Change the target segment. Maybe your initial assumptions about your target customers were wrong. Check to see if there might be additional customer segments and repeat the experiment on different segments.
3. Modify the offer (your value proposition). This includes not only experimenting with setting different price levels, but also adding extra value and removing non-essential value from your main offer.

Mark Joyner in his book *The Irresistible Offer: How to sell Your Product or Service in 3 Seconds or Less* (2005) suggested a great approach for assessing the attractiveness of your offer. If you find yourself in a situation where you have to update your core value proposition, it might be helpful to use this approach. I've slightly upgraded it to be more suitable for startups in the market fit verification stage (see Table 24). Evaluate each of those seven touchstones of your offer and decide what you could improve. If it's realistic, proceed with modifying your offer and get ready to repeat the market fit experiment.

Table 24. Offer attractiveness assessment

How good is the offer	Evaluation 1 - 10	Possible to improve
How obvious is the problem your offer solves?	1 .... 10 (unclear) (totally obvious)	
How important is the need your offer satisfies?	1 .... 10 (no need) (vitally important)	
How common is a solution to the problem?	1 .... 10 (get anywhere) (get only here)	
Can you show the return on investment for the customer?	1 .... 10 (can't at all) (quite easily)	
How emotional is the offer? How appealing is it?	1 .... 10 (stone heart) (soul touching)	
How timely is the offer? Was it shown at the right time?	1 .... 10 (don't need it) (need it now)	
How good is your offer compared to competitors?	1 .... 10 (we are losers) (we are best)	

 Validate the target segments with the most potential

We have already discussed what you should know about your ideal target customer (see Chapter 3: Segmentation and potential market size). Before starting your problem-solution-market fit experiments, you should have already created your target customer archetype (the template can be downloaded from www.EvolutionCurve.com). A customer archetype combines everything you know about your "most typical" customers into either one or a few complete profiles. Remember, you are looking for ideal customers who:

- Not only have a problem but are aware of having it
- Have been actively searching for a solution
- Are using some kind "home-made" solution
- Have or are able to acquire a budget to buy a solution

In this step, you are trying to determine if there are enough customers to create a sizable business opportunity. You should define the number of customers and the size of the potential business (possible sales volume and profit) in advance and compare these numbers with your factual findings through experiments. It might be as simple as identifying how many potential customers showed the initiative to buy or pre-order your product during market fit verification. To determine if there are enough customers to create a sizable business opportunity, be sure you can answer these top 10 questions:

1. Is there a market? Is the problem or need highly important to a large number of people? Is this number lower or higher than you expected,?

2. Is the market growing significantly with strong growth potential? If not, then maybe the market size is static or even decreasing? You definitely don't want to bet all of your success on a market that is decreasing.

3. Do you have proof from your experiments that customers will buy repeatedly and refer others to do the same?

4. Did some segments respond better, faster, or with larger orders than others? Did any new segments emerge, or should any be eliminated?

5. Can you describe a day in the life of a typical customer so you know how to pitch your product better?

6. How much do you know about your customers in terms of what they read, trade shows they attend, celebrities they follow, and where they look for new product information?

7. Who are your competitors? Which of them has emerged unexpectedly?

8. How is your offer better and unique compared to all alternatives in the market?

9. Can you draw a sales pipeline or funnel, showing how customers are acquired?

10. What are your expected marketing costs and what tasks need to be completed to reach your target customers?

Based on your findings you should update your target customer archetypes. Initially, you were able to create customer archetypes based on statistics about customers' demographics and behavior, using insights based on Google Trends, Google Insights, scientific and industry reports, studies, news, discussions on Facebook and other social network groups, and maybe even researching your competitors' customers. While conducting your experiments, try to find an opportunity to interview people who are similar to your potential customers so you can understand who they are, what they do, what they want, and how they behave. It's very important to continue to update your customer archetype as you learn more over time. This will have a great payback as you'll be able to implement more effective marketing tactics to reach your customers and sell them your product.

Update your business model according to findings

If you found that you should target a different customer segment, you should update that in your Business Model Canvas. Another important update is related to experiment results that end up changing your initial assumptions. You should replace your previous assumptions in your business model with any newly discovered facts. Usually, after finalizing the problem-solution-market fit, the business model might have some major changes:

- You might have found and validated customers' new problems and product features that would lead to you updating your value proposition.

- If you found the minimum feature set that resonates with customers, it might influence not only the value proposition, but other parts of your business model (for example, cost structure, strategic partnerships, jobs, and activities).

- If you learned facts that changed how you define your target customers, it's obvious that you should review customer segments, the value proposition, sales channels, and the ways you will create a relationship with customers.

- Furthermore, target customer validation should lead you to insights about average order size, customer lifetime value, sales closing rate, profit margin, and others. Review your business model and update it according to your findings.

 Recommended reading

1. Ash Maurya. *Running Lean: Iterate from Plan A to a Plan That Works.*
2. Eric Ries. *The Lean Startup: How Today's Entrepreneurs Use Continuous Innovation to Create Radically Successful Businesses*
3. Steve Blank, Bob Dorf. *The Startup Owner's Manual: The Step-by-Step Guide for Building a Great Company*
4. Dan Olsen. *The Lean Product Playbook: How to Innovate with Minimum Viable Products and Rapid Customer Feedback*

11. Create a strong positioning statement

WHY IT IS NEEDED

A positioning statement is a short description of your target customers and a clear picture of how you want those customers to perceive you. Though it may sound like a promotional statement, this is actually an internal tool. Every decision you make related to your startup development has to be aligned and integrated with your positioning statement. An effective positioning statement is a very powerful guideline for your whole marketing activity and helps to maintain focus on the essence of who your customers are and why they should buy from you. Customers don't care about your startup as much as you do. You need to be able to answer the question from them, "Why should I buy from you?" If you can't answer the question, how do you expect customers to be able to figure it out on their own?

Positioning is the very core of your marketing strategy. If you don't have a clear positioning statement, it means you have no real marketing strategy!

HOW TO DO IT

01 — **Define the Target Segment**
Focus only on the main group of customers if you want to succeed in positioning

02 — **Find Differentiation Point**
Describe how differently you deliver value to customers compared to your competitors

03 — **Provide the Proof**
Provide the proof and clear reasons why customers should believe in you

04 — **Craft the Positioning Statement**
Create one sentence to explain the value you bring to your target customers

05 — **Create positioning slogan**
Put the very essence into few words that will go everywhere together with your brand

Define the group of target customers and the main competitors who serve them

The good news is that you've already made the first step towards effective positioning: you have already defined and verified your target customer. If you validated a few different customer groups, you should create separate positioning statements for each of them. Start by identifying your main target customer group and focus on them. Later on, you can develop additional positioning statements for your secondary targets.

It's always a good idea to compare yourself to your main competitors before crafting a positioning statement. Experience shows that comparing the value you deliver to customers versus your competitors might influence how much effort you need to put into marketing (Figure 25 and 26). A competition map helps objectively identify your main competitors and helps you foresee how any competitive situation will develop. For instance, if a competitor is delivering great value and puts a lot of effort in marketing, he'll probably increase his market share in the long run. On the contrary, if even the market leader is underserving his customers (delivers low value compared to price and alternative solutions in the market) and his marketing activity doesn't show many initiatives, he'll most likely lose his market leading position.

Figure 25. Competition map based on average price, delivered value, and marketing

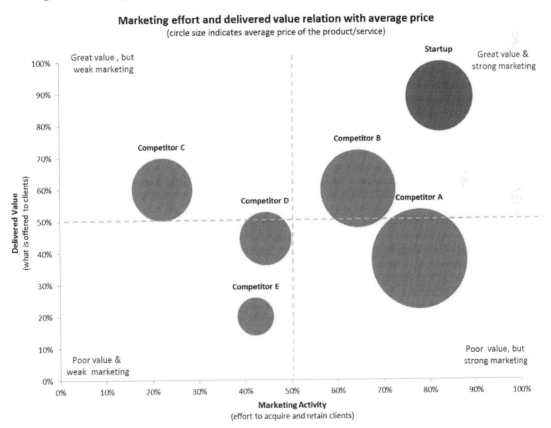

If you'd like to create similar competition maps for your business, download a set of templates at www.evolutioncurve.com and you will find this spreadsheet with instructions on how to use it.

Figure 26. Competition map based on revenue, delivered value, and marketing activity

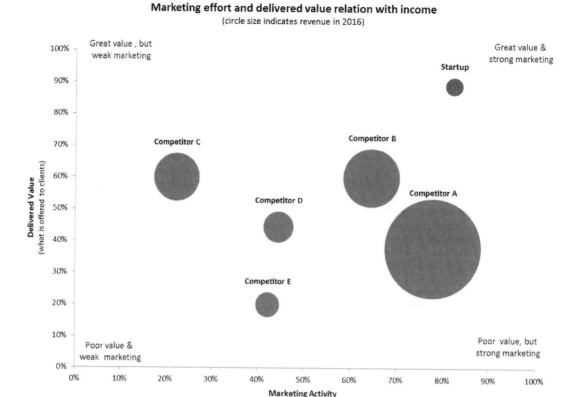

Marketing effort and delivered value relation with income
(circle size indicates revenue in 2016)

 Find your differentiation point that is important for your target customers

You can develop your positioning strategy in a variety of ways, but the main thing is to find the point of differentiation that is meaningful for your target customers. The point of differentiation usually describes how your brand delivers benefits to customers in ways that set you apart from your competitors. A positioning statement can be built on one or more of the following elements:

1. *Customer benefits*. I always recommend placing the customer benefits aspect in the beginning of the positioning statement because customers are looking first to see what's in it for them. If you can tell customers about the unique and valuable benefit they can get only from you, that would be a very appealing point of differentiation. Furthermore, startups focus their business on solving customer problems and creating gain for them. Thus, if you already have problem-solution-market fit, include it when you craft your point of differentiation.

- **CliClap** - *"Add your Call to Action to any Content"*
- **Clubio** – "DJ booking platform"
- **Chef Koochooloo** – *"Teaching kids math, science, and geography through cooking"*

2. *Product characteristics*. This strategy basically focuses on the product character-istics, and in most cases, it is not as effective as focusing on benefits. For most startups, it seems like it would be relatively easy to create, but in fact, it is difficult to differentiate your product unless it has such innovative and unique character-istics that can't be copied by competitors. If your product characteristics are not that innovative or unique, you'll end up communicating characteristics that can be delivered by your competitors as well. It obviously makes no sense to write a positioning statement that helps your competitors.

   - ***Duracell Batteries*** – *"No battery is stronger longer"* indicates that the battery is the leading product in its product class for durability.
   - ***Brushee*** - *"A Disposable Toothbrush with 3 in 1 Convenience."* It explains that Brushee has toothpaste in the bristles, a toothpick, and floss.

3. *Pricing*. This is a common (but not always effective) positioning approach that compares different aspects of quality and price. In many product categories, there are brands that deliberately try to offer more in terms of service, features, or performance. They charge more, partly to cover higher costs and partly to let the consumers believe that the product is of higher quality. Undoubtedly there is an opposite positioning possibility which focuses on a low cost-low price strat-egy. But such a decision is very dangerous unless you are the cost leader and have a strategy to maintain the lowest costs in the industry.

4. *Use, application, or packaging*. Basically, this type of positioning is used for the second or third level position for the brand in order to expand the brand's mar-ket. As an example, a gift packaging service can transform any product or service into a gift, therefore you might sometimes be selling your product as gift solution. Positioning all features of an application or its use is often used for introducing the product to new segments in the same market or when entering absolutely new markets. Basically, it says that product can be used in different ways, for dif-ferent purposes, or maybe on specific occasions.

5. *Product class*. Positioning by product class sometimes consists of promoting two products that lie in the same product class. By promoting two related products simultaneously, the positioning of both is improved. This type of positioning can be quite effective because a business gains more consumer exposure by offering a product that works with, or has a relation to, the initial product that customers may already know and trust. You don't need to have two products of your own if

you wish to use this type of positioning approach. Often, especially in the innovative startup business, the competition for a particular product comes from outside the product class. Thus you can choose to compare your product or service with a totally different category, but one that is well known as a main current solution or has such attributes which can help explain your positioning message instantly.

- **UNLOQ Systems** – "Passwordless security" offers organizations the ability to increase their cybersecurity by using multifactor authentication and eliminating passwords, the weakest link.

6. *Cultural symbols*. In today's world, many advertisers are using well recognizable cultural symbols to differentiate their brands from competitors. The essential task is to identify something that is very meaningful to your target customers that your competitors are not yet using and associate this symbol with your brand.

- **AirView** – "*Uber for drones*" started with this positioning slogan which instantly explained the main value proposition, which is the option to request drones on demand.

- **PropShelf** - "*Bloomberg for real estate in India*" is a data-driven platform with a database of more than 50,000 brokers and 1.2 million secondary real estate market listings across various cities in India.

7. *Customers*. Positioning could be built associating the product with a particular user or group of users. Usually, this is a simple and easy-to-understand statement: if you are a similar person, the product is right for you. But this type of positioning lacks reasoning as to why the customer actually should choose the product. Therefore, this type of positioning is often strengthened by combining it with additional aspects of positioning to add more weight to the purchase decision.

- **Arbunize** – "*for professionals who want to control their personal brand and become more successful.*" This is a platform where everybody can create their professionally designed resumes including infographics, videos, endorsements, and much more. The solution is truly outstanding compared to standard resumes, therefore Arbunize appeals to professionals for whom having a great resume is highly important.

- **TheNextOffer** – "for freshers to become professional" is another startup related to the employment industry, but it targets graduates who are searching for their first job.

- **AxBizz** – "CRO tool for marketers and conversion rate experts." Because of the CRO abbreviation, not everyone might understand what this company offers, but that might be okay because they have developed a conversion rate technical analysis and optimization tool for online marketers. If someone doesn't understand what CRO means, that person probably doesn't need what AzBizz provides.

8. *Competitors*. This type of positioning strategy refers to the relationship of your product or service with one or more of your competitors. In some cases, the competitor can be the dominant aspect of the positioning strategy of the startup, especially if your startup solves the same problem or satisfies the same need which has been abandoned by the well-known market leader (your competitor). Thought it might be highly effective, you should be very cautious about choosing this aspect of positioning. Some countries have strict regulations for using the competitors' name in your marketing means and running comparative advertising. Comparing yourself with competitors may cause you another pitfall: some of your target customers might choose the competitor instead of you, just because you named the alternative solution in your positioning message or advertising. So, the competitor will say thank you!

- **Avis** – *"We try harder"* targets the market leader (Hertz), by implying that they are lazy and complacent, particularly in the area of customer service.

- **Apple Computer** – *"Everything is easier on a Mac"* is targeting IBM style computers, highlighting that the Mac is much simpler and easier to use.

What makes your startup brand stand apart from all other alternatives (including indirect competitors)? Think about the services your company offers of which you are most proud and confident. If it provides a meaningful value for your target customers, that might be a good start for developing your point of differentiation.

 Provide proof as to why they should trust you.

It's not enough to find your point of differentiation, you must prove it! How can you back up your positioning statement with proof? What is the main reason the customer should believe you? This could mean anything from showing your process and sharing data statements to providing a risk-free guarantee to prove that your statement and proposition is genuine.

Make a list of at least three strong reasons to believe in you. Which of those reasons are:

- Shortest and easiest to understand?
- Strongest and prove your credibility best?
- Most sustainable and hardest to copy by competitors?
- Simplest to integrate into your positioning statement?

⚠ Craft your positioning statement in one sentence

Here is the formula for writing an effective positioning statement:

For [insert target customer], the [insert your startup Brand] is the [insert point of differentiation] among all [insert frame of reference or competitors] because [insert reason to believe].

The wording of your positioning statement doesn't have to match this template exactly. But if you want your positioning to be effective, it must contain all five of the components in brackets. Your positioning statement should be written for the average reader. Pretend that you are going to meet a potential customer in the elevator and he asks what business you are in. Your positioning statement should be short, easy to understand, and memorable.

Write down at least few different versions of your positioning statement. Review and update them. Share the draft versions with your colleagues and clients. Find the one which resonates with your target customers the most. To create an effective positioning statement might be a tough challenge, but don't give up. Visit www.evolutioncurve.com/templates and download a worksheet to help you create an effective positioning statement for your startup. Strong positioning statement will save you a lot of work, time, and marketing budget in the future.

CliClap is a content engagement platform providing B2B SMEs with the most advanced and cost effective solution for growing their business through content marketing. We do so by empowering businesses to seamlessly track, engage, and convert leads from ANY content they share, even when sharing third party content.

Just to be clear about what exactly *CliClap* does, it allows you to:

- easily add your own call-to-action to any content you share, even third party content
- customize your call-to-action with your brand name, logo, and colors
- link to your own content or even to your product's landing pages
- do all of this absolutely FREE

As we see in Table 25, *CliClap's* positioning statement has all the components. Yes, we could argue about how to make the point of differentiation and the reason to believe simpler, shorter and more direct, but generally, this positioning statement serves as a great guidance for internal use and the whole marketing strategy.

Table 25. Components of the CliClap positioning statement

Target customer	B2B SMEs, that stands for business-to-business, small and medium enterprises
Startup brand	CliClap
Point of differentiation	most advanced and cost-effective solution for growing their business through content marketing
Frame of reference or competitors	content engagement platform
Reason to believe	by empowering businesses to seamlessly track, engage, and convert leads from ANY content they share, even when sharing third party content

 Create your positioning slogan

A positioning slogan is the very essence of your brand promise stated in two or three words and reinforcing your brand logo. It might not explain the whole positioning idea at once, but should help potential customers to understand what your product is about, what value they could get, and why should they buy from you.

Here is a handy checklist for creating a positioning slogan (you can download this Excel worksheet at www.evolutioncurve.com/templates):

1. Does it differentiate your brand from competitors and other alternatives?

2. Is it focused on your main target customers?

3. Does it identify your brand's unique value to your customers?

4. Is your brand promise believable and credible?

5. Is it easy to understand and remember?

6. Is it consistent in all areas of your business?

7. Is it hard to copy? Can only your brand own it?

8. Is it positioned for long-term success and leaves potential for growth?

9. Will it withstand counterattacks from your competitors?

10. Will it help you to make marketing more effective?

The easiest test to evaluate your positioning slogan is to substitute another brand name in your slogan. If you can do this without losing or gaining much, the slogan is worth absolutely nothing. And, you don't need a worthless slogan, that's for sure! If, for example, CliClap would have chosen *"the most cost-effective way to drive traffic to your site,"* that would be a worthless slogan, because the same could be used by anybody else who drives traffic at low or no cost at all. It wouldn't matter if it was an online advertising agency, a PR agency, a link exchange system, or whatever:

- *"**CliClap**—the most cost-effective way to drive traffic to your site"*
- *"**X advertising agency**—the most cost-effective way to drive traffic to your site"*
- *"**X PR agency**—the most cost-effective way to drive traffic to your site"*
- *"**X link exchange platform**—the most cost-effective way to drive traffic to your site"*

Branding is about putting the brand in the consumer's mind along with its main point of differentiation. If the positioning slogan doesn't reveal the difference in a specific way, most of your marketing budget and efforts will be wasted.

Once you come up with few possible slogans, show them to potential customers or at least your friends and listen to their opinion. The main validation rule here is to check if other people quickly grasp the right impression about how your startup is different and why or in what circumstances they should choose you.

I didn't ask Arie and Yonatan for their official and public positioning statement. If it exists, potential customers can clearly see it without asking. Actually, I visited their website and found three statements that could claim to be positioning statements:

- *"Turn your curated content and earned media into leads and opportunities with the click of a button!"*
- *"Add your Call to Action to any Content"*
- *"The most cost-effective way to drive traffic to your site."*

The good thing is that the *CliClap* guys think from a customer perspective and try to communicate what benefits their customers will receive. The problem is that there is not one strong and consistent positioning statement that would have a high score based on the criteria we have discussed. Evaluating each of those potential positioning slogans and putting a score by each criterion (Table 26), it becomes obvious how good each of those statements is (the maximum evaluation total score is 100%. In reality, anything above 80% is quite good and can be implemented, if no better options are found).

Table 26. Evaluation of positioning statement alternatives

	Criterion (score from 1 to 10)	Turn your curated content and earned media into leads and opportunities with the click of a button!	Add your Call to Action to any Content	The most cost-effective way to drive traffic to your site.
1	Does it differentiate the brand from other alternatives?	9	10	2
2	Is it focused on the main target customers?	9	10	8
3	Does it identify the brand's unique value to customers?	9	10	1
4	Is the brand promise believable and credible?	5	6	4
5	Is it easy to understand and remember?	1	10	4
6	Is it consistent in all areas of the business?	4	8	5
7	Is it hard to copy? Can only the brand own it?	2	5	1
8	Is it for long-term success and does it leave potential for growth?	4	10	7
9	Will it withstand counterattacks from competitors?	5	7	5
10	Will it help to make marketing more effective?	1	10	6
	Total score	49%	86%	43%

 Recommended reading

1. Al Ries, Jack Trout. *Positioning: The Battle for Your Mind*
2. Philip Kotler, Gary Armstrong. *Principles of Marketing*
3. Jim Joseph. *The Experience Effect: Engage Your Customers with a Consistent and Memorable Brand Experience*
4. Pat Flynn. *Will It Fly?: How to Test Your Next Business Idea So You Don't Waste Your Time and Money*

12. Testing communication and distribution channels

WHY IT IS NEEDED

By now, you should already have an offer your target customers will love and will buy at a certain price. Now it's time to find ways to reach those target customers and show them your offer. Marketing communication channels, also known as media, are the delivery vehicle for your message and can be anything from advertising, personal selling, direct marketing, sponsorship, communication, promotion, and public relations. Successful marketing happens when you send the right message to the right market using an effective communication channel.

Some people might think that testing communications channels take too much time and it would be better to focus on sales and a high coverage marketing plan. But, if potential investors were to ask you how exactly you plan to use the marketing budget and how many sales you expect to drive in, how would you answer? Do you know how many customers you could reach through different channels? How much would it cost you per customer? What if you are planning to invest your own money? Would you be willing to do this blindly or based just on assumptions?

More than 91% of startups who took part in the research acknowledged that the time they invested in testing communication channels paid off very well. These rapidly developing startups found three major benefits:

1. Avoids wasting huge marketing budgets on doubtful tools and channels.

2. Helps to find the most effective communication channels and messages, thus the big marketing plan (which is built later) has much higher than expected ROI.

3. Testing your communication channels doesn't stop you from driving sales. Contrary to opinion, it doesn't waste time but is a methodical and well-proven way of finding the most effective sales mechanisms and driving initial traction (actual sales).

 Decide on distribution strategy

Distribution channels are one of key marketing elements that explain how you'll reach your customers and deliver your product or service to them. Companies can sell through a single distribution channel or through multiple channels. These may include wholesalers or distributors, value-added resellers (VAR), retail networks, consultants, dealers, sales agents, and direct selling through the Internet, catalogs, sales teams, and physical retail shops. Each distribution channel can have a few levels, but three of them are the most common.

1. Producer → Customer

   Producer sells directly to customers. This distribution channel has no intermediary levels, thus the producer can keep the higher profit margin. But customer reach is limited by the possibilities and efforts of the producer, factory outlet store, online sales page. Actually, this is one of the major strategies for early stage startups—if you want to get feedback from the customer, you must be close to him. Having a short distribution channel allows faster response and pivoting possibilities.

Therefore, if you are not sure about your product and value proposition yet, this might be the distribution strategy you should start with.

2. Producer → Retailer → Customer

Producers sell their products directly to large retailers who then sell them to the final consumers. The producer gets money only when the product is sold to the final customer. Early stage startups should seriously consider this option. The customers already know the retailer and visit his online or physical shops, thus you don't have to spend your money on bringing traffic. Most retailers have good credibility and are constantly trying to improve the customer experience, which will be helpful to the producer.

3. Producer → Wholesaler → Retailer → Customer

A wholesaler typically buys and stores large quantities of several producers' goods and then breaks them into bulk deliveries to supply retailers with smaller quantities. For small retailers with limited order quantities, the use of wholesalers makes economic sense. For producers, this type of channel provides very large market coverage. Usually, most wholesalers are not eager to work with startups whose products are still not well known in the market. But this distribution strategy might be a key success factor in the growth stage when you have solid traction and all of your hypotheses have been verified.

When deciding on your distribution strategy, focus on the needs of your end-users and what you actually need more: faster feedback or larger market coverage. Right now, the most important thing is how you plan to grow sales in the near future. Here are few suggestions that worked very well for most startups who participated in my global research on startups:

- You must build your own specialized sales team including yourself as a founder to contact target customers, get feedback, and close deals directly

- If users need personalized service and you already have the product-market fit, you can create a local dealer network or reseller program to provide that service

- If your users prefer to buy online, you can create an e-commerce website or landing page and sell directly

- If you need higher coverage, you can also sell to another online retailer or distributor that can offer your product on their sites (online and physical).

TSS the sports shop is based in Egypt and has become the market leader for official and licensed football merchandise in the MEA region (Middle East and African countries). Their growth was not out of investments or because they started big. They became market leaders because they were the pioneer retailers of this very specific merchandise in the region. Kareem Elkady, the founder of *TSS the sports shop*, remembers that they started very small by buying around 10 products from Amazon at the consumer price, and, after shipping and customs, their cost had doubled the market price globally. But they chose to list those products for sale at a loss through a Facebook page because their vision from the beginning was to build a reliable and trustworthy brand name. Once the products started selling and the founders got confirmation from the real market that there is a demand, they started finding suppliers and contacting them.

Next, they started contacting football clubs directly after considerable research on the Web and tools like LinkedIn. *TSS the sports shop* did not hesitate to talk to the biggest football clubs because they knew that this was the only way to grow. Talking to the most well-known football clubs and major suppliers in the world, they presented their current performance and achievements, historical and potential growth data and numbers, and their plan to market and sell products with a famous sports brand. Not everyone was welcoming at first, but after upgrading their presentation resources and website interface with the highest quality, and by being persistent about achieving their objectives, *TSS the sports shop* was able to work with the biggest global suppliers and form partnerships with the most famous clubs. The clubs themselves benefit from such an arrangement by starting to have their presence in the MEA region, even though it is via a start-up.

 Make a draft of your sales pipeline or sales funnel

A sales pipeline is a great sales tool that helps you understand your sales process, increase your sales, and make you confident about your data. Therefore, a sales pipeline is extremely important for startups. Somebody might argue that there is a difference between sales pipeline and sales funnel, but generally, the idea is the same. Both reveal how close the potential customer is to becoming a real and even repeat customer. The sales pipeline defines steps to be taken by the seller, while the sales funnel concept looks at the steps to be taken by the buyer.

Table 27. Most common stages of sales pipeline and funnel

Sales pipeline	Sales funnel
1. Initial contact	1. Website visitor
2. Qualification	2. Sign-up for trial or gift
3. Meeting	3. Login or download
4. Proposal	4. Active user
5. Close	5. Paying user
	6. Evangelist

A traditional business (where sales are mainly done by personal selling) would most likely use something similar to the standard sales pipeline stages (Figure 27). Each potential client has an attribute in the seller's CRM (customer relationship management) database defining how hot (close to actual sales) the lead is. The sales manager's task is to grow his client's portfolio by a number of leads (potential clients) and their stage in the pipeline (move each client closer to actual sale as possible).

Figure 27. Example of standard sales pipeline

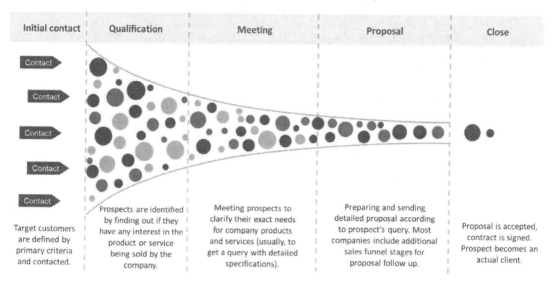

An online business where most of the sales are done with marketing automation tools more often focuses on the sales funnel instead of the sales pipeline. This concept illustrates the idea that every sale begins with a very large number of potential customers (for example, landing page visitors) and ends with a much smaller number of people who actually make a purchase. Stages might be different depending on the marketing strategy and business specifics, but the most common stages of a sales funnel are illustrated in Figure 28.

Figure 28. Example of sales funnel

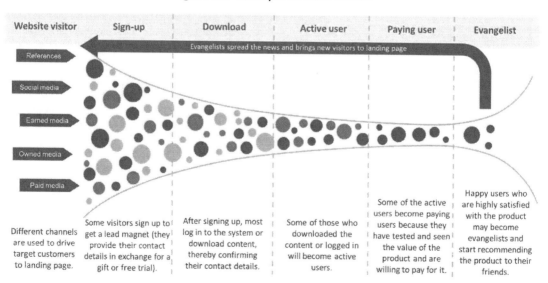

Choose which concept is closer to your situation: if you plan active personal sales, you should draw your estimated sales pipeline. If you plan to use various marketing channels and tools to bring customers to you, a sales funnel would be a more convenient choice. By the way, it would be wise to set up Google Analytics goals on your website for the significant stages of your sales funnel. This will provide you with meaningful insights and will help with your channel verification hypotheses.

As my research showed, nearly all of the fastest growing startups have been tracking and constantly improving the conversion rate of each sales pipeline or sales funnel stage. A few checkpoint examples are provided in Table 28. If you want to consistently improve your sales, you must raise and check the hypotheses related to your sales pipeline or funnel.

Table 28. Physical and online channel checkpoint examples

Physical channel checkpoint examples	Online checkpoint examples
✓ One of five potential clients will buy if they have a chance to talk to the CEO or a member of the board ✓ We can sell our product within a month after the first meeting ✓ Customers will use our service at least three times in six months	✓ At least 20% of website visitors will sign up ✓ More than 70% of signup visitors will log in to their account ✓ Average session duration will be 2.5 minutes per visit ✓ 30% will become paying users after trial period
✓ An average order will be around $5,000 ✓ One out of ten clients will actually recommend us to others	✓ Every new customer invites three friends who signup

 Make the list of potential channels

You should already have a few channels that you've used during your problem-solution-market fit hypotheses verification. In addition, you could spy a little bit on your competitors and see what channels they are using. Studying your competitors is important because doing so lets you know what tactics are already working in your niche and on which marketing channels. Would any of those channels be suitable for you as well? Save your time and use effective spy tools (such as SpyFu, SemRush, BuzzSumo), especially if your competitors use online communication channels.

It's important to keep in mind that even if your product or service is sold via physical distribution channels, customers still search for information about such products online. Therefore, you should at least think about basic online channels to generate awareness and to provide product information. As a rule of thumb, it almost always includes a website, a digital form of your selling material (brochures, catalogs, instructions), a targeted social media presence, and some kind of growth engine (viral, sticky or paid) to attract more potential clients to your physical distribution channel. You can download a worksheet with more than 100 communication channels for you to review and brainstorm what might be suitable in your situation (www.evolutioncurve.com/templates).

Although the main objective in marketing is to maximize profit through the satisfaction of consumer needs, it is also important to keep intermediate objectives in mind as well. Nowadays, consumers have so many products to spend their money on. These products might be direct competitors or alternatives to your solution. Hence, marketing is becoming increasingly difficult. Following are the main objectives of your marketing program:

1. *To reach a certain level of awareness.* In order for a product or a service to be sold successfully, it is first necessary to ensure that as many target customers as possible know about its existence in the market. Some say that good products do not need marketing because they are being purchased anyway. However, if just a small portion of the market knows about your product, then your sales volumes won't bring a smile to your face.

2. *To become favorable.* To earn the favor of your target consumers is the next step following popularity. What is the point if the consumers are only just aware of a certain good or service? If they don't feel that they should favor this brand, producer, or service provider, then the likelihood of the customer turning towards the associated company when the need arises is very low. This objective is not equally relevant to all companies. If a company is producing cheap products that are aimed at users who make a choice based solely on price, almost or completely disregarding other aspects, then the price will be the determining factor if this product is favorable compared to alternatives. But for most startups, becoming favorable is one of the essential tasks.

3. *To earn the trust of target customers.* This is one of the more important and more relevant objectives. This objective often reflects the company that provides meaningful, important, or expensive goods or services within the market. There are also some paradoxical situations in the market: a customer prefers one brand to the other, but when they have to choose, they pick something completely different. This happens in situations when a given company is planning its marketing communication and does not evaluate the fact that the consumer favors one trademark over the other based on one set of criteria, but when it comes down to actually purchasing, another set of criteria is used. This might be seen among some startups as well: target customers like the product provided by a startup, but when it comes to paying money, some of them stay with the old and trusted alternative, even though they favor the new product. Building trust is essential and you have already laid foundations of it if you created a strong positioning statement (as you probably remember, proof and reason to believe is one of core elements in positioning statement).

4. *To encourage customers to try a product.* When consumers are buying a lot of products, especially more expensive ones or the ones that they are used to, they consider their choice for a longer period of time. Once they have thought it over, they come to a decision concerning the purchase or they simply do not consider any alternatives at all and buy out of habit. Your goal is to build a customer's habit to buy your product without comparing it too much with other alternatives. That is why startups quite often encourage customers to try their product for free or even create "forever free" versions of the product in order to attach to the customer and build a stronger habit.

5. *To encourage customers to buy the product.* This is the main and most widespread objective in marketing communication. It is not the only one, as mentioned earlier. Some companies have recently announced that the main objective of their marketing strategy is greater and more profitable sales. However, a significant portion of their marketing communication is not aimed at the achievement of this objective. Sometimes, their communication lacks a call to action and their advertising becomes focused on strengthening the brand and nothing else. This might strengthen the brand, but if the aim is to sell right now, this objective has to be present within the entire marketing promotion campaign.

6. *To encourage repeat purchases.* It is no secret that it is much easier to sell a good or service to a current customer and it is cheaper than attracting new clients. Therefore, a smart and skillful marketing specialist will always think through the possibilities in communication with the customers, who have already purchased the company's products or have made use of its services (or at least already tried the product). The objective for future purchases is also included. For instance, if a consumer purchases a camera, a smart salesperson will certainly offer a convenient case, a memory card with more space for storage, a battery charger, and other accessories to go with the camera. Sometimes, the marketing strategies of certain companies are based on this exact objective. The consumers are being lured in with especially attractive offers and the company generates profit by selling additional products. Might that be a suitable strategy for you as well?

7. *To get clients recommending your product.* The best and most effective advertising happens when the company's goods or services are recommended by satisfied clients. That's why we have talked about early adopter evangelists during validation of your target customer. If the product is good, customers will be more inclined to recommend it, but that does not mean that they will always do it. You should determine the ways and means to stimulate recommendations by satisfied customers. There are two different approaches in this situation, but it usually depends on the individual situation when determining which one to use. Sometimes, clients are encouraged to recommend the product by implementing

financial and material stimuli. But advocates of the other approach state that it might be unethical to reward clients for their recommendations because the sincerity of such customer action is put in doubt.

Now it's time for you to do your homework. Take the list of potential communication channels and fill in Table 29. Before starting to test any channel, you should have a clear vision about what you expect from this channel (*Goal*), how you will measure the results (*Metrics*), how much money you can allocate for this channel (*Budget*).

Table 29.   List of potential communication channels

Channel	Goal	Metrics	Budget	Expectations and Comments

 Test channels in small batches

When you're just starting your marketing communication, it's important that you keep things simple. Don't spread yourself too thin. It might be a good idea to pick just one marketing channel for the moment. Instead of investing months to plan and research, lean startup encourages you to develop assumptions and quickly test them in the marketplace. Instead of developing big plans and investing the vast majority of your marketing budget in one or two initiatives, break your budget into smaller pieces and test a variety of ideas. In the long run, you definitely don't want to rely on a single marketing channel even if it showed the best results. The reason is obvious: if that marketing channel changes its rules or suspends your account, your business could be ruined. Therefore, when you start seeing results, consider simultaneously working on another marketing channel as soon as possible.

Experiment not only with different channels but also test different content, calls-to-action, designs, and other attributes in the same channel. Testing with different options will give you a better sense of how your target customers respond to your marketing so that you can focus your energy and budget on those channels and tactics that work best. For example, if customers tell you certain images get them more interested in your products, find more of those images and test your assumptions once again. By doing this, you can adjust and find those marketing channels and messages that work best for your brand.

Steve Blank and Bob Dorf (2014) recommend that you buy $500 worth of AdWords and see if they'll drive customers representing five or ten times that amount in potential revenue to the site or app and at least get them to register. Test at least two different headlines and as many calls to action, carefully monitoring the performance of each. Drop ineffective ones and refine the best.

It's not a good idea to commit to long-term marketing campaigns on any channel at the very beginning. Pick a variety of banners and develop different ads. Within one or two weeks, look at the results to measure which ads send the most traffic to your site and which ads result in better conversions. Compare the traffic and conversion rates relative to the money you spent. Which network is sending more customers? Do particular ads have higher click-through and conversion rates? Which ads perform best on both networks?

Here is an example of just three experiment tasks that can be run one after another or even simultaneously if there is significant traffic on the website. Let's say we have a typical situation where a startup introduces some kind of new product. Chances are low that we would try to sell the new innovative product to people who know nothing about us and our product. It would be better to educate potential customers first about the product and the benefits and only then try to sell them the product. Therefore, we should use different marketing communication channels and set different goals. Look through the experiment cards below and identify what communication channels are used and what goals are set for each of them.

Table 30. Experiment example No.1

EXPERIMENT TASK NO.1	
Experiment: TARGETED TRAFFIC TO LANDING PAGE	Responsible: ____XX____ Starting date: ____XX____
We believe that it is possible to acquire a significant number of quality visitors (targeted customers) to our website at a price of $0.30 per visitor	
In order to check that, we will run advertising campaigns on 3 channels (Google Adwords, Facebook, Twitter) for 3 weeks. In addition, we will try 2 different banner designs and 4 different calls to actions in all channels	
We will measure these results by average CPC (cost per click) and total amount of visitors who spent at least 0:45 seconds on our landing page (which is enough time to read the main message and to view our introduction video)	
The hypothesis will be confirmed if at the end of the experiment we find a way to drive at least 100 targeted visitors per day on average, spending not more than $ 0.30 per visitor.	
If the hypothesis is confirmed this will allow us to have at least 3,000 targeted visitors with less than a $900 monthly marketing budget. Having confirmed this, we can proceed with testing the next stage of our sales funnel: email submission rate (signup for follow-up). If the hypothesis is rejected: a) we will try the same channels but with totally different banner designs and messages, if CTR (click through rate) in our campaigns was lower than 2%	
b) we will look for additional communication channels (with possibly lower CPC or larger reach) and test them with the best-performed banner designs and messages (if CTR in our campaigns was higher than 2%).	

Table 31. Experiment example No.2

EXPERIMENT TASK NO.2	
Experiment: SIGNUP FOR FOLLOW UP	Responsible: ___XX___ Starting date: ___XX___
We believe that at least 20% of our website visitors will provide their email address in exchange for a gift (coupon to try our product for free).	
In order to check that, we will run A/B testing of our website and show each version of the website to 500 visitors. According to the results of experiment No.1, we can expect to have 3,000 visitors per month. This will allow us to run 3 A/B tests per month, thus we will test: • 2 different layouts of our website, • 2 different design concepts of our website, • 2 different call-to-actions.	
We will measure these results by conversion rate (the number of submitted email addresses divided by the number of total visitors).	
The hypothesis will be confirmed if we find a way to achieve 20% or higher conversion rate.	
If the hypothesis is confirmed this will allow us to capture leads (contacts of target customers) very effectively. Having confirmed this, we can increase our marketing budget to drive more targeted traffic to our website and proceed with testing the next stage of our sales funnel: effectiveness of e-mail follow-up campaigns (click through rate to our sales page). If the hypothesis is rejected we will continue A/B testing with additional versions of the website (design, layout, call-to-action) and check if there is a difference in conversion rates depending on the channel which generates traffic to our website.	

Table 32. Experiment example No.3

EXPERIMENT TASK NO.3	
Experiment - SALES AFTER EMAIL CAMPAIGNS	Responsible: ___XX___ Starting date: ___XX___
We believe that after reaching out potential clients with an email campaign, at least 7% of them will order our main product via sales page or phone call.	
In order to check that, we will create three main email campaigns (3, 5, and 7 emails) and will send them to our potential clients who submitted their email address for follow up. Each campaign will be sent to 1,000 potential clients. In order to have better results, we will use marketing automation tools to send the emails.	
We will measure these results by campaign overall conversion rate (the number of orders divided by a number of email addresses to which the campaign was activated). In addition, we will watch three major indicators which determine the overall conversion rate: email open rate, email link click through rate, and sales page conversion rate.	
The hypothesis will be confirmed if we find a way to reach at least 7% campaign overall conversion rate.	

If the hypothesis is confirmed this will prove that we have a profitable business model: $900 monthly marketing budget will bring us at least 600 email signups from 3,000 visitors which will result in more than 40 sales (estimated sales profit $2,000). We'll continue to do further experiments looking for the ways to scale up our business.

If the hypothesis is not confirmed we'll check possibilities to improve email subjects (to increase email open rate), a copy of the email (to increase link click-through rate), and will run A/B tests of main sales page (to increase its conversion rate).

Now it's your turn to test your communication channels. This is not a do-it-once-and-forget-it kind of task. A true marketer will be looking for more efficient, cost-effective, and higher reach, larger scale communication channels and tactics to combine them. There is worksheet available at www.evolutioncurve.com/templates which helps to track the effectiveness of your sales pipeline or funnel and review the most common types of hypotheses for communication and distribution channels. I periodically update it to help startup founders stay on track and find the most effective marketing channels for their business.

It's 5 to 10 times cheaper (depending on business model and industry) to keep a loyal customer than to attract a new one. It would be wise to invest some of your time to keep your current customers happy and loyal to your product or brand. Therefore, you should think about communication channels that help you maintain a relationship with your current customers. There are two main areas that you should consider critical for your business success: customer feedback and loyalty programs.

How will you get feedback from your customers who already bought your product or service?

- *Customer feedback and complaints*. Get proactive about customer service issues. If any customer is unhappy with your product, service, or any other aspect of your business, how will you know that? It's much better if they spill out all their negative feedback and bad emotion on you rather than on your potential clients. Do you have a system to collect customer feedback? Maybe it would be wise to add a customer feedback phone number on your every product, put a form on your website, and monitor customer feedbacks on social networks? Don't hide! Fix their problems as soon as possible and make them happy as far as it is reasonable and right. All of your other potential customers should see that you are a responsible company and don't hide from problems.

- *Customer satisfaction survey*. You could plan to check the customers' experience and satisfaction via regular surveys (printed, online, phone call). The goal here is to understand how you could improve the overall experience of your customers, so don't be afraid to get some negative feedback. This is the only way you'll find out how to improve. By the way, try to avoid closed questions. You'll get much more value from open questions (for example, "what could we do to make you happier with our services?," "if your friend would ask your opinion about our product or service, what would you say?," "what issues have you faced in purchasing or using our product?").

- *Check-in calls* mean planning to call every customer, or every third, fifth, tenth customer, once per certain period of time just to thank them for being with you and using your products or services. In addition, you could ask how they like your product and include more specific questions about product features, functions or any other aspects of your business that might help to develop your startup faster.

- *Pro-active communication.* If your product is innovative, you might consider the possibility of sharing a newsletter, personal mail, event, etc., to show how customers are making the most of the product. This would help educate your customers as well as give you an opportunity to collect some feedback (for example, in what particular situations are customers are most happy about using your product, what new ways of using your product have they found which might be useful for other users).

- *Face and body detection technologies* today can already be used to automatically evaluate customer satisfaction. FaceMedia, one of the startups I met during my global research, offers an automated customer satisfaction score component that enables free-standing cameras (linked to the Faceboard Retail platform) to capture real-time data about consumer perceptions of the retail environment and their interactions with the staff. It provides the ability to calculate and determine the satisfaction score of customers in real-time without any surveys, manual observation, or video review. According to FaceMedia, automated customer satisfaction scores through facial detection and analysis works with 95% of branch visitors without direct interaction. *Results of the satisfaction scoring were verified by an independent market research agency, TNS Global. Technologies are being developed fast, and we shall see even more advanced and precise solutions in the near future.*

 Update your business model according to your findings

Now it's time to review your business model once again. Pay most of your attention to those parts of the business model which define your communication and distribution channels, revenue streams, and costs. It's quite possible that you'll have to reject some channels you initially thought would be effective and to add new ones which performed well during your experiments. These changes might dramatically influence your cost structure and revenue streams.

Ankota, a US-based company, has developed software for managing a home care business and for monitoring patients in between visits from their home care professionals.

Ankota has tested mostly inbound marketing channels by sharing useful information in their blog and e-books with the hope that potential customers will see it and get in contact with the company. It's been a good way to grow and learn, but the founders of *Ankota* have learned that they can only get initial leads, not actual sales through these channels. Therefore, they decided to combine it with outbound marketing initiatives in order to actively reach potential customers who were indicated as initial leads. Though it was not a dramatic change, their business model had to be updated, including direct marketing channels and additional costs.

 Recommended reading

1. Steve Blank, Bob Dorf. *The Startup Owner's Manual: The Step-by-Step Guide for Building a Great Company*
2. Gabriel Weinberg, *Justin Mares. Traction: How Any Startup Can Achieve Explosive Customer Growth*
3. Dan Olsen. *The Lean Product Playbook: How to Innovate with Minimum Viable Products and Rapid Customer Feedback*

13. Evaluating profit and growth potential

WHY IT IS NEEDED

It seems obvious that you need to evaluate profit and business growth if you want to create a profitable and scalable business. Unfortunately, too many startup founders go crazy with excitement when they get market validation and start seeing some traction and the money coming in. My global research on startups showed that two out of three startups (68.4% to be precise) who dream about growth hacking have not estimated what that growth might look like. But the fact is that those startups who have achieved meaningful results in their business growth made a weighted decision on what growth directions to choose. They were successful because they had a great expansion to multiple foreign markets or adapted their product for different segments of the current market and tremendously increased their sales. These successful startups evaluated how much profit they could earn in different scenarios. They also evaluated their growth potential in different markets using different marketing channels. So, that's the distinction between a dream about growth and a plan for how to achieve it!

Startup entrepreneurs and investors may have different appetites for profit margins and business growth potential. The main goal at this point is to determine if you should proceed with your business idea or not. In order to make a weighted decision, as those successful startups did, you should estimate your profit and growth potential and evaluate if there are any possibilities to make those numbers more attractive.

HOW TO DO IT

01 — Estimate Your Profit Margin
Identify the easiest and most rational ways to increase your profit margin

02 — Estimate the Market Reach
Calculate how many customers you can reach with your chosen channels

03 — Check Effectiveness of Sales Funnel
Set clear conversion metrics to measure how effective your sales funnel is in each stage

04 — Update Your Business Model
Review your business model and make necessary changes according to your findings

05 — Confirm the Final Business Model
The final business model is actually the starting point for your real business model

 Estimate profit margin and possibilities to increase it

To estimate your profit margin and any possibilities to increase it, you should keep in mind the three main numbers that determine your profit margin:

1. *Average production costs per product or service unit* should definitely be included in calculations of your potential profit, but how these costs could be reduced is more of a production issue rather than a marketing issue

2. *Average income per* sale is a number that most startups usually pay attention to. It only includes the price of their product, although it doesn't really represent the true number. (We'll talk more about the importance of up-sell, cross-sell,

and other strategies helping to increase the average income per sale in future chapters.)

3. *Average marketing costs per sale* show how much money you have to invest in order to make one sale (sometimes it is called "customer acquisition costs" or "marketing costs per customer").

Because average income per sale depends directly on the price level, you should be aware of how the price level affects the volume of your sales and total profit. Usually, the higher the price, the fewer customers who are willing to buy the product. It's not always the case, but I won't overwhelm you with the theory of demand elasticity. At a minimum, you should know these two simple, but yet very valuable formulas, and use them together with factual data from your market fit or channel verification experiments:

- *Formula (1)* shows how much total sales should increase if you apply a certain discount and want to keep the same profit (it's obvious that if you apply a discount and your sales volume doesn't increase, you are losing your profit, so there is no sense in providing a discount)
- *Formula (2)* shows the opposite case calculation. If you decided to increase the price (even though some customers might think it's too expensive and won't buy your product), the formula indicates how much you can allow your sales volume to decrease and still have the same profit (selling fewer units, but at higher price can result in even a higher total profit)

If you plan to run a sales promotion based on a discount or you pay out commissions to partners selling your product, evaluate the results of this formula and decide how likely it is to have such sales volume increase due to a particular discount or commission payout:

$$TS = (\frac{x}{PM - x}) \times 100 \tag{1}$$

In this formula, TS is total sales, x is the discount (%) and PM is the profit margin (%) before reducing price

As an example, if your profit margin is 30% and you decide to reduce the price by 10% (as a sales promotion discount or even set a regular price level), your sales should increase at least by 50% if you want to keep the same profit. If your total sales increase more than 50%, it means you will earn a higher profit and this discount is reasonable from an economic sense.

$$TS = (\frac{10\%}{30\% - 10\%}) \times 100 = 50\%$$

Keep in mind that we're not talking here about strategic decisions (for example, if you are a cost leader, thus will always try to provide a lower price than your competitors, or if you are a premium brand that can't be priced too low). This formula shows a plain black and white answer about what would be more profitable to you based on numbers, not opinions.

If you are considering the possibility of increasing the price, here is the formula (2) which you should evaluate:

$$TS = (\frac{y}{PM + y}) \times 100 \qquad (2)$$

In this formula, TS is total sales, y is the price increase (%), and PM is the profit margin (%) before the increase in price.

Let's use the same example: your profit margin is 30% but you decide to increase the price by 10%. If you want to keep the same profit, your sales shouldn't fall more than 25%.

$$TS = (\frac{10\%}{30\% + 10\%}) \times 100 = 25\%$$

These formulas can be very valuable for early stage startups during market fit verification. To make it easier for you, I've created a simple worksheet that you can access online and estimate various discount and price increase scenarios. If you run the same go-to-market experiment but with different prices, you could collect factual data as shown in Table 33. That would allow you to make a reasoned decision to set up the price level. Make a quick calculation with one formula and assess how realistic it is to have higher sales volume than the formula showed.

Table 33. Marketing costs per customer acquisition

Price	$9.99	$12.99	$14.99	$19.95
Visits (potential customers)	1,000	1,000	1,000	1,000
Marketing budget	$500	$500	$500	$500
Cost per lead	$0.50	$0.50	$0.50	$0.50
Sales volume	100	60	55	20
Conversion rate	10%	6%	5.5%	2%
Cost per sale	$5.00	$8.33	$9.09	$25.00
Total profit earned	$499.00	$279.60	$324.50	-$101.00

Average marketing costs per sale is another very important component for your profit calculation. There are many articles and even books about optimizing your average lead or sales cost (I highly recommend *Startup Owners Manual* by Dorf and Blank to learn more about this topic). But one thing should be kept in mind: marketing communication today is more complicated than ever before. It's not enough to calculate your marketing costs per one advertising or sales channel to decide whether your communication channel is cost effective. You should focus on the effectiveness of entire sales funnel or sales pipeline. As we have already discussed, different communication channels might have different goals in your marketing strategy (not every marketing channel will try to sell your product at once, so it's not correct to evaluate the effectiveness of a communication channel based on generated sales). After running a number of experiments using different channels and messages, you should come up with the average costs of customer acquisition through the entire sales funnel or pipeline. Take those costs into account for your estimated profit. In the next steps, we'll talk how you could come up with ideas for optimizing these costs.

 Estimate the potential reach of your target market

Ask yourself a simple question: which of your tested communication channels are scalable? How large is the target audience you can reach with these channels? If your target market is 1,000,000 but your tested channels can reach at maximum 100,000 potential customers, you still have work to do. It's not a tragedy if you proceed with the implementation of your business model, but it just means that you have only found a way to reach 10% of your total target market. So if you are making any assumptions about your business potential, you should be careful. You still don't know how to reach remaining 90% of your target customers and don't have a clue how much it would cost you. It might be a good idea to continue experiments with new communication channels and add them to your marketing strategy if they are confirmed.

 Check the effectiveness of your sales funnel/pipeline

Do you have clear conversion metrics for each stage of your sales funnel or sales pipeline? What is the industry standard and how you compare to it? Is the overall effectiveness of your sales funnel/pipeline satisfactory? Can you be profitable at this overall conversion rate? Can you improve it?

It's much easier to answer these questions if you have your sales funnel/pipeline with conversion metrics in front of you. An example in shown in Table 34 (you can download this spreadsheet at www.evolutioncurve.com/templates).

Table 34. Initial sales funnel conversion rates

Action in sales funnel Stage		Conversion		Potential Customers	
		Overall	Converted	Lost	
Stage 1	Visit the website	100.0%	100.0%	100,000	--
Stage 2	Sign up for free trial	15.0%	15.00%	15,000	85,000
Stage 3	Activate free trial	80.0%	12.00%	12,000	3,000
Stage 4	Buy the product	20.0%	2.40%	2,400	9,600
Stage 5	Repeat purchase	40.0%	0.96%	960	1,440

Where is the bottleneck in this sales funnel? At which stage will you lose most of the potential customers? Looking at this sales funnel it's obvious that there are some problems with Stage 2 (15% conversion with 85,000 potential customers lost) and Stage 4 (12% conversion with 10,560 potential customers lost). The overall effectiveness of this sales funnel is only 1.44% which means that only 1,440 potential customers out of 100,000 are buying the product, and only 576 become loyal customers (and make repeat purchases). What conclusions could you draw out of these facts?

Let's say this startup is selling a digital product (with fixed one-time production costs and no variable costs) at a price of $14.99 and cost per lead is $0.50 (the same numbers from the previous example). It means that we'll have to spend $50,000 to get 100,000 visitors to the landing page, but finally, we'll sell our product only to 1,440 customers which will bring us $21,585 in income and $8,634 from repeated purchases. Not a good deal! We spend $50,000 to earn only $30,219!

For most business, 85,000 potential customers is quite a significant number so we need to think about how to stop losing so many leads. Without any other additional information, we can assume that there might be two general ways to increase the conversion at this stage:

- Optimize the landing page. Make it more appealing and more effective at guiding visitors to sign up for the free trial (solution: update the landing page and run A/B tests)
- Increase the quality of traffic to the landing page. It's quite possible that most of those visitors are not truly your targeted customers (solution: check which channels bring visitors with the best conversion for signup, try to find new channels to reach target customers, and reduce spending on ineffective channels).

If we want to increase the conversion purchase after the free trial, we might consider:

- Talking to a customer who doesn't buy it and clarify the main reasons for their decision

- Improving the process of follow up during the free trial and after it is over (put more effort in direct communication with the potential customer)
- Revising the offer (maybe potential customers would be more willing to buy a bit different package) and think about implementing a down-sell strategy for those who don't buy after the full sequence of follow-up.

Let's say after a few experiments and changes, we succeed in achieving higher conversions at these stages (see Table 35). Now the overall sales funnel conversion is 3,.52% and 1.41% for repeat purchases. This now means that in driving 100,000 visitors to the website, we make $52,764 in initial sales and $21,105 in repeat sales ($73,869 in total). If it's possible to keep the same $0.50 cost per lead, it means we found a profitable business model for our digital product). Investing $50,000 to drive traffic to the sales funnel brings $73,869 in revenue.

Table 35. Improved sales funnel conversion rates

Action in sales funnel Stage		Conversion		Potential Customers	
		Overall	Converted	Lost	
Stage 1	Visit the website	100.0%	100.0%	100,000	-
Stage 2	Sign up for free trial	20.0%	20.00%	20,000	80,000
Stage 3	Activate free trial	80.0%	16.00%	16,000	4,000
Stage 4	Buy the product	22.0%	3.52%	3,520	12,480
Stage 5	Repeat purchase	40.0%	1.41%	1,408	2,112

Increasing the efficiency of your sales funnel/pipeline takes ongoing effort. Even when you do the market launch (introduce your product to the entire targeted market instead of just running tests in particular market segments), you should always keep an eye on your overall conversion rate and the ways to increase it. Due to their specifics and costs structure, different sales channels support different products and price levels. It means that not all channels will be effective and suitable for your product. Try to keep your sales funnel/pipeline clear of ineffective channels.

 Do the final check-up of your business model

Once you estimate the effectiveness of your sales funnel/pipeline using a different combination of communication channels, it's time to decide if the validated business model is attractive enough to proceed. If there are any stops, don't ignore them, but don't worry about them too much. Fill your business model KPI (key performance indicator) scorecard based on the findings of your continuous series of experiments.

Table 36 how an example of a startup's financial forecast based on few main indicators. You can choose more indicators for estimating your profit potential, but these should definitely be included:

- Customer acquisition costs—the cost on average for you to get one client
- Product variable costs—the cost for you to produce and deliver an average order
- Average revenue per sale—the revenue a customer pays per average order
- Expected number of sales—a forecast, not a guess, about your future sales (for example, if you plan to double your marketing budget for acquiring new customers and have solid proof that your sales funnel/pipeline is scalable, you might forecast double sales)
- Operational costs—your startup's fixed costs that you will have to pay independent of the volume of your sales. It means that even if you have no sales, you will bear these costs anyway. That's why successful startups go as lean as possible in their early stages.

Table 36. Example of a startup's financial forecast

KPI (Key Performance Indicators)	Scenario		
	Pessimistic	Realistic	Optimistic
Customer acquisition costs	15	12	9
Product variable costs	3,5	3	2,5
Average revenue per sale	20	21	25

REALISTIC	Forecast for 24 months (by quarters)							
	1st	2nd	3rd	4th	5th	6th	7th	8th
Expected number of sales	100	150	300	500	1000	1500	3000	3500
Marketing expenses	1.200	1.800	3.600	6.000	12.000	18.000	36.000	42.000
Product variable cost total	300	450	900	1.500	3.000	4.500	9.000	10.500
Sales revenue	2.100	3.150	6.300	10.500	21.000	31.500	63.000	73.500
Sales profit	**600**	**900**	**1.800**	**3.000**	**6.000**	**9.000**	**18.000**	**21.000**
Ongoing expenses	2.000	2.000	2.000	2.000	2.000	2.000	2.000	2.000
Net profit (Cash burn)	**-1.400**	**-1.100**	**-200**	**1.000**	**4.000**	**7.000**	**16.000**	**19.000**
Accumulated profit (loss)	-1.400	-2.500	-2.700	-1.700	2.300	9.300	25.300	44.300

Source: Available for download at www.evolutioncurve.com/templates

Even if your financial forecast table looks great, here are a few major consideration for the final checkup of your business idea:

- Is there big enough market that's waiting for your product? Have you estimated sales potential in units and total revenue? Have you verified demand, average purchase volume, and purchase frequency hypotheses? How many new customers per year you will attract?

- Do you have a confirmed and sustainable revenue model? Is your pricing validated by market (target customers)? Have you tested at least few different price levels and value propositions?

- Have you estimated all channel costs and conversion rates? Have you set up an effective sales funnel/pipeline to have an acceptable cost for customer acquisition? Can you scale communication channels to reach all target markets and still be profitable? What is your customer lifetime value and the cost of customer switching that you might have to pay in order to get the customer?

- What is your customer retention rate? Do they make repeat purchases? Is there a significant viral effect? So your customers bring new customers?

- What are the basic operating costs of the business? What is your cash burn rate and when will you achieve your break-even point?

- Does this estimation and forecasting show a scalable and profitable business? Would such a business be able to generate substantial exit value (in case if you expect to create a buyable startup)?

It's great if you were successful in finding a profitable and scalable business model. But it's not reasonable to follow up with a business idea that has fatal flaws that you don't know how to solve. I support the optimistic attitude that there are no problems impossible to solve, we just haven't figured out how to solve them yet. But it's not wise to make major investments of time and money if you still have unsolved fatal flaws. Here are just a few examples which should stop you from further expansion of your current business model and redirect your focus to do the homework of improving and reinventing your business model:

- Customer acquisition or channel costs are too high, rendering the company unprofitable

- In order to be profitable, the company needs more customers than it's possible to reach

- The sales funnel/pipeline is too long and with low conversion rates, making the cost of sales too high

- If the business model depends on repeat sales, but too few customers make repeat purchases, and there is no way to increase this conversion

- Despite all efforts, customers aren't recommending the product to others and there is no possibility of getting additional customers through a viral effect

 Confirm your final business model or make a pivot

Let's be honest, *final* here does not really mean *final*. If you find meaningful facts while developing your business, you obviously shouldn't ignore them. But, in general, at the current stage, you should already have a validated business model. If you don't have it yet, or if there are some doubts, repeat some of the previous tasks and re-check your hypotheses with different variables and aspects. It's highly recommended that you have the validated business model before proceeding to the next chapter where we will discuss main aspects of marketing strategy.

 Recommended reading

1. Steve Blank, Bob Dorf. *The Startup Owner's Manual: The Step-by-Step Guide for Building a Great Company*
2. Philip Kotler, Gary Armstrong. *Principles of Marketing*

14. Develop alternative marketing strategies

WHY IT IS NEEDED

Generally speaking, there could be different forms of marketing strategy, but three essential questions should be answered in any form of marketing strategy:

1. What are you selling?
2. To whom are you selling?
3. How are you selling?

Obviously, your product or service is what you are selling and the definition of your target customer answers to whom you are selling. You have already designed your problem-solution-market fit, possibly with many pivots. For early-stage startups, many experts agree that feedback is more important than customers. The faster a startup can resolve customer objections and improve the product according to the market demand, the higher the possibility of achieving success in the long run. So, if you've done your homework right, you should already have at least a concept of a market confirmed product. But there still may be major pivots because of the remaining aspect of your marketing strategy—that is, how are you selling—will determine your overall success. If you've already tested some communication and distribution channels, you have partially answered the question of how to sell.

More than 87% of the successful startups that I interviewed during my global research on startups fall in one of two categories:

1. One portion of the successful startups was focused on development based on raising funds from investors. They had a clear marketing strategy that defined how investments would be used in marketing and what results they expected. But they didn't just actively pitch their idea and seek the attention of potential investors. They had a plan B, an alternative marketing strategy. Those successful startups had a clear strategy for what they would do if there were no funds raised for some period of time. Waiting was not a strategy. They were ready to implement (and some of them actually implemented) an alternative marketing strategy that didn't require as much funding as their primary strategy.

2. Another portion of the successful startups was bootstrapping. The growth of the startup was dictated by the amount of funds the founders initially had and any additional revenue they could generate. This group of startups didn't depend on the availability of additional funds. They had more or less clarified their marketing strategy to allow them to increase the speed at which they could grow only if some extra funds became available. The founders took the time to think through the possibilities of getting a grant or credit on favorable conditions, or if a new partner with meaningful funding joined the startup. Scaling faster and then outrunning the competition were the main goals of this alternative strategy.

So we can conclude that there is no difference if you are bootstrapping or fundraising. Having an alternative marketing strategy can increase your chances of success and help foresee possibilities in advance.

 Indicate the relationship of your product to the market

Defining the playground for your marketing strategy brings more clarity and simplicity in strategic decisions. As Steve Blank and Bob Dorf (2014) reminded us, there are four possible product-to-market strategies (Figure 29).

Figure 29. Product development strategies

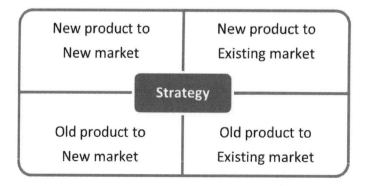

- *New product to new market*—In this scenario, customers don't yet have an idea about your product and don't know if they need it, therefore put your main efforts into explaining what problem your product solves and what benefits customers will get from using it. Customer education will be the main focus of your marketing communication. If you have a great communication reach, you might become a leader in this product category, the one who comes to the customer's mind when a product category is mentioned.

- *New product to existing market*—Customers are aware of the problem or specific need, but they are accustomed to older solutions. Your marketing communication should be based on comparing your product to your main competitors and explaining what additional value your product delivers, how some features are different, and why your product would be the best choice. Al Ries and Jack Trout (2001) call this strategy a front attack (openly out-competing the market leader) or flank attack (out-competing the market leader by some features or aspects).

- *Old product to new market*—This is a situation where existing products are used in new ways to solve new problems, satisfy new needs, or to serve new target segments. The main marketing communication task is to stress that your product can be used in another way to solve new problems and satisfy new needs. Old products may already have a good reputation in the existing market and a wise marketer will always try to think how it could be used in the new market. Prepare to explain why your product is better than any new emerging alternative (innovative products and services).

- *Old products to existing market*—As a rule, there is not much innovation and startup effort in selling old products in existing markets. Startups rarely fall in this category, unless we take fast growth as the main criterion for defining what a startup is. Such a situation might emerge when a business model focused on fast growth is applied: the old product is sold in the existing market and the main marketing efforts are focused on taking the largest share of the market as possible.

 Set strategic direction of your growth

Imagine that your target market can be defined as a cube where the volume of the cube shows the total market size. The larger the cube, the larger your market. The cube has three dimensions (Figure 30) which indicate the growth possibilities and the overall size of the cube:

1. Market penetration indicates how many target customers are already using the product (they might not be using your product, but your competitors)

2. Average purchase size is the average amount of money spent on one purchase

3. The average rate of purchase shows how many times target customer buys the product during the period (for example, per 12 months).

Multiply the actual value of those three numbers and you'll know the size of your current market (total sales per year). If you want to find out the size of the potential market, simply multiply the maximum value of all dimensions, and you'll get an assessment of how large the market could still grow. If there is a big difference between current and potential market size, you should strategically focus your marketing efforts on any of these three dimensions:

- Attract new customers who are not using this product yet (if your customer acquisition costs are relatively small)

- Encourage your customers to purchase a product more often (if it is applicable and you have a solid customer base)

- Increase the size of the average purchase; in other words, once the customer decides to buy, try to sell him more (it's is called up-sell and we'll talk about it later).

Figure 30. Strategic directions of sales growth

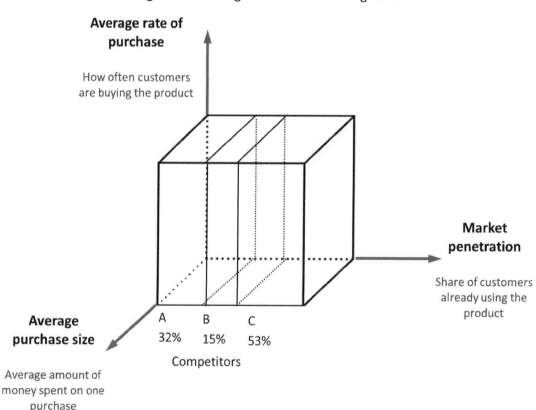

If you see that the current market size is close to its potential (though it's quite a rare scenario in a startup business case), taking market share from a particular competitor might be your strategic decision. As Figure 30 shows, competitor C has the largest market share (53%), so maybe it would be possible to find a niche where his clients are underserved and to prepare your offer for these clients in order to lure them. It would be a strategic decision to focus your marketing efforts and business growth expectations on competitor C targeting by his particular client group.

Each situation is individual and your strategic decision regarding business growth should be well reasoned. You can set your goals to increase all dimensions of the market cube and even target particular client, but be aware: the more targets you have, the harder it is to hit them.

 Write down your main marketing strategy in seven sentences

As J.C. Levinson (2007) suggests, guerrilla marketers create a strategy in seven simple sentences. If you are just an early stage startup, there is no need for a comprehensive marketing plan that lists projected goals in great detail for the next five years. Today, the guerrillas know what it takes to win with their marketing and they win with a very high margin. These seven sentences can make or break your marketing strategy, so always keep them in your mind and top of mind:

1. *The purpose of your marketing.* This is the introduction to your seven sentence strategy where you should describe what exactly you want your potential customer to do. All your marketing strategy should be directed towards that goal— to encourage the customer to perform an action you want. If your marketing's sole purpose is to create awareness of some kind global issue, it's a bad goal, because it leads nowhere. A slightly better example of your marketing purpose would be to generate traffic to your business website in order to gain visitors and potential sales. But maybe you also want to increase the number of phone calls, trial downloads, or free or paid signups? Just name it and be specific: what exactly you want the customer to do?

2. *How you will achieve this purpose.* This is going to provide a quick outline of the way you intend to achieve this purpose. How will you accomplish your targeted goals? What makes your product or service more desirable compared to others? It is well known that people buy benefits, not features. This sentence should explain what your product or service does that sets it apart from the others and makes it a benefit to your client/customer (remember the positioning statement which we have already discussed).

3. *Your target market.* This should be self-explanatory, but some people forget to think about this part of their marketing. A generalization isn't going to get you

the same benefits as a pinpoint accurate description of your target market. Casting a fishing rod into an ocean without any research on the area could get you a few bites, but knowing a specific area with fish that love the bait you're using could get you hundreds of bites.

4. *The marketing weapon you will use.* This should be a short list of whatever marketing tools you'll use. General ideas are good, but again, targeted ideas are great. Remember that you should always think about what can and will work the best for your business.

5. *Your niche, your position, and what you stand for.* The niche is pretty close to your target market but slightly different. The position you talk about is geared towards explaining why your product or service is needed and what your company stands for. If you're a plumber, it's obvious that your market is the plumbing industry, but your niche may be the elderly who are too weak to fix the problems themselves.

6. *The identity of your business.* There could be many things that your startup stands for but remember that an identity and your image are two completely different things. The image of your company is an outsider's impression about you and your startup. Your identity is what you're known for and what you want people to remember about you. Identity is described just in few words that represent your core values and explain what you stand for.

7. *Your budget.* If you are just starting a business, you should budget only a specific amount of money for the initial stage and then foresee how your marketing will be funded from the revenue it brings in. Generally, most small businesses will allocate a specific percentage of their budget and will hold true to it. Your budget can be anywhere from 3% to 50% (or even more) depending on how much money you want to put into it and how good you estimate your ROI (return on investment) to be. Typically, when startups choose growth instead of profit and they spend more than they earn. Such scalable startups as Airbnb and Uber share gift coupons to boost the enrollment of new users in new markets: they encourage current users to invite their friends by giving a gift (meaningful discount or voucher sometimes $10—20 value). It's obvious that AirBnB and Uber get a negative income stream with this type of activity (they spend more than they earn), but that's a strategic decision. They take a loss in the short term expecting to earn profit later because the average customer lifetime value is much greater than the cost of the gift. We'll talk more about sticky, viral and paid growth engines a bit later.

I would love to be able to share an example of a marketing strategy of a real case startup that I met during my journey of writing this book. But most companies consider their marketing strategy as too sensitive to be publically shared. Therefore, let me share my own strategy with you. While writing this book and having so many personal interviews with startups, it was suggested that I create a series of online video courses for startups. These courses would help startup founders build their profitable and scalable business faster by effectively aligning marketing activities. My marketing strategy for these online courses could look like the one in Table 37.

Table 37. Example of main marketing strategy in seven sentences

Purpose	Target customers enroll in comprehensive online courses at a price range of $997 - $2,999
How to achieve it	Lead magnets will generate sign ups to free online mini-courses that will solve one or more painful problems related to startup marketing and will deliver tangible value right during the course. Then I will show them what other problems could be solved in my comprehensive online courses and how these courses help start-ups to build a profitable and scalable business faster. Strategic calls (video conference via Skype) could be used for onboarding high ticket customers at the final stage.
Target market	Early stage startups who have innovative ideas, but are still searching for how to build a profitable and scalable business, and have no resources or don't want to spend them on hiring profes-sional marketers or consultants at this early stage.
Marketing weapons	Lead magnets (templates and spreadsheets for startup marketing, free online courses, webinars), virality boost tools (for example Maitre App, Pay with a tweet), social media advertising, contex-tual advertising, blogging and guest blogging, guest speaking at startup events, email marketing automation, affiliate marketing partnerships, free e-books, and other useful giveaways.
Niche	Comprehensive startup marketing online courses with six months mentoring and one-on-one consulting.
Identity	Expertise, individual, and in-depth approach
Budget	$2,000 starting budget, 20% of revenue will go for marketing

What I've learned through my own practice and through my interviews is that the best way to keep this seven-point strategy alive is to keep it in one paragraph and keep it in front of you every day.

 Define your alternative marketing strategy in seven sentences

If you just finished writing down your main marketing strategy, I'd suggest you take a break and have a cup of tea or coffee or a nice walk in the fresh air. After your break, review your marketing strategy and share it with your colleagues, mentors, or at least some friends to get an external opinion. Once you feel comfortable with your market-ing strategy, prepare your possible alternative strategy.

If we continue with the example of my online courses, the marketing strategy could look like the one in Table 38. It is built on the assumption that for most startups, the price ($997 - $2,999) might be too expensive. So what could I do if the market experiment proves the assumption to be true, but I still want to market the course to startups? I made one major change (individual consulting and mentoring were removed) that allowed us to reduce the price. As a result, I also had to adjust the other elements of the marketing strategy.

Table 38. Example of alternative marketing strategy in seven sentences

Purpose	Target customers enroll in comprehensive online courses at a price range $239 - $497
How to achieve it	Lead magnets will generate signups for free online mini-courses that will solve one or more painful problems related to startup marketing and will deliver tangible value during the course. Then, I will show them what other problems could be solved in the comprehensive online courses and how these courses help startups to build a profitable and scalable business faster.
Target market	Early stage startups that have innovative ideas, but are still searching for how to build a profitable and scalable business, and have no resources or don't want to spend them on hiring professional marketers or consultants at this early stage.
Marketing weapons	Lead magnets (templates and spreadsheets for startup marketing, free online courses, webinars), virality boost tools (for example, Maitre App, Pay with a tweet), social media advertising, contextual advertising, blogging and guest blogging, email marketing automation, affiliate marketing partnerships, free e-books and other useful giveaways.
Niche	Step-by-step startup marketing courses online with self-assessment and progress tracking tool
Identity	Expertise, clarity, and simplicity
Budget	$1,000 starting budget, 30% of revenue will go for marketing

As we have already discussed, if you are fundraising, it would be wise to have an effective marketing strategy in case the fundraising takes much longer than you expected. If you are bootstrapping, turn on your creativity and think what strategy you could employ for faster growth if you had more resources (money, time, skills).

 Update your business model according to your findings

Once you've defined your main marketing strategy, don't forget to review your Business Model Canvas or Lean Canvas. If you gained important insights and your business model has changed even slightly, update the canvas in order not to lose track of your thoughts.

Recommended reading

1. Jay Conrad Levinson, Jeannie Levinson, Amy Levinson. *Guerrilla Marketing, 4th edition*: *Easy and Inexpensive Strategies for Making Big Profits from Your Small Business*
2. Al Ries, Jack Trout. *Marketing Warfare*
3. Philip Kotler, Gary Armstrong. *Principles of Marketing*
4. Richard Rumelt. *Good Strategy Bad Strategy*: *The Difference and Why It Matters*

This stage of the Startup Evolution Curve is finished once you have a validated business model and a clear marketing strategy. Your business model should be based not on assumptions, but on factual data from tests in a real market with your real potential clients. Through hypotheses verification, you should have developed the structure of your sales funnel/pipeline to constantly bring the same level of profitable sales.

Once you have discovered how to scale your business model, you can confidently proceed to the next stage of your startup evolution (Fundraising or Product Launch depending on which is more important in your case). Proceeding to the Fundraising stage, you will already have a validated business model and your startup will be much more interesting to potential investors. But that is not the only thing needed for successful fundraising. The sane investor will want to have a clear picture of why you need a particular amount of investment and how it will help you to scale the business. So, if you did your homework in this stage, you'll have an answer to this question as well.

If you plan to develop your startup by bootstrapping, you can proceed to Product launch and plan the next steps for how to effectively take your market share.

Stage 3. Fundraising

Fundraising is not as easy and exciting as most early stage startups would like to think. In fact, it is one of the most frustrating periods in your startup development because you need to search for money while still keep your startup going and growing. If you are a small team and your startup is in the very early stage, fundraising efforts will likely consume far more time than you'd expect. Sadly, there is no proven shortcut to this process unless you are really lucky and investors come to you at the right time. Luck, as someone said, is at the crossroads of opportunity and preparedness. This book is a marketing manual for startups, therefore we won't dive in the very depth of fundraising strategies, tactics, and skill development. The major tasks for marketing are to help you be prepared to meet investors and to increase your chances of meeting the right investor at the right time.

The main goals of this stage are to:

- Set fundraising milestones
- Create fundraising material
- Become visible to investors

If you clearly set up your fundraising milestones, you'll know the best time to start talking to investors. Well-crafted fundraising material will make communicating with investors much more effective. Being visible will definitely increase your chances of not only being spotted by potential investors but will also provide you with some advantages when you start negotiating.

15. Startups challenges and the fundraising process

WHY IT IS NEEDED

If you are responsible for marketing, it would be difficult to contribute to successful fundraising without understanding the whole fundraising process. In order to prepare winning fundraising materials and to become visible for potential investors, you should at least have a clue what to expect.

During the summer of 2016 *InnMind*, a Swiss – Eurasian startup and investors platform, conducted a study of investors' behavior and decision-making process. *InnMind* interviewed hundreds of investors (venture capital firms, institutional investors, and business angels) from the USA, Canada, Europe, Russia, India, etc. in order to learn how they make decisions on investing in startups. The study showed that the majority of the investors don't insist on a detailed business plan prepared by the startup. Moreover, many of them do not consider the format of the information provided by the startup as important. It could be a presentation, canvas, executive summary, or any other relevant form. The most important information for investors is to get proof that the founders understand their business, know the market and their competitors, have the clear idea on how to bring their product to the market and generate profit, and can clearly explain this to the investor. More than 60% of the investors emphasized that the first sign they look for in the founders is motivation. They want to see very strong motivation to succeed and the deep commitment of the founders: the more a founder invested in the startup (time, money, efforts, etc.) the more likely he is to receive an investment. Before risking their investment in a startup, investors want to see that the founders also take risks.

HOW TO DO IT

01 Learn Different Types of Investors
Investors are not all equally valuable even if they bring the same investment

02 Turn on Fundraising Mindset
It's easy to talk about, but not as easy to get mentally prepared. Get used to it!

03 Get Ready for the Process
Fundraising is a continuous process, not something that can be done only once

Be familiar with the different types of investors

Not every investor is equally valuable for you even if they bring the same amount of cash. We'll talk about different sources of funding for your startup business later but first, it is helpful for you to understand that you will meet different types of investors, including but not limited to the following:

- Investors who don't understand what you do at all, but will have their own opinion and assumptions about your product and business. Don't waste your time. Just talk about facts and the new hypotheses you want to have checked, but not just about their opinions and assumptions.

- Investors who don't have the money and don't intend to invest, but still want to show off as active in the market. Don't waste your time!

- These investors want to know every tiny detail about what you will be doing for the next three or five years, even though you both know that you can't predict the future and make such a forecast. Explain your plan and the conditions under which the plan is built. Don't get involved in little tiny details, because a startup is not a regular business. You'll face many pivots in your business.

- Investors who give you great feedback and would be able to help you, but they want to invest only if someone else invests in you as well. Great! Find out as much as possible about their doubts. Are they related to your startup or is it just some limitation in their policy? Strengthen your efforts to find additional investors and maintain a relationship with these investors.

- Investors who are extremely helpful and want you to succeed, but yet they want you to achieve greater traction before they invest. That is awesome! You have entered into a good relationship with your future partner and found out that your business has a particular problem. Go and solve it. Listen to investor's advice and get more traction.

- Investors who want to invest but don't agree with your valuation and would like to get more equity than you were ready to propose. Not a problem, but don't hurry to sign a deal. First of all, ask how they arrived at their valuation. Are there any serious facts or issues? Maybe it would be wise to dig deeper and make some essential changes in your startup to get a higher valuation before fundraising. Secondly, seek outside advice and prepare to defend your offer. Thirdly, don't close the door for other investors; go to meetings with other investor and listen to their offers.

- Investors who are interested in your business, but doubt you, as the founder, or your team. ... tThis will feel like it's a little bit personal. Instead of getting angry, ask them to state their perceptions of you or your team. Maybe there are some reasonable concerns and you should make some changes. But, if you don't get sound arguments, don't take it personally. Why should you bother with somebody's opinion who has no arguments to back it up? Seek for other opportunities with other investors.

Once you are in contact with a potential investor, the sooner you identify which type he belongs to, the sooner you'll be able to reap the benefit of your relationship. During my global research on startups, I met Batukhan Taluy, founder of *Uservision* in Turkey. He had secured an investment proposal of $1 million in return for 60% of shares in his company. However, after considering his options, Batukhan realized that *Uservision* doesn't need that amount of capital. He also realized that they can minimize development and ongoing costs, so he decided not to go through with this option. It was hard to say no, but it was a logical decision. The know-how and the networking with industry professionals were more important than the funding for this startup. *Uservision* provides advanced user experience testing solutions for mobile applications. Marketers, developers, product managers, and UX designers are the main clients for *Uservision*, but Turkey may not be the best market for growth selling such a solution. Therefore, the founders had a clear vision, that potential investors should be able to help them to enter the global market.

 ## Turn on fundraising mindset

It's easy to talk about, but maybe not so simple to get mentally ready for the whole process. The fundraising mindset centers around a few main ideas:

- Fundraising is a process that takes time and is not as easy as you would like it to be. Therefore, you should start networking and developing relationships even earlier than you start the actual fundraising process. Keep your eyes open and try not to miss opportunities to get in contact with or make connections with potential investors.

- You will gain experience at every meeting. You will probably be rejected many times. But that's how you learn. Figure out what mistakes you're making or why you're being rejected. Then, update your fundraising material or even the business model itself if the reasons for the rejections are serious enough and concern the core of your business model. Just remember, ending the meeting with rejection from investor's side is not the end of your story. It's just a lesson to be learned and next day you'll be better at fundraising.

Get used to analyzing what you've heard during your meetings. Sometimes you'll hear very valuable and frank advice, sometimes you'll get straightforward critics, sometimes you might get personal remarks, and so on. Develop a habit of writing down all the questions you were asked and comments you heard during the meetings. Revisit them the next day and draw some conclusions about HOW TO DO IT better the next time.

Get ready for a continuous fundraising process

For most startups, fundraising is not something that can be done only once and then forgotten. It's a process which has different stages, strategies, and tactics. Here is the general outline what the fundraising process looks like:

1. *Create your fundraising materials*. Basically, this means doing your homework. It doesn't make sense to go fundraising if you have nothing to show and nothing to prove the potential of your business idea. As we have discussed, you can build a valuable relationship without any fundraising material, but if you want to seek investment in your startup, you must do your homework first.

2. *Set up fundraising milestones*. For each milestone, be absolutely sure when you need the money, how much you need, why you need it, and how much time you'll have to raise this amount.

3. *Network and build relationships*. If up until now networking was suggested as a recommendation, now it is an essential activity. Startups will seldom get funded without serious networking, so don't bet your success on luck. Actively and consistently build valuable relationships.

4. *Collect initial offers and choose with whom to proceed*. It's not a lot of fun to only have one proposal to choose from. So put your efforts into trying to meet as many potential investors as possible and collect their offers. It's obvious that the more offers you get, the better the odds for you.

5. *Sign a term sheet before drafting and managing the legal process*. If you feel confident about one of the offers you received, gain agreement on the term sheet before working on the final offer.

6. *Close the deal and receive funds*. It's probably the most anticipated moment, but fundraising doesn't end here. By accepting investments, you agreed to follow particular conditions.

7. *Act according to agreed to conditions and report to investors*. This step is quite often underestimated as not very important, but that's not the case. If you don't act according to the agreement, you might lose the investment you attracted and might not get the next release of funding of cash, in the case of a tranche investment. Investors talk to each other and if you don't meet your obligations or spoil your relationship with your current investor, it will be much harder for you to succeed in the next round of fundraising.

8. *Know when to start preparing for the next round*. Scalable startups don't limit themselves to a single round of investment. They want to achieve rapid growth

and tremendously high valuation. Therefore they go for at least few fundraising rounds which might include: seed round, angel round, series A round, series B round, series X round. The main target of scalable and buyable startups might be the Exit strategy: to sell the company to one of industry giants (M & A strategy, which stands for Merge and Acquisition) or through IPO (Initial Public Offering).

To go for fundraising, you need to achieve particular milestones, otherwise, none of the investors will get interested in your business idea. Seed rounds are easy as you essentially raise money to conduct an experiment. That experiment has to have worked and indicate profitable scalability in order to go to a Series A investment, which is much harder. If you were not able to achieve market validation after consuming your seed investment, your chances of getting to another round are very low. Chances will also be low if you ask for an unrealistic amount of money. Investors will think that you don't know what it takes to get to the next milestone efficiently.

The story of Tail illustrates the right mindset for fundraising. Tail is an app that, along with a fashionable clip, helps customers take better care of their dog. This startup is addressing a huge market with significant potential. According to the Euromonitor International report, *Pet Industry 2016,* there are about 86 million dogs in the European Union with a market value that exceeds €32.2 billion with 2.7% annual growth. *Tail* is targeting not only Europe but also the global market, which is unbelievably huge. Another opportunity indicator is the exploding wearable technology market, including technologies such as GoPro or iWatch among others, with a whopping CARG of 35% through 2020. The *Tail* commercialization strategy assumes Poland and Slovakia as the testing and initial entry market (testing MVP), followed by entrance into the UK, France, Germany, and Sweden. Once they establish a presence in these markets, the US and other overseas markets will be addressed.

Even though there is no actual income yet, multiple revenue streams are foreseen. For example, sales of *Tail* hardware and app, a subscription-based service, advertising within the app, sales of accumulated big data to insurance companies, pet supply stores, veterinary service, and more. The main competitor Whistle (GPS and Activity tracker) has raised $21 million in two rounds from nine investors but is still trying to conquer this market. It's important to note that *Tail,* even though they are addressing a highly lucrative potential market, were not funded on the spot. They had to achieve multiple milestones in fundraising to develop their startup:

- Initial investment of founders: €20,000
- Investment from Deutsche Telekom Venture Fund GmbH: €80,000

- Investment from Platinum Incubator Seed sp. z.o.o.: €100,000
- EU subsidy of Horizon 2020 in the topic "Open Disruptive Innovation Scheme" for research and development as well as for commercialization plan: €50,000.
- Now they are preparing for next investment round size of €500,000 at an expected post-money valuation of €2.5 million.

The *Tail* founders are not just lucky guys who got the attention of investors. They have worked consistently, step-by-step towards the next development milestone. With this persistent effort, *Tail* succeeded in overcoming the odds (a 3% success rate!) to secure Phase 1 of a high-profile public funding scheme SME Instrument, part of the European Commission's Horizon 2020 Program. The SME Instrument is an incentive that seeks to boost the best strategic plans of the most innovative SMEs in the advanced technology sector in Europe. An SMEI phase 1 grant for the project's comprehensive feasibility analysis is a tremendous investment for this company, but more importantly, it paves the way to much higher odds to secure the second phase of the program with a grant of up to €2.5 million towards commercialization of the *Tail* platform. So, don't expect fundraising to be easy and fun! Be ready to work hard and stay persistent if you really believe in your idea.

 ### Recommended reading

1. Carlos Espinal. *Fundraising Field Guide*: *A Startup Founder's Handbook for Venture Capital*
2. Alejandro Cremades. *The Art of Startup Fundraising*: *Pitching Investors, Negotiating the Deal, and Everything Else Entrepreneurs Need to Know*
3. Belsito Mike. *Startup Seed Funding for the Rest of Us*: *How to Raise $1 Million for Your Startup - Even Outside of Silicon Valley*

16. Setting up fundraising milestones

WHY IT IS NEEDED

The first step in preparing to communicate with potential investors is to determine what your cash requirements are over time. The easiest way to do this is by visualizing your company's cash burn rate and projected development milestones. Basically, this means you know how much money you burn (or use) each month developing your startup and how much time is needed to achieve each particular milestones of your project. By checking the remaining cash balance in your account you will have a clear view of how far you can go.

Therefore, if you set up your startup development milestones first, it will be much easier to communicate with investors and explain to them what amount of investment you need, for what purpose and when you need it. Having a clear picture of your investment needs will make the whole fundraising process more consistent, smooth, and with much greater chance of success.

HOW TO DO IT

01

Identify Key Milestones
Set your market, product, funding, human resources, and other milestones

02

Estimate Your Financial Needs
Determine what resources you need to achieve your next key milestone

03

Decide When to Start Fundraising
Bear in mind that even if you have potential investors, it still takes time to close the deal

04

Define Your Preferred Conditions
Be sure you know what you are looking for before you start fundraising

 Identify the key milestones of your startup development

Unlike the typical financial goals of any newly established company (that is, sustainable revenue and profit margin), startup milestones are specific events. Usually, they mark the most important points in a startup's history, such as validating problem-solution-market fit, creating a prototype, hiring key employees, launching the product, getting a certain number of customers, and first revenues. Planning for these milestones allows you to focus on what you will be working on and put all your efforts into achieving them. Identifying and planning milestones also makes you think when and in what order you and your team should try to execute something. Following are the general types of milestones:

- *Market milestones* (first customers, price verification, distribution channel verification etc.). These milestones can be defined as gaining proof from market that, for instance, you can effectively reach a target audience of at least 1 million customers, that the product is useful to particular segments (gaining first 100 paying customers), that there is market (gaining first $100,000 in revenue), the business is scalable (growing to $1 million revenue per year), etc.

- *Product milestones* are related to prototype production, product launch, and updates. The examples could be building a working prototype, delivering the first batch of product to retailers, or introducing an upgraded version of the initial product providing some kind major enabler.

- *Human resources milestones* are attached to hiring or otherwise onboarding key people that will make a strong impact on your startup. Building a full management team would an example of a human resource milestone.

- *Funding milestones* include not just the fundraising rounds (contrary to widespread opinion), but significant proof that your startup is ready for fundraising. For instance, the proof that your business idea is worth of potential investors' attention, the proof that you are ready to talk to and negotiate with investors, and the proof that you are efficient with money (you know how to use funds to get the maximum result and you actually do that).

All investors seek to minimize risk without losing the opportunity to invest in a hot startup with huge potential. Investors are looking for the least risky point at which to invest. Therefore, the best time for a startup to seek funding is either right before or right after achieving key milestones. It depends on your chosen potential investor's attitude. In any case be sure your fundraising strategy uses these milestones to your benefit without getting caught between them with no cash in reserve. Some fundraising experts advise that you should try to raise as much money as you can. There is, of course, a contrary opinion: you should not try to raise more money than you actually need to complete your key milestones and become a self-sustainable company (start earning a profit). The argument is simple: the more money you raise, the more equity investors will require in exchange.

Once you have a clear picture of your key milestones laid out on a timeline, you should be able to find a variety of points when you could start the fundraising process more efficiently and with a clear perspective how much money, for what purpose, and when it will be needed to develop your startup.

Figure 31. Fundraising milestone example

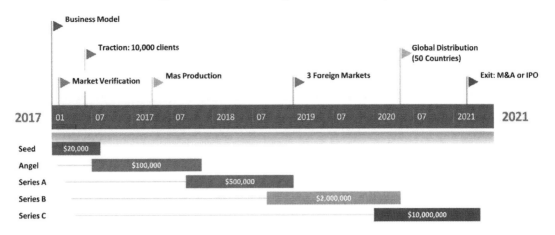

 ? Estimate your financial needs relatively to key milestones

An investor may not necessarily know the exact amount your business will need to grow to the next key milestone. Therefore, you should calculate how much money you will need to achieve each of the key milestones. Investors usually rely on your ability to make and communicate your financial plans. If they can't rely on that, they don't invest! The reasonable investor will review your cash needs relative to your stated goals (the milestones you want to achieve) and check the structure of your monthly cash burn rate (the amount of money you spend each month). Investors might make weighted assumptions about ways to reduce your cash burn rate. Therefore, be ready for a scenario where you will be offered a smaller amount than you are seeking in order to achieve your next key milestone. Usually, this form of communications works quite well:

"This is what I need: {ideal amount of investment you estimated to be sufficient to achieve the next major milestones} to achieve {major milestones you are targeting}, but this is what I can accomplish {one or two smaller, but yet meaningful milestones} with this {smaller amount} investment."

Decide on the right time to start fundraising

If you are not a bootstrapper, probably the best time to start fundraising was yesterday! The process of when you start looking for investors until you close the deal and get funds into your account may take quite a long time. During my global research on startups, I found several cases where quite interesting startups (with market validation and prototypes ready) were not able to get funded for a year or even more. It's not unusual for the early stage startup round to take up to eight months from having the initial meetings until you close the deal. Just keep in mind that a lot of work must be done before any investor will agree to meet you. A study by Tom Eisenmann (2015) showed that it takes 12.5 weeks on average from meeting until the deal is closed in early stage investment rounds. There's no doubt that your chance of success and the time required depends heavily on your communication, networking, and fundraising skills. The main task for you now is to estimate when you should start meeting with your chosen potential investors in order not to stall the development of your startup. You definitely don't want to get into the situation where you run out of money without achieving key milestones.

 Define your preferred conditions

Not all investors and investment conditions are equally good. So be sure you know what you are looking for. Even though it's just a guideline, it's always good to know in advance what investment conditions would satisfy you. Special attention should be paid to tranche investments as they are quite popular among investors who are ready to fund a startup but still want to minimize their risk if the upcoming milestones are not met.

Typical tranche investment is similar to the investor giving you half of the investment once the deal is signed, and half the investment when your revenue reaches a predefined amount. Most investors think that such approach is a good tool to motivate founders to reach a milestone and reduce the risk of their investment. However, trenches can be damaging in the long run, especially if milestones are not met or the startup lacks just a bit to meet them. This might demotivate founders if these situations are not discussed in advance. Another danger is related to reduced creativity. If the chosen milestone is easily achievable, this might limit the creativity of the whole team as nothing forces them to think how to grow the business faster. Tranche investment also might be a signal that maybe the investor is not ready for a full commitment or that there are some unaddressed doubts, neither of which is good.

If you find a deal for tranche investments, here is what you should consider:

- Agree on simple and clear milestones without any possible interpretations and unexpected conditions.
- Reduce the amount of money and set a closer-term milestone to be achieved (discuss the possibility of setting smaller milestones instead of one major one).
- Define what help you can and should not expect from the investors (for example, if you need an investor with good connections to enter new market and you set the milestone related to export revenue, but the investor won't take enough time to help you with his connections, technically the milestone might not be completed and that will be your responsibility).

During the negotiation process with investors, all these conditions might be put under question and modified. But at least you will have a clear vision and be able to declare your preferences and expectations to investors who become interested in your startup.

 Recommended reading

1. Carlos Espinal. *Fundraising Field Guide*: *A Startup Founder's Handbook for Venture Capital*

17. Bootstrapping or be ready for plan B

WHY IT IS NEEDED

The main advantages of bootstrapping are that you remain the boss of your startup, you are not accountable to anybody else, and you are 100% responsible for the results you get. That's probably one of the main reasons why bootstrapped startups usually get relatively quick validation from the market about their business idea. It's simple: there isn't time for the long game! If you chose to bootstrap your startup, that's great! You deserve sincere respect for taking full responsibility for your success. This chapter should help make sure you don't miss a chance to use the momentum and scale your business.

Sometimes bootstrapping is done not by choice, you might literally have no other option. Maybe you have a truly great idea as to how to solve a painful problem, but the solution requires more financial assets than you currently have. When you are just starting out with an innovative business idea, you're not at the point where a bank or investor would be willing to invest in you. The main task in this situation is to speed up your startup development as quickly as possible to become more attractive in the eyes of potential investors and financial partners. We have already talked about problem-solution-market fit, which is an essential part of your startup development. During my global research on startups, I learned that almost all of them had to finish this stage on bootstrapping and only then were they able to get funded from investors or lenders. This means that, even if you plan to build your startup with fundraising, you'll have to do your homework (get market validation) and invest at least some of your own money. Otherwise, if you don't have enough faith in your business to risk your own money, why should anyone else risk theirs?

In this chapter, I recommend a few actionable steps and ideas on how to survive the bootstrapping phase and not to miss the momentum for scaling your business up and taking it to another level.

01 — Evaluate Your Financial Capabilities
Estimate which milestones you can achieve with your current resources

02 — Build Foundations for Marketing
Bear in mind that the stronger your marketing is, the more chances you have for success

03 — Boost Your Sales Manually
Be ready to do some things manually, especially when your budget is close to zero

04 — Don't Lose the Momentum
Think about how you could use the momentum and scale your business

 Evaluate your financial capabilities

First of all, begin by doing a thorough inventory of your assets (financial and otherwise) that you could use to develop your business idea. You don't have to use them for your startup, but it's always good to know what you have in your reserve. You are likely to uncover resources you might even don't know you had including savings accounts, investments, equity in real estate, retirement and insurance accounts, passive income streams, vehicles, equipment, valuable collections, etc. You may decide to sell some assets for cash or to use them as a pledge for a loan. Try to estimate how much cash you could accumulate from your assets.

If you plan to go for fundraising, you should already have defined at least your key milestones which we discussed in the previous chapter. Now comes the moment of truth. Check which milestones you could achieve with whatever amount of cash you are able to accumulate. What are the chances that your startup will become more interesting for investors and lenders after achieving those milestones? If the odds are good enough, you should proceed towards those milestones. Otherwise, don't hurry, but instead reassess your business idea, key milestones, and possibility acquiring funds. Joe Garza (2016) from Founders Institute states that too many promising startups have failed because the founders neglected to make informed decisions with their limited funds or utilize their available resources to their full potential.

Let's look at *TestingTime* as an example. *TestingTime* is a Swiss-based startup providing an online recruiting service for test users. From 2013 until the end of 2014, *TestingTime* was bootstrapped as a side project. In 2013, it generated €10,000 in revenue, while in 2014 revenue reached €100,000. At this point, the founders knew they had a valid business model and founded a company to onboard the third co-founder. Now, all of the co-founders were working full time on *TestingTime*. The startup kept bootstrapping until mid-2015 when they raised nearly €850,000 in the seed round. *TestingTime* ended 2015 with €300,000 in revenue and close to €1 million in 2016. They could have continued bootstrapping but accepted a seed investment instead. As Reto Lämmler, one of the co-founders explained, they saw that for faster growth they needed to hire a team, but at the moment they couldn't afford it using only the revenue they have generated.

 Build strong foundations for your marketing

If there is no strong marketing, then your success in the market and with investors will be determined more by accident than by design. While it's true, it's also sad to admit that too many startups fall into the trap of thinking that they will take care of marketing once they get funded or have the product created. It doesn't cost much money (if anything at all) to do most of the essential homework in startup marketing. If you do all the tasks of Feasibility Study and Hypotheses and Experiments stages you'll have a much greater chance of success. Here are few additional tips which might be helpful:

- Make your brand name easy to spell, memorable, and engaging. If users can't spell and remember your brand name, they won't be able to find it when searching for your products or services and won't be able to share it with others.

- Once you create a strong positioning statement, make it clear and appealing in your written and visual communication to your consumers. Make your startup look like a leading company in the market or at least in the niche. Test this communication on social media and check to see if you are attracting your target customer segments and how strongly they are engaging.

- After choosing which channels you wish to be visible, establish a strong relationship with a journalist who writes articles related to your industry. A good relationship with a journalist in particular channel might save you a substantial amount of your marketing budget, so it's worth it to invest some time in building real relationships.

- Establish yourself as an industry expert and be ready to talk not only about your startup and product but about the whole field in which you are solving customer problems. Showing that you are a worthy source of knowledge will serve you when you are trying to attract more attention from journalists.

- Social media is no longer the free advertising channel as it was some time ago. The audience reach in most social network platforms is quite low unless you boost it with at least a minor budget. Whether you'll invest some money in this communication channel or not, while you're bootstrapping it's important to be active and consistent with your posts. Don't brag about yourself and don't post worthless old news. Try to make your posts fun and engaging for your followers. Most social platforms are built in such a way that the more engaging your posts are, the larger the audience you'll reach.

 Boost your sales and traction manually

Sales and traction are the most important indicators of startup success, especially if you are bootstrapping. If there are no sales, you get no money. Your cash burn rate becomes the only indicator of how much time you have to change the situation until your startup story is over. If there is no traction, it means there is no significant proof from the market that what you are doing is important for your target customers, therefore, none of the reasonable investors will take your startup seriously. Here are few ideas from startup bootstrappers on how to generate sales and traction without wasting too much of your money:

- A good value proposition and a strong positioning statement are the essential factors of your success in sales and fundraising. That's why we've discussed this topic at the beginning of this book. Prepare marketing material with your main value proposition and test how potential customers perceive what you are offering. You should have done that in the Hypotheses and Experiments stage. If you haven't developed and validated your value proposition, don't ask me what advertising would be most effective for you. The answer will be simple: None, because you don't know what you are selling, to whom you are selling, and why should they buy from you. Don't waste your money on advertising and PR until you have these answers!

- No matter what you are selling, create a website and provide valuable content to attract more target customers. Even if you sell your product in a physical store, it is more than likely your potential customers are looking online for information about your product. Become visible for them and don't just rely on "hope marketing" (which basically means "I hope they will get interested when they see my product"). Develop your website in the way it generates you leads of potential customers whether it's submitted via email or a phone call, becoming a follower on one of the social platforms, or even visiting your physical store.

- When you are just starting and your marketing budget is close to zero, put your main efforts towards direct marketing. Get in contact with potential customers personally, which is much more respectful and effective than just cold calling or emailing SPAM. Take it from this perspective: instead of fishing (waiting for the clients to come to you), go hunting (choose the most prospective clients and take targeted actions to get them on board). Don't forget to ask your early adopters for positive testimonials for your product as this will definitely help to establish your startup's reputation.

- Leverage your network. Find partners, influencers, and other experts in your market. Approach them with a well-crafted proposal to promote your product. You will have to put some effort into creating a separate value proposition for influencers as you'll have to show them what benefit they will get for promoting your product. Sometimes free sample and building good relations or offering an affiliate commission could be enough. Don't limit yourself to these standard approaches, think more creatively from the perspective of your product, the problem you solve, or the specific market.

 ## Don't lose the momentum

It doesn't matter if you are bootstrapping by your own choice or forced by circumstances, you should regularly ask yourself how you could scale your business and take it to another level. Here are few questions you should consider:

- What could help you to grow your business faster? What is it? Any kind of resources, new valuable connections, distribution, access anything else?
- Does it cost money or time? Is it related to additional funding or you could go for it you're your current assets?
- How could you grow your business if you would have 10 times as much cash?

This simple exercise will help you to spot the momentum and move to the next step. If you remain without external funding (it doesn't necessary have to be from investors) for too long, you may be unable to take advantage of opportunities to grow your business.

I'd like to share the story of SlideModel for inspiration and encouragement. Julian Magnone started *SlideModel* as a spin-off and presented it as a case study for his final MBA thesis, after investigating different startup development methodologies introduced by Eric Ries, Steve Blank, Ash Maurya, Rita McGrath, and others. *SlideModel* emerged as a spin-off of another product (SlideOnline.com) and after successfully running an MVP with a couple of iterations to validate the hypothesis they had formulated, the product started to generate revenue. Then, German Viera, an engineer with a strong background in technology and business, joined the project and the company was incorporated.

Even though *SlideModel* was bootstrapped in a garage in Montevideo, Uruguay (South America), it was a profitable business from the very beginning. They started providing presentation templates for individuals and businesses and reached 120,000 subscribers in 2 years, now serving companies around the globe in more than 100 countries. And even now they stay lean and modest by having just a very small office in Uruguay with a virtual structure. So who said that large investments are necessary to build a profitable and scalable business?

 Recommended reading

1. Marcus Gibson, Greg Gianforte. *Bootstrapping Your Business*: *Start and Grow a Successful Company with Almost No Money*
2. Eric Karjaluoto. *Speak Human*: *Outmarket the Big Guys by Getting Personal*
3. K.A DeWolf. *Bootstrapping Entrepreneur*: *100 Free Online Tools for Startups and First-Time Entrepreneurs*

18. Choosing the best funding source

WHY IT IS IMPORTANT

The excuse that you can't start a business because you don't have money is not valid anymore. A tremendous number of startups need funding at different stages. Their financial needs, development goals, and overall business risks are very different. On the other side, there is a huge amount of money waiting for good investment opportunities. You just need to know what funding sources are available and which of them would be most suitable in your case.

During my global research on startups, I found one very common mistake that early stage startups tend to do when going for fundraising for the first time. Most of them try to spread the news about themselves as wide as possible and approach all possible funding sources. Such fundraising efforts mostly end up as a terrible waste of time if you don't do your homework first. You already know about the fundraising process and should have foreseen your startup development milestones. Now it's about time to get acquainted with different startup funding sources and decide which of them you will use to achieve the particular milestones of your startup development. Even if you are bootstrapping and currently don't see the need for outside investment, this chapter might be useful for you when you decide to scale your business.

01 Personal Savings or Loan
Be ready to fund with your own savings, if you want investors to take you seriously

02 Business Income in Advance
Determine if it would be possible to get an advance payment for your products

03 Crowd Funding Platform
Get your first customers and funding by generating cash for product pre-orders

04 Angel Investors and Seed Firms
Consider this option if your startups is in seed stage, but already has some proof of viability

05 Accelerators and Incubators
Know the difference between accelerators and incubators and chose wisely

06 Venture Capital Funds
Narrow the type of VCs you are targeting and focus your efforts purposefully

07 Other Possible Sources
Consider other options like a side business, grants, contests, or vendor financing

 Personal savings or loan

Most investors and your future partners will take you more seriously if you invest at least some amount of your personal assets. Said another way, if you don't invest money in your project, why should anybody else do that? Sure, that's no big deal if you believe in your business idea and have some savings, but what should you do if you don't have any assets? Here are few possibilities on how to get initial funding on your own:

- *Selling your assets* that you don't really need anymore. Selling them might help you at least partly cover your initial costs (for example, to create low fidelity prototypes and test some initial hypotheses).

- *Family and friends* usually believe in you much more than any bank. Maybe they will support your idea financially without waiting until you have real customers and revenue. Borrowing from friends and family is an interesting alternative as you can come to an agreement faster than with any bank and maybe have low or even no-interest credit. It is recommended that these commitments be done in writing with some kind of condition (for example, maybe you will be obligated to return the loan from your salary or any other sources after you get funded by the investor, or you will convert the loan into equity at a particular development stage and etc.).

- *The personal loan* might be a solution if you have an excellent credit history. If your startup isn't a company yet, you can try talk to the bank and get a personal credit. You'll have to be able to present how the loan will be spent and what income sources you have to cover your financial obligation. If your startup has no income and your personal income is too low, you might seem too risky to the bank and you won't get the loan.

- *Peer-to-peer lending platforms* might be considered as a small business loan alternative if they are available for you. A peer-to-peer lending platform is a financial marketplace which connects people willing to lend their money to people—and sometimes companies—who want to get a loan. This is not a crowdfunding platform. You'll have to pay back the loan with interest that might be higher than in a bank. The difference is that you won't owe a single amount to a bank, but many small amounts to a lot of people.

- *Credit cards* usually have a high interest rate, therefore it's not very wise to overuse them. But, if you need cash to make progress in your startup and become more interesting to potential investors, this option should be considered as well. Actually, there are specific credit cards designed for entrepreneurs. Call to your bank to talk about possible options.

 Business income in advance

Selling your products before they are launched is an often overlooked yet highly effective way to raise the money needed for financing your business. Personally, I like this most because it has a double benefit! If you can successfully run at least some pre-orders of your product, this not only allows you to collect some money but also validates the market hypotheses. Stay focused on real sales during your experiments, and run the pre-order campaign once the prototype is introduced.

Even a non-standard startup such as Eematico has been successful for more than two years by focusing on business income in advance. Eematico is an organization in Romania that leads innovation of educational programs (not software) aimed at developing life skills in children for the 21st century. In their first two years, the team has managed to create more than 600 hours of educational activities as well as full sets of specific materials for more than 190 different activities. Programs and activities are being sold to thousands of children. The key success factor was selling their services and products early on, as soon as they were viable. This allowed them to develop educational programs with 9 modules of 4 weekly lessons each, while only investing the money for just the first module. Once *Eematico* designed the concept, they made presentations of the materials and pitched them to individual clients as well as to kindergartens. As soon as contracts started signing, Eematico created the whole program.

 Crowdfunding platforms

One of the funding sources that startup founders are becoming more interested in is crowdfunding via online platforms. However, these platforms can be of two different types:

1. *Cash for product pre-orders* (for example, Kickstarter, IndieGoGo). This is one of the newer ways of funding a startup or just a new product. The general idea is that anyone can contribute money to help a business or project that they believe in. You can create a crowdfunding campaign by putting up a detailed description of your business, your main goals, a definition of the target audience, and the amount of funding you need and for what purpose. The more appealing you present your idea, the greater the chances you'll get funded. But don't expect miracles to happen! If you want to receive, you must give something back. Usually, it's called pledges—your promise of what you'll give for a particular amount of donation. To offer your product as a pledge is one of the best solutions: your greatest fans will be the first to get your awesome product before it's in the market and you'll get a confirmation as to whether your product is worth that amount of money (this will help you to define pricing level for the future).

2. *Cash for equity* (for example, AngelList, Seedrs, Crowdcube, Crowdbnk). These platforms allow contributors to provide you cash in exchange for a share of your company ownership. Literally, supporters are becoming investors and shareholders of your company, with all the rights and duties. These platforms differ from each other by how they structure the investment into your company and the locations where they can operate.

To get more information about opportunities on these platforms, visit them and check out their downloadable materials and intro videos. One thing you should be clear about is that you should not expect to use any crowdfunding platform as a stand-alone solution. If you want to get funded, you'll have to put some effort into promoting your crowdfunding campaign instead of trusting your luck and attracting random visitors to the chosen platform.

 Angel investors and seed firms

This is one of the most popular options for startup seed funding. Angel investors are wealthy individuals with significant experience and networks in a particular industry giving their own money to a startup project (typical investment might be $25,000-100,000). Angel investors usually allow you to keep control over your company, but they oftentimes want a large portion of your equity, meaning when you make money, they also make money. Angel investors can give you not only seed money but valuable mentorship when it's needed. They use their network connections to make your startup grow and start earning revenue faster. Although these investors can have a strong personal interest in your project, they have busy lives and other investments, so you will not always be able to rely on them for the support you need. Most early stage startups don't limit themselves to working with one angel investors and try to attract several of them to have stronger overall support.

Seed firms are small venture capital funds that have professional, savvy investors and pursue investments on a full-time basis. The usual investment amount ranges from $250,000 to $1 million in a startup, therefore they have a greater financial interest in your success. The advantage is that seed firms have more money to give you later if needed. The downside of working with this type of investor is that seed firms may not always be the best experts in your industry plus they are involved and many other deals, but they might be willing to have control over your business decisions.

 Startup accelerators and incubators

You might consider the possibility of applying to accelerators and incubators. There are plenty of them and their conditions are very different. Usually, an accelerator works with startups for a short and specific amount of time (90—120 days is most common). Accelerators also can offer startups a specific amount of capital (in most cases, it might be up to $20,000). In exchange for their guidance, capital, and some particular services, most accelerators require anywhere from 3 to 8% ownership of your company. Joining the accelerator is still not an all-inclusive solution to your startup funding. The main goal is to prepare your startup to raise larger amounts of capital. Accelerators try to grow the size and value of a startup as fast as possible and prepare it for an initial round of funding.

Incubators focus less on quick growth and help startups with mentorship often lasting more than a year. Usually, incubators do not provide upfront capital like accelerators and take little to no equity in your company. Many incubators are funded by grants through universities, allowing them to provide their services without taking some equity out of your startup. It's far more difficult to get into the incubator because many startups are willing to get in there and receive help without losing part of their ownership. An incubator most likely won't give funds to develop your startup, but being inside the incubator might help you to develop your startup much faster and attract investors from other sources.

 ## Venture capital funds (VCs)

A venture capital (VC) fund is a professional group that looks specifically to fund startups. VC typically provides funding for early-stage, high-potential, and growth companies seeking to generate a return through an eventual realization event such an IPO (Initial Public Offering) or selling the company in any other way. This type of investor holds a lot of money available to invest in startups, but there are a few major downsides as well. Venture capital typically looks for larger opportunities that are more likely to be stable. It means that your startup should have a strong team and a need for few million dollars to scale effectively. To secure their investments, these funds might require having some level of control in your startup.

If you decide that VCs funding fits your strategy and you want to achieve success in fundraising, first of all, you should narrow the type of VC you are targeting. VCs are of different types and sizes. They can be categorized along a few main dimensions: size and purpose of the typical investment, location, and industry sector. Generally, there are few main types of VCs based on the purpose of the investment:

1. Early stage financing:
   - Seed financing is usually a small amount that enables a company to get a start-up loan
   - The purpose of start-up financing is to finish the development of products or services
   - First stage financing is used when the company has spent starting capital and needs funds for taking business activities to full-scale
2. Expansion financing:
   - Second-stage financing is used to begin a startup's expansion in a particular way
   - Bridge financing may be provided as a short-term, interest-only finance option as well as a form of monetary assistance to companies willing to employ the IPO as a major business strategy.

3. Acquisition/buyout financing (even though it is not a VC fund by itself, it might be worth to have this financial solution in mind):

- Acquisition financing assists in acquiring a certain part of or an entire company
- Management or, so- called leveraged buyout, financing helps a particular management group to acquire a particular product of even another company

Once you have narrowed down the list of targeted VCs, look at their most recent investments. Research how many investments they have made, what types of companies they invested in, and if they specialize in a specific sector or geographic location. Try to estimate the size of their investments, if possible. If your business closely matches with their most recent investments, that might be a good signal to proceed with figuring out how to approach these particular VCs.

 Other possible sources

We have looked through all major possibilities of where your startup could get funded. But, if your fantasy is without limits, there may be some other, not so common possibilities:

- *Side businesses* (your other business activity) can generate some revenue and fund your startup. It's quite similar to funding a startup from your own assets, but in this case, if your startup is an established company, maybe you can provide some other services or products to earn cash for the main project?
- *Grants* could be a great gift if your business focuses on a scientific or research-oriented field. This financial aid is usually provided by governments to support particular causes. It might be worth some effort to research what grants you could apply for. For example, *ERES Biotechnology* got a $30,000 grant from the government of Turkey to find new and simple solutions for specific biotech problems. Their academic background was a large part of their success, but they didn't stop after getting this grant. *ERES Biotechnology* actively sells their other services and products to the global market in order to raise money for further development.
- *Winning a contest* might sound something like "OK, win a lottery and then launch your business." There are many startup events, pitches or business plan competitions, and entrepreneurship fostering programs and contests where startups can win cash or other valuable prizes like professional services, free of charge. These events are taking place all over the world, for example, the Wolves Summit in Poland recently gave away $100,000 ($25,000 in cash and $75,000 in investment).

- *Vendor financing* could help if you need tangible products for reselling or for using as components in your production. Many manufacturers and distributors can agree to defer your payment until these products are sold by you. This can't be treated as a long-term financial solution but could help you to save money for a few months (depending on your creditworthiness, industry standards, and your negotiation skills).

- *Purchase order financing* can solve the most common scaling problem faced by startups: they can't accept a large order because they don't have enough funds to build and deliver such a large amount of product. Companies providing purchase order financing service will often pay the required funds directly to the supplier, providing you the opportunity to complete the huge order.

- *Factoring accounts receivables* help startups to get cash on sales immediately, rather than waiting for 30 to 60 days or longer for payment. Through this process, a service provider will front you the money on invoices that have been billed out, which you then pay back once the customer has settled its bill.

 Recommended reading

1. Brad Feld, Jason Mendelson. *Venture Deals: Be Smarter Than Your Lawyer and Venture Capitalist*

2. Andrew Romans. *The Entrepreneurial Bible to Venture Capital: Inside Secrets From the Leaders in the Startup Game*

3. Visit crowdfunding platforms and check their provided guides and statistics

19. Creating winning fundraising material

WHY IS IT NEEDED?

When it comes to fundraising, many founders get such an uncomfortable feeling. It's almost like they are back in school and have to go in front of the classroom to show how well they've learned the subject and to answer teacher's tricky questions. That's because they are not sure how well they did their homework and what questions the teacher will ask. The good thing about fundraising is that you can prepare well in advance and feel confident about your investor pitching.

If you could know what investors have in mind when evaluating the company and making a decision whether to fund you or not, you would feel far more confident. Investors rarely have time to read long business plans, so the first impression becomes more and more important.

But it's not enough just to have a great elevator pitch. The times when VC investors were chasing potential unicorns is already gone. Today, most of them are looking for sustainable businesses which have proof that they can be profitable and scalable. Therefore, if you prepare and optimize your fundraising materials and address key issues, you'll have a much greater chance to start negotiation and get funded.

HOW TO DO IT

 Elevator pitch

The main goal of an elevator pitch is to get those miracle words, "I'd like to know more," from a potential investor. Experience shows that the structure of the positioning statement is one of the most effective forms to start your elevator pitch. Thus, your success mostly depends on the very essence of your business idea, but not in the form of the pitch.

Start crafting your elevator pitch with your one sentence positioning statement. Then add another sentence explaining what you've already achieved (provide proof of your business model). The third sentence should define what you are looking for in terms of investors and your (what kind of investors you are seeking and what would you expect from them).

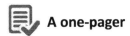 **A one-pager**

The one-pager mostly is used I two general ways. The first and most often is the case when you send an introductory email or message to the potential investor via startup networking platform or professional social network like Linkedin. Your one-pager goes as an attachment. Another case for using your one-pager is after the potential investor heard your "elevator pitch" and said he'd like to know more. But that's quite a rare case, because... well, how many times per day you "ride the elevator with potential" investors?... If you are not a maniac you are trying to meet investors in startup events, which are not taking place every day. Therefore you might try reaching investors by phone and giving them your "elevator pitch."

Summing up, your one-pager should be nearly a work of art that represents your business idea, brand, tone, and even your personality. It will be your most often used piece of fundraising material because you'll have to reach as more potential investors as possible at the beginning stage in order to find the best partner for your startup. The one-pager should:

- contain all the critical facts about your company, but still remain minimalistic
- be of high quality, by all means, therefore you might consider hiring a freelance designer to make you one-pager visually outstanding
- prepared in a mobile-device-friendly format, convenient to send and read via mobile

 Investor presentation and the pitch

Introducing your business idea verbally (pitching) will require a simplified presentation with fewer details compared to the pitch deck which you will hand to potential investors. The main focus during the pitch should be on you and your verbal communication. So, a very detailed and overloaded presentation won't give the potential investors much of an opportunity to listen to you. Most of them will just run through the presentation and get bored.

There are different recommendations as to what aspects should be included in your investor presentation, but my research revealed that these seven points should be covered:

1. *Problem* – Remind investors about the main problem your product is designed to solve and explain why a solution is so important and urgent. Prove it by showing the main findings from your experiments validating the problem.

2. *Solution* - Show the product or at least use screenshots, sketches, prototypes or photos. Show your experiment findings to confirm that customers agree it solves the problem and they are ready to pay for it (market verification).

3. *Customer workflow* (with and without your proposed solution)—This is optional, but if your solution is innovative, the simplified customer journey map will help investors to better understand the essence of the product and your business specifics.

4. *Market overview* - The total addressable and target market size, key players, competitors, possible partners, your competitive advantage, and differentiation. Review what you've already done in the Feasibility Study stage and what new findings came through during the Hypotheses and Experiments stage.

5. *Financials* - Share your financial situation and plans for the future (including key milestones).Investors want to be sure that you will use their funds effectively. Usually, this section requires you to also highlight how you will make money and when the invested funds will be paid back, which might be difficult to define. But if you don't have an idea about the investment payback conditions and timing, it would be the same as offering to buy a lottery ticket and hoping to win a jackpot at some time. Why should investors trust their money to you instead of buying one or two well-known lottery tickets?

6. *Achievements*—Provide the evidence about your progress, including an overview of what you've already done and how it made your startup stronger. The most successful investor pitches are those where startups show that they are doing great, are earning money, and huge profits are close at hand. All you need is a certain amount of investment for certain activities to build or scale the business.

7. *Team members*—Introduce your key players and prove why you and your team can make this happen.

Pitch deck as a stand-alone presentation

This presentation is called a *stand-alone* solution because it is designed so that any investor reading it will fully understand your idea and business model. The main purpose of the pitch deck is to cover all important aspects of your startup business in such way that potential investors can review it in less than five minutes. Actually, as Kim-Mai Cutler shared in his article on TechCrunch, investors spend only 3:44 minutes on average to review each startup's pitch deck. Therefore, your pitch deck should not be designed to close the investment deal, but to get investors interested and move you to the next stage to discuss additional aspects and possible partnerships.

It's obvious that this presentation should have a cover page and summary. You'll have more chances to get investors interested if your cover page includes the unique benefit for investors or your positioning statement rather than just a startup's name. Usually, the summary is the next page after the cover and shows the crucial information that you provide to potential investors. This page needs to be marked as confidential, especially if you have some data that should not be revealed to anyone other than the investors.

Other sections to include in the presentation are:

1. *Target Market* - Define your target segments (especially early adopters - evangelists) in less than 10 words and include an image or two to better visualize your target customer's profile.

2. *Problem* - Clearly identify a real and huge problem in less than 10 words so that investors can see you are addressing a real and current need.

3. *Solution* - Simply explain what your solution addresses the problem you've described. Don't go into too much detail yet, but show your quantifiable solution benefits, if possible.

4. *Market Analysis*—Show the size of the potential target market (domestic and global), how fast it is growing (% and actual numbers), and who is already working in it (competitor market share).

5. *Unique selling proposition (USP)*—Explain why your solution is the best choice for target customers (no brag, no fluff, just proven value proposition). Sometimes, what makes your offer unique to customers is called your *secret sauce*.

6. *Marketing Plan*—Explain the main aspect of how you'll communicate your USP to the target market, what the sales funnel/pipeline will look like, what tools you will use, and what conversion rates are expected (don't forget to prove your numbers by experiment results, for example).

7. *Business model*—One of the best ways is to show your business model or Lean Canvas with some explanations.

8. *Traction*—Basically, you have to provide proof of the concept and the best way to do that is to show that your startup is getting traction which will lead to revenue and profits (for example, how many customers and distribution partners you have, what is your presence in media, and does it drive qualified leads to you).

9. *Competitor analysis*—Show the best available alternative solutions of the problem for customers and prove how your USP is better. If you can't find alternative solutions in the market, maybe the problem you are addressing is not a problem at all and nobody cares about solving it?

10. *Intellectual property*—List all of the intellectual property you own that helps to strengthen your USP and the whole business model (for example, patents, trademarks, copyrights, domains, special know-how, etc.).

11. *Team*—Introduce founders, executives, advisors, investors, and key people who are involved in the startup. Try to show how each of them contributes to your startup success and how their input will be valuable in the future.

12. *Milestones*—Show completed and targeted milestones of your startup development. Try to prove that you've already done a meaningful amount of work and that you clearly know what to do next to create a profitable and scalable business.

13. *Financial data*—Provide key indicators such as your cash burn rate, revenue, customer acquisition costs, profit margin, etc. Be very thoughtful with the content, as investors will probably spend the most time on this section.

14. *Risk management*—Be honest with potential investors and show what risks you see and how you are prepared to deal with them. You should already have foreseen all that in Chapter 4: Business model and fatal flaws.

15. *Offer for investors*—Explain how much money you are requesting, what are your general terms (this one is optional because you might want to offer different conditions to different investors), what those funds will be used for, what is your exit strategy and why it is realistic.

References and contact details should be final slides of your pitch deck. It's up to you to decide where to show the list of statistics and research sources on which your assumptions are based. You can put links in particular presentation where such facts are mentioned or you can provide the list of references at the end of the presentation. In any case, it will provide additional credibility.

 Online profiles and media

Now it's time for your startup to become more visible that investors can spot you. Register your startup on major startup-investor matchmaking platforms like AngelList, F6S, *InnMind*, and others meaningful platforms that are typically used to learn more about your startup (you can download a list of such platforms at www.evolutioncurve.com). I wouldn't just sit and wait for a miracle to happen (investors knocking at your door), but creating professional and appealing profiles on these platforms is a very important step. Even if you reach investors directly, most of them will check to see what public information is available about your startup. Therefore, it's important to be visible and credible.

Try to get noticed by the media and save the links to posts, articles, and podcasts where your startup is mentioned. It might serve as a proof of traction and that your startup is doing something meaningful and a new trend is coming. Investors want to see more than just a PDF or PowerPoint presentation about your startup (all those fundraising materials we've talked still remain extremely important), or a mention in media, they also want to see unique videos about your startup. For example, you could prepare the introduction video, the MVP presentation video, the backstage video made in your workshop, and team introduction videos. Just name it! Investors like video, because they can see much more than in a static presentation. They can see your passion, involvement, and progress over time. Check out startup video storytelling platform like VentureCondo. It might be a good place to start uploading your videos and creating your startup video story so it will be visible to many VC investors.

 ## Financial assumptions model and cap table

The investor is not a Santa Claus ready to give you expensive gifts just because you were a good person during the year. Once you ask an investor to become your partner and tell them about your funding requirements, be prepared to show your financial assumptions and current ownership situation (cap table) in detail. Even if you are not an accountant, as a startup founder you should always be ready to discuss the following:

- *Cash burn rate*—The amount of money you burn through each month (which you should have evaluated it in Chapter 7: Financial assessments and updated it in the Hypotheses and Experiments stage).
- *Aggregated investment*—The amount of funding you have already raised.
- Cap table - Equity distribution among your team members.
- *Option pool*—The reserve of equity which is a remuneration for your existing and future employees, directors, and advisors. There is no rule of thumb, but in most cases, the option pool ranges from 5% to 20% depending on the company's stage and upcoming hiring needs.
- *Round size* - The amount of money you are raising to achieve your stated milestones.
- *Pre-money valuation* - The worth of your startup company prior to the new investment coming in.
- *Post-money valuation* - The sum of the pre-money valuation plus the round size.

If you are not good at finances, I'd suggest preparing your financial assumptions with the help of a mentor, consultant, or at least a freelancer who can guide you through the process of completing blank templates and preparing a professional financial assumption set. Also, you can check out the financial assumption templates available at www.evolutioncurve.com.

During my global research on startups, I met Matthew Maly. Matthew has written five science books and spent thirty years developing the sophisticated technology that went into his app. His startup, PsyClue, graduated from the Founders Space accelerator but was still searching for seed investment. From a marketing perspective, I found Psy-Clue to be an alternative to a psychologist (at some level) that you can have in your pocket at any time. It is a "self-help" or "psychological" smartphone app where you type in your interpersonal problem, the app asks three questions, and you find the solution to your problem by entering answers into the app.

Matthew shared many of the misgivings he felt during the fundraising process. Even though his startup was based on well-grounded technology and had graduated from an accelerator, he still was not able to find seed investment. Instead, he received a feedback that he should not be the one who pitches the idea to investors because he was 57 years old and he had no MBA! Many of the suggestions he got from potential investors were shallow and not relevant.

Once I saw the initial PsyClue investor pitch deck, it became clear why there were misunderstandings and miscommunications between the startup founders and potential investors. Holding a Ph.D. degree and being a scientist myself, I understand Matthew's passion to spend most of the time during the pitch on the technological solution. But as a marketer, I noticed that his pitch deck missed many major points we talk about in this chapter. The pitch didn't provide the investors with the information most relevant to them. There was no proof about market fit and the business model was based on a doubtful monetization solution.

I can't guarantee that preparing a pitch according to guidelines listed above will open the doors to all investors, but your chance of success will definitely increase. Coming back to PsyClue case, instead of asking investors to support tens of thousands of dollars for MVP development and then somehow developing business, the founders could go to the market and get some facts from experiments. As we've discussed in Chapter 9: Creating minimal viable products: purposes and types, it›s not necessary to code a full app or to build a final product to get initial feedback from early adopters. For instance, there could be a very simple app that just sends messages to Matthew's computer and he sends his answers back to users. This simple app would allow him to run an experiment with one or more selected potential target users. Matthew himself could temporarily become the app that asks the right questions. After running this experiment for a week or two, the founders of PsyClue could gather decent feedback from at least 100 potential users. He could even let investors try the app during the pitch to get a sense if it delivers the promised value. That would help demonstrate the strength of the problem and solution itself, without even needing the app. If at least half of those test users would say that the app is super useful (or would even say they would purchase the app), PsyClue founders would have a serious proof for investors. How do you think their fundraising chances would change then?

 **Recommended reading**

1. Mark Peter Davis. *The Fundraising Rules*
2. Evan Baehr, *Evan Loomis. Get Backed*: *Craft Your Story, Build the Perfect Pitch Deck, and Launch the Venture of Your Dreams*

20. Determining the value of your startup

WHY IT IS NEEDED

We have already talked about your fundraising milestones. You should have at least rough estimates of the amount of money you'll need and when you'll need to raise it to develop your startup successfully. The problem is that not all investors will agree with your opinion. The funding investors are willing to provide to you will depend not only on how well your startup has been developed up until now but also on how much equity they will get for their investment. This is directly related to the pre-money valuation of your startup. If you start raising money based on the valuation of your startup, the whole process will take less time and you will be able to get back to your direct business development work sooner. Furthermore, understanding how the valuation of a startup works is important for planning your exit strategy. Most startup founders get their revenue not from profit or salary, but from selling their equity. Obviously, the price of your startup stocks will directly depend on the valuation of your startup. So let's review how the value of startups is determined.

HOW TO DO IT

01 Learn How Businesses are Valuated
Become familiar with business valuation methods to have background knowledge

02 Specifics of Startup Valuation
Use top-down and bottom-up approaches to estimate the valuation of your startup

03 Maximize Your Valuation
Find the ways to increase your startup's pre-money valuation to get better proposals

Classic approach to business valuation

There are few main methods for business valuation which have been used for a long time. Even though startup valuation is done in a bit different way, it's good to know the background of how the value of companies is usually determined. This might help you better understand investors during the negotiation and reach a mutually beneficial agreement.

- *The Discounted Cash Flow* is based on valuing a project or company using the concept of the time value of money. Basically speaking, cash in the future is less valuable compared to cash today. All future cash flows are estimated and discounted by using the cost of capital to calculate their present values. The sum of all future cash flows (incoming and outgoing) is the net present value, which is taken as the value or price of the cash flow in the future. This method is widely used in investment finance, real estate development, corporate financial management, and patent valuation.

- *Valuation using multiples* expresses the market value of an asset relative to a key statistic that is assumed to relate to that value. This method requires you to identify comparable assets and obtain market values for these assets, convert these market values into standardized values relative to a key statistic, and finally, apply the valuation multiple to the key statistic of the asset.

- *The First Chicago method* is a context-specific business valuation approach mostly used by venture capital and private equity investors. It combines elements of discounted cash flow valuation and multiples-based valuation. This method takes into account payouts to the holder of specific investments through the holding period under various scenarios (for example, best case, base case, worst case).

- *The Market and Transaction Comparable* method looks at similar or comparable transactions where the acquisition target has a similar business model and similar client base to the company being evaluated

- *The Asset-Based Valuation* (for example, Book Value) method is based on the original cost of the asset less any depreciation, amortization, or impairment costs made against the asset. Usually, a company's book value is its total assets minus intangible assets and liabilities, but book value may also include goodwill or intangible assets.

- *The Liquidation value* method is based on the likely price of an asset when it is allowed insufficient time to sell on the open market, thereby reducing its exposure to potential buyers. Liquidation value is typically lower than fair market value.

Valuing a startup is quite different from valuing established companies. Because of the high level of risk and often little or no revenues, traditional quantitative valuation methods are of little use. Startup valuations are largely determined based on qualitative attributes.

Main principles of startup valuation

Generally, there are two main approaches to startup valuation:

1. *The top-down* approach is when an early-stage investor tries to estimate what the likely exit size could be for a company in a similar sector. Then he judges how much equity his fund should have in the company to reach his targeted return on investment. If an investor knows what percentage they own after they put their money in and they can guess the exit value of your company, they can divide the size of investment by the percentage of equity and get a cash-on-cash multiple of what their investment will give them.

2. *The bottom-up* approach basically takes the average entry valuation for companies of a particular type and stage. Investors typically see and value startups relative to entry averages. The entry average used by the bottom-up approach is based on a figure that will likely give investors a meaningful return on an exit for the industry in question. During negotiations, investors might offer a similar proposal to the top-down approach, estimating what amount of money your startup might need to achieve in order to hit particular growth targets and thus, how much your startup is worth at the current stage.

It's better to keep in mind that investors will consider both where similar deals in the same sector are being priced and the amounts of recent exits. Both of these factors can dramatically affect the valuation of your startup. Therefore, you should check what valuations are in the market before you speak to investors. Try to find other startups like yours that have already raised money and see if they'll share with you what valuation they were given and how much they raised at a similar stage as yours. It's very important to keep track of news in your industry, which might occasionally give you the meaningful information to update or revise your valuations.

You can also check various online calculators to roughly estimate your startup valuation and possible equity split. If you are bootstrapping or yet in an early stage, but there are few co-founders, you might want to check the Slicing Pie concept and online tool. It is a universal, one-size-fits all model that creates a perfectly fair equity split in an early-stage, bootstrapped startup company. Cayenne Consulting provides a high-tech startup valuation estimator where you can answer 25 questions and get an approximate valuation range for your startup. This is a great tool especially because it makes to think through if you have done all your homework or are just dreaming about unicorns. This estimator can show $0 as your startup's pre-money value. What a wake-up call that would be!

 ### How to maximize your valuation

External investors, such as VCs and angel investors, will use a pre-money valuation to determine how much equity to demand in return for their cash. Therefore, you want a high, pre-money valuation while investors want a low, pre-money valuation. The more arguments you have to prove a higher pre-money valuation of your startup, the better the chances you'll keep more equity in your hands. Investors will be willing to pay more for your company if it is in a hot sector, has a great management team, a functioning product, traction, and a sustainable competitive advantage. Your startup valuation could also be much lower than the sector average if margins in the sector are getting low and you are just starting, competition is increasing and you have no solid differentiation, your management team has no track record, there are some technical issues with your product, you are running out of cash, or have other problems.

Generally, there are four main factors (Figure 32) that influence your startup's pre-money valuation: performance of your startup, market specifics, competing funding offers, and negotiation skills. Pay attention to all these factors while working on your fundraising materials.

Figure 32. Factors influencing startups pre-money valuation

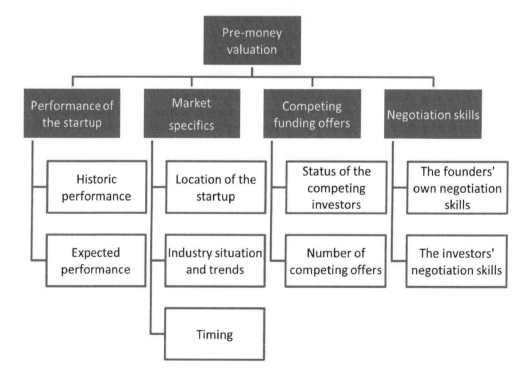

It's obvious that if the startup makes good revenue or even profit, the company is really valuable. The paradox is that some startups get a really high valuation with no significant traction yet. This is because investors evaluate not only the results you have achieved so far but also your expected performance in the future. Therefore, confidence and the right arguments also help to get a higher valuation, but without proven traction, no level of confidence or convincing arguments will create a miracle.

Figure 33. Average seed valuation by regions

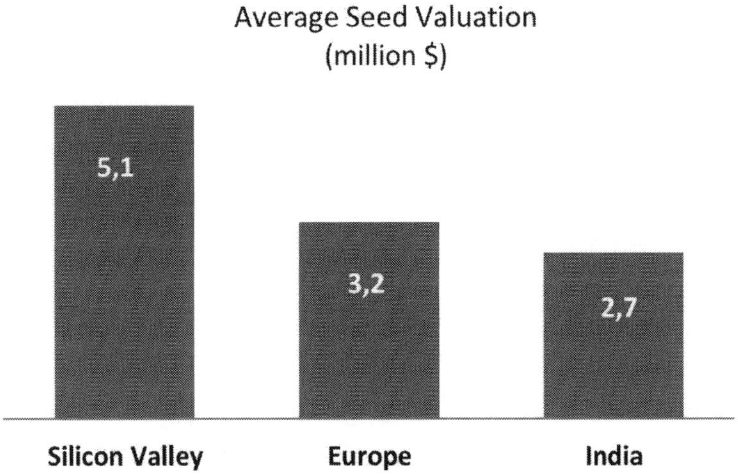

Average Seed Valuation
(million $)

Source: https://angel.co/valuations

Historical data shows that startups in particular locations tend to get higher seed evaluation compared to startups founded in other locations. We won't get too deep into the specifics of why and how such differences arise, but the fact is, that if your startup is situated in Silicon Valley, you can expect higher average initial evaluation than if you were based in Europe or India. You can check AngelList for more statistical data about average valuations.

Mark Suster (2016) surveyed 150 VCs and announced the results at the very beginning of 2016. He asked investors which statement best describes their mood going into 2016. His findings showed that 82% of surveyed VCs were concerned about the future. Obviously, your pitching would face at least some extra resistance and increased caution with such general mood in the market. Therefore, you are likely to get a lower pre-money valuation from potential investors. The same can be said about timing: if you are running out of cash and time is pressing, don't expect as high a pre-money valuation as you would get if you had a solid cash reserve and didn't need the funds so soon.

Competition for funding offers is another very interesting aspect that sometimes remains underestimated. You, as a founder, can get investors to compete, bid, and

Figure 34. VCs opinion about future perspectives

82% of VCs expressed concern going into 2016

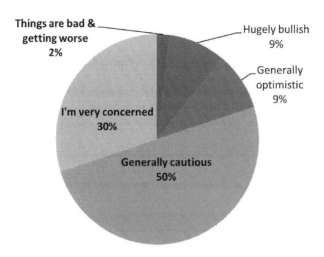

Source: Mark Suster, Upfront VC analysis 2016

maybe even form alliances. Sometimes the news that a well-known business angel or VC fund became interested in your startup might bring other investors to your door or at least make them more receptive. That is why it is so important to have a clear and structured fundraising process. Your goal is not just to wait until you get one or two offers, but to have established clear calls for fundraising with the exact dates when the deal should be closed. Having this process structured will help you in two ways:

1. Potential investors will see how well organized you are.

2. Showing that you have alternatives can encourage competition and you will get better deals (the status of the competing investors is far more important than the number of offers you receive).

Negotiation skills are also important in fundraising. There is no one-size-fits-all formula for setting the value of your startup and each potential investor can have different goals, investment policies, and rules. The good news is that you don't have to rely solely on your own personal communication and negotiation skills. Your advisory board members (if you already have such) can come in very handy. You're already on-boarded investors from previous fundraising rounds who share a common goal with you. They want to have as high a pre-money valuation as possible because they are already shareholders of your company and want to keep a relatively large part of their equity. If it is your first fundraising round, seek out mentors and specialized consultants. If you have a mentor, you can expect to receive his advice free-of-charge. There are also consultants of different levels and their fees are not necessarily high. If you are just starting the first fundraising round, getting professional help to back up your assumptions on the pre-money valuation could very useful when you sit down to the negotiation table with potential investors.

A startup's valuation is largely dictated by the market forces and many other factors in the industry. Therefore investors will take a deep dive into your business model, cost structure, marketing strategy, market size, competitors, and other aspects. Most investors don't have any problem paying the right price for equity, they just seek to avoid high-risk investments with a dubious potential for return. The best way to prove your company's value and its potential is to show that people want your product, they are willing to pay for it, and the market is growing.

 Recommended reading

1. Carlos Espinal. *Fundraising Field Guide*: *A Startup Founder's Handbook for Venture Capital*
2. Poland Stephen R. *Founder's Pocket Guide: Startup Valuation (Founder's Pocket Guide Book 1)*
3. Alex Wilmerding and Aspatore Books Staff. *Term Sheets & Valuations: A Line by Line Look at the Intricacies of Term Sheets & Valuations (Bigwig Briefs)*

21. Consistent targeted actions

WHY IT IS NEEDED

Contacting more investors will get you more meetings, but it won't necessarily get you more money or better deals. DocSend and Tom Eisenmann (2015) did a study of 200 funded startups that raised $360 million in total. According to the results, if you do everything right, you'll likely have to contact 20 to 30 investors to get funded. The good news is that you don't need to contact hundreds. (Realistically, if you talked to 100 investors and none of them decides to fund you, there is definitely a serious problem in your business idea, your team, the whole industry, or even you!) In any case, it doesn't make sense to continue arranging new meetings with potential investors until you solve the core problems with your startup. Then you can focus your efforts on the quality of your connection to the investors.

Sometimes it's just plain luck to get a good offer for funding your startup just by being at the right place at the right time. I don't refute that, but do you want to count on plain luck? The better you prepare yourself, the better your odds will be. The more targeted actions you take and the more effort you put into them, the more chance you'll have to strike a good fundraising deal.

HOW TO DO IT

01 Focus on Building a Business
Consistently do everything you can to build a profitable and scalable business

02 Leverage and Automate
Try to leverage and automate your business as much as possible

03 Become Visible to Investors
Instead of only relying on your personal network, build your targeted online presence

04 Create a List of 30 to 50 Investors
Keep in mind that time is limited, so you should focus your efforts on targeted investors

05 Set the Right Mindset
Put yourself out there and meet with different investors before making a final deal

06 Reach Out to Targeted Investors
Instead of cold emails, try to find people who can connect you with your target investors

🏛 Focus on building a profitable and scalable business

This is the main reason you will get funded or not. You must do everything you can to build a profitable and scalable business. Define a business that is open-ended and continuously improving. If you are building your startup on a one-time sales concept (selling to the customer once), it probably won't be a very scalable business. It would be much more attractive if your customers keep making repeat purchases and referring you to their friends. But don't try to solve every customer problem at the same time.

Build a strategy for continuous innovation, while offering follow-on, complementary solutions to grow your revenues.

Investors like business ideas that are based on solid market research from outside experts, especially if these experts forecast a billion dollar opportunity. This type of startup is much more likely to be scalable and investment worthy. You don't necessarily have to hire expensive outside consultants if you are able to follow the guidelines we've discussed in the previous stages, Feasibility Study, Hypotheses, and Experiments.

Collokia, is a machine learning-based, collaboration platform with commercial offices in the USA and development offices in Uruguay and Hungary. They initially raised $500,000 in seed money and one year later has secured an additional $1.3 million in seed funding, led by software giant Globant and Fundo Pitanga, a Brazilian venture capital firm. It wasn't that difficult, mainly because of the contacts and reputation of the team. But Pablo Brenner, founder of *Collokia*, acknowledged that raising funds for global innovation from outside the USA is very difficult, as most local and regional VCs prefer investing in well-proven business models, and not in innovative technologies. So the spectrum of potential investors became very narrow even for such a well-established startup as *Collokia*. Therefore, you must be ready for the same challenges: prepare proofs of your business concept and focus on building a profitable and scalable business from the very beginning.

Leverage and automate your business to the maximum

Every startup should know that there are certain things they have to do that don't scale. But once you have figured out your processes, try to leverage and automate your business as much as possible. This will help your business scale faster (maybe even without additional money) and save you time, which you can use for building relationships and meeting investors. Following are main areas where you should constantly look for automation and leverage possibilities:

- *Production and delivery automation.* A startup that is labor intensive is not very scalable. Start looking at technology and outsourcing to automate your production and outsourcing before you begin to scale the business. If you still need additional employees to scale the production, building online training videos and clearly documenting processes is the least what you can do.

- *Marketing automation.* Focus on automating your sales funnel/pipeline and use leverages to reach more potential customers. Direct marketing is highly useful at the initial stage when you need to get feedback from customers, but generally, it's not scalable (except e-mail marketing automation, which we'll discuss later).

- *Revenue stream automation* leads to consideration about licensing and franchising. All of your resources, including time and energy, are limited, thus you probably won't be able to take on all the markets in the world (if you think you can, you might be overestimating your capabilities or your business model targets to a rather low volume market which won't be very interesting for angel investors and VCs). Many markets already have major players. It's up to you whether you want to compete with them or to make them you partners which, actually, can be much more effective for scaling than trying to out-compete them. Consider all possible partnerships forms including exclusive distribution, licensing, and franchising.

Startups who have found ways to grow the business by automating and leveraging production, marketing, and revenue streams will be far more attractive to any investor.

 Become visible and regularly update your online presence

Try to become more visible on larger and smaller online platforms for startups like Angel List, F6S, Startup Valley, *InnMind*, etc. Create your profile, submit projects, product photos, and upload videos. Some of them are large and well know while others are for niche prop projects and target a specific sector or geographical market (you can download the list of investor platforms at www.evolutioncurve.com). It doesn't require much time to create your profile and to post few updates when they are available. These platforms just on their own won't necessarily bring you investors, but once you get in contact with your targeted investors, don't miss an opportunity to show that you are a serious startup and your professional profile is available almost everywhere. There are two totally different scenarios after you send your one-pager or pitch deck to potential investors. In one case, they might get slightly interested and decide to look and see what other information is available about you online or they might feel that your startup is being listed on too many platforms or not enough platforms.

If you want to create a good profile, look at the startups being featured on AngelList. Don't copy them, but get an idea on how to improve yours. Also, a good idea is to check startups in your sector who succeeded in fundraising and were featured in media. If you know something about Google remarketing, you might consider keeping your full pitch deck and additional information for investors on your own website. You can put a link to this website in your profile on all platforms. You can create a remarketing (sometimes called retargeting) campaign addressing just visitors to your website. In this way, you would have a chance to remind potential investors about your startup when they visit your website. Set up it once and it won't need any extra maintenance work.

Find out where your target investors are active, what they read, what they watch, and what they post. And especially, find out what events they attend and make sure you are there! Don't go overboard on sales, but be polite and subtle. Highlight your startup and your progress, reveal the opportunity for investors, and put out your call to action.

The goal here is not to strike a fundraising deal right then and there, but to increase the awareness of your startups and start building a relationship with potential partners.

 ### Create a list of 30 to 50 targeted investors

A good idea is to start by making a list at least 30 investors you would be happy to work with as well as a list of at least 30 investors to whom your pitch should be highly interesting. Find the match between those two lists and come up with a list of between 30 and 50 investors you'll try to reach. List them in the priority according to your own preference. Just keep in mind that time is limited, thus you should focus your efforts and don't spread yourself too thin. As we have already discussed, if none of them will agree to invest, something may be wrong with what you're pitching or how you are developing your startup. Take their feedback seriously and make needed changes (at least in the pitch) before contacting other investors.

 ### Set the right mindset for fundraising

The main mindset for successful fundraising is to be willing to put yourself out there to meet anyone in the first place. Even though you don't need to talk to hundreds of investors, it's still a numbers game. Usually, it is advisable to have at least several meetings with different investors before making a final decision on the partnership.

Decide which of the founders will be responsible for fundraising and meeting investors, while others make sure the business performs well *during the fundraising* process. Being a good storyteller helps people to remember you and initiate discussions. So it might be wise to see who among your founders is the best story teller. Start building personal relationships with potential investors, partners, and people who might connect you to them today, even if you are not fundraising yet.

Perseverance and patience are two of the best personal traits needed for fundraising. Rejections will happen and the hurt might feel personal. Just anticipate rejection in advance and don't be upset when it happens. Just keep going!

The best time to raise money is when you don't need it because you are able to walk away if the deal is not good enough for you. Having your startup development and fundraising milestones defined will help you know when to walk away. If you face a situation when an investor asks for more than 25% of your equity, you should be very careful. If you give up too much of your equity and control over the decision making too early, future investors might have strong doubts about your capabilities to successfully develop the business. Don't get involved with the wrong people either, even if their financial proposal looks great. Sometimes it's better to refuse an offer rather than to take the money and obligate yourself to work with people whom you don't like or whose values are too different from yours.

Reach out your target investors daily

Once you have created a list of 30 to 50 target investors and ranked them according to your preference, you should start to focus on the top 5 angel investors or VCs you'd love to work with. Don't be in too big a hurry to contact them with cold email or regular online form submissions. These approaches have some chance of success, but not much.

The best way to approach an investor is to identify a specific partner, principal, or employee in the investor's company. Find them in your network and get to know them: check their Linkedin profile, read their blog and tweets, and see if they were featured in media. A good idea would be to get an introduction from another founder who has been funded by them or another third party who has had recent and frequent contact with the target investor. It's not always as difficult as it may seem. For instance, you could make the first connection by recording a personal video where you address them individually (say their name and explain why you are seeking their attention rather than another investor). Furthermore, in the same video, you could reveal how you took your previous funding round and hit all the milestones agreed with your earlier investors. Then you can explain how the amount of the current round will help you reach the next stage of your startup, when you plan to raise additional funds, and what they could expect in terms of the valuation of your company, thus, the benefit of becoming an investor for the current stage.

Once you start receiving calls for meetings, try to schedule meetings with a few investors on the same day. Such meeting organization will help to create artificial urgency and make you look more important (as opposed to just another startup) in the eyes of investors. Don't be arrogant with them (actually don't be arrogant with anyone). During your meetings with investors, try to have a discussion with them instead of pitching them. This is not a pitching competition. You are looking for partners and if you are sitting at the same table, it means you have at least some interests in common.

 Recommended reading

1. Carlos Espinal. *Fundraising Field Guide*: *A Startup Founder's Handbook for Venture Capital*
2. Alejandro Cremades. *The Art of Startup Fundraising*: *Pitching Investors, Negotiating the Deal, and Everything Else Entrepreneurs Need to Know*
3. Evan Baehr, Evan Loomis. *Get Backed: Craft Your Story, Build the Perfect Pitch Deck, and Launch the Venture of Your Dreams*
4. Mark Peter Davis. *The Fundraising Rules*

You've done a great job from a marketing perspective if you have set clear fundraising milestones, prepared fundraising material, and become visible for investors through your personal network, various online startup platforms, and maybe even media. Your next tasks depend on what stage you are in and which fundraising round you are going for.

If you have raised funds for your product launch, the next stage of Startup Evolution Curve is right for you. We'll talk about how to effectively to launch your product or service into the market, why it is different from a regular business launch, and how to improve your sales economy, even if you haven't started yet. If you are already in the market and have significant traction, I assume you have been raising money for scaling your business. Well, you can run through the next chapter, maybe catch one or two more ideas on how to improve your presence and performance in the market and focus on a further topic - Stage 5 "Growth Hacking"

Stage 4. Product Launch

Startups are not big companies. It's no secret that there are not many big and successful launches for startups. Startups tend to address customers' needs in a new way, offer innovative solutions, and employ new business models. Startups are usually in the market far earlier than when the product is ready for launch. In this stage, we'll talk about what has to be done after you have confirmed all the main hypotheses, attracted enough funds to scale your product manufacturing or service provision, and determined your marketing. Now it's time to introduce your product or service to the market.

Building a brand identity will allow you to avoid competing just on price and will help you to connect with your customers. Identifying customer touchpoints will help you to create more appealing—or even irresistible—offers and prepare a more effective marketing plan. Up-sell and cross-sell strategies will help you to increase your average order value and customer lifetime value, which, in turn, will create increased revenue and profit. A down-sell strategy could come in handy if you realize that certain customer segments won't buy your main offer and it can be downgraded. Your one-page marketing plan will show you a full picture of what needs to be done to communicate your offers successfully and achieve your main marketing goal.

Startups never stop testing and measuring. Once you stop learning, you stop progressing. You should keep this same attitude, even when your product is already launched in the market.

The main goals of this stage are to:

- Craft an irresistible offer
- Plan how to communicate it
- Execute-Measure-Learn

22. Myth of the Big Boom launch

WHY IT IS NEEDED

Too many startups still count on big launches. My global research on startups showed that 46.2% of startups expected that a big launch will help them, even though they were yet to find significant traction in the market. Wrong! They'll just burn more money and waste time! We discussed this earlier in the chapter about most dangerous mistakes in startup marketing. Traditional businesses often do big launches and implement expensive market entry strategies because it's more or less certain to have a positive payback. Sometimes, even small businesses conduct big launches with good results. But startups are not traditional businesses.

In early 2009, Sean Ellis (2009) shared the fact that more than 80% of startup big launches fail and nothing has essentially changed since then. Startups are being built on assumptions which first must be tested in the market. It's crazy to count on a big launch until you have at least found your product-market fit, identified your ideal clients (early adopter-evangelists), and tested your marketing communication (messages and channels). Most startup launches fail for a few reasons: wrong product, wrong target customers, wrong value proposition or communication channel, or even errors in the whole process.

Imagine if somebody would offer to cross-sell your product together with theirs. Let's say their product will be sold in a bundle with a free trial of your product. If customers like it, they can upgrade it to a paid version. Their commission fee for a new user (no matter if it is a trial or paid) is $10. That means that you'll have to pay for each new registered user gained through the partnership. The partner is ready to commit to one million new sales, which means one million new users for you. Not bad, right? Such a launch would require investing $10 minimum per user. Let's assume your product is priced at $8 and your average customer lifetime value is estimated to be $18 (you don't have solid facts, just estimates). What would you do? Even if you can do an effective up-sell and achieve your estimated average customer lifetime value ($18), you earn a nice $8 million profit. If you aren't able to do the up-sell, but all trial users purchase your basic paid version, you'll be minus $2 million. If none of the new users become your paid users, you'll lose $10 million and probably go out of business. So, that's a big launch. In most cases, the situation is even more difficult. In this example, you know that you'll at least get a solid number of trial users. But in most big launches, the only number that is clear at the beginning is how much you'll spend, but not what return you'll get. Want to go for it and risk your (not investor's) money? Or would you prefer to prepare a bit better and minimize your risk?

01 Plan and Do Things That Don't Scale
Instead of dreaming about a big launch, make sure it works well on a smaller scale

02 Double Check Once Again
Review how your target segments, value propositions, and channels are aligned

03 Review Actual Sales Findings
Don't stop collecting data after the market fit is found; make decisions based on facts

04 Check for Errors in the Process
Go through the whole process manually by yourself to prevent errors

 Plan and do things that don't scale

There are two points of view on things that don't scale. First of all, there are things that initially must be done manually and can't or shouldn't be automated. This viewpoint was elaborated by Paul Graham (2013). Secondly, there are things that can't be easily increased or multiplied; basically, they prevent you from scaling your business.

French startup Aladom was launched in 2008 as a marketplace for home services (including house cleaning, tutoring, childcare, senior care, gardening, etc.). After 3 years of operation, they were able to list 100,000 services providers and to find a viable business model based on B2B revenue. But first, they had to do things that don't scale. Being a market place they had the chicken and egg problem. Aladom founders realized that the people looking for jobs where the most active people on their website. So, Aladom worked on getting job offers from companies instead of wasting money on large-scale advertising or a big book launch. Aladom worked on collecting job offers directly from their B2B customers using integration or XML feeds. Then those offers were presented to people looking for jobs on the website. Visitors were happy with the service (they found many job opportunities) and with word of mouth advertising, Aladom was able to get more and more people registering on the platform. With many registered users and companies, Aladom has solved their chicken and egg problem. Now they are scaling their business and launching in new geographical markets.

Instead of dreaming about a big launch, first of all, you should do all tasks in Stage 2: Hypotheses and Experiments. They cover most of the things Paul Graham (2013) recommended that you focus your attention on:

- Focus on a narrow, but yet profitable market niche. Once you find your product-market fit, scale it in the niche and look for the ways to extend it into other market segments or totally new markets.
- Reach customers manually, get their feedback, and improve (product, service, communication, etc.)
- Solve customer's problem manually and then find a solution for automating it. Don't build high-end things and solutions that nobody wants.
- Make your customers happy, show personal interest in their situation, and become their consultant instead of just another seller.
- Get rid of the unnecessary. This applies to everything: wrong customer segments, vague and miserable products, useless activity (builds no value, neither for the customer nor for you).

If you have already reviewed all of those elements, check if there is anything which might stop you from scaling your business four very rapid growth. If there is at least one thing that doesn't scale, you definitely can't go for the big launch. What happens if you drive huge traffic to your website or physical store, but there is something that needs to be done manually or requires too much time? That's your bottleneck for growing your business. You can't scale your business until you remove anything that can't be scaled. Review all your business processes and identify your limitations. You should come with the limitations which are important to scaling your business as shown by example in Table 39. The next step is to estimate the current level of each limitation and check how easily you could upgrade these limitations.

Table 39. Example of limitation factors

Limitations	Server	Autoresponder	Customer Support	Individual VIP course
Current level	~ 5,000 visitors at a time	10,000 email addresses	up to 100 per day	up to 10 per day
Possibility to increase	No limits	up to 200,000	up to 500 per day	up to 50 per day

Let's use the example at the beginning of this chapter where someone offers you a chance to acquire one million users. But this time, you did your homework. You have solid facts from real market experiments that your conversion rate and customer lifetime value is good enough to earn a nice profit. But if you don't know your business limitations (for example, how many customers you can serve per day), you might get into serious trouble and waste your money.

 Double check segments, value proposition, and channels

Let's assume you've built a product customers love and are willing to pay for it. If not, you should get back to hypotheses and experiments to do some extra homework. If you don't have a great product, it makes no sense to put your efforts and money in launching your product into the market. In the best case, you'll achieve medium results, but most likely it will be a failure. Creating an effective marketing plan requires you to know not only what promotional tactics could work best in your case, but you also need to know such basics as what target group to talk to, what to say, and how to say it. This is not an issue if you have already verified all major hypotheses and confirmed:

1. WHOM are you selling to (customer segments)—Who are your early adopters-evangelists, where they can be found, and what's important for them?

2. WHAT you are selling (value proposition)—What will you offer to customers as your core value proposition and why would customers be willing to get to the next stages of your sales funnel/pipeline (what are your smaller value propositions in order to build customer's trust)?

3. HOW are you selling (communication channels)—How customers will be reached, which channels will be used for what purpose, (just remember that not all channels are equally good and suitable for sales promotions)?

 Record and review actual sales findings

When startups try to automate and scale their sales (that is, launch products into the market) most of them get far fewer sales than expected. This is mainly caused by the fact that startups haven't found early evangelists and were trying to sell to target segment that is too general. Or, perhaps something went wrong with other components of the business model.

When you run experiments, you collect data and make decisions based on facts. Don't stop doing that when you have found your product-market fit and verified your business model. Be ready to keep this practice when you launch your product into the market. Technically, you are in the market starting with the first day you showed your product and made it available for purchase. Launching into the market means that you are looking for ways to change your manual sales efforts into automated and scalable ones.

The main tasks while still testing the product in the market (manual sales) and before automating and scaling sales include:

- Save the contact details of potential customers who showed interest in your product, (you can use bitrix24, awesome and free online CRM, to track the record of your leads and sales).
- Collect their opinion about the product and why they chose it (this may be very helpful when you are crafting your irresistible offer and advertising).
- If customers don't buy your product, ask why. If you ask this question you might notice a pattern in answers and find a way to improve the product or your sales process.
- Ask your target customers who bought your product (or at least are highly interested in it), what they are reading, what websites they are visiting, and what people or brands they are following on social networks. The goal is to get as much information as possible about potential communication channels through which you'll be able to reach these and similar customers in the future when your sales get automated and scaled.

 Check for errors in the whole business process

You don't have to be a super innovative startup based on high-end technologies to get errors in the process. Some of those errors can literally kill your business. A few years ago I had a client who was not a startup. It was a security company based in London which asked us to help with their online marketing, including SEO. We've spent a significant amount of money and much of our time to make this company visible online and drive qualified traffic to their website. The company even became organically visible among the top three in UK Google results for "door supervision" and a few other specific keywords related to security services. The website traffic increased tremendously and a few hundred visitors clicked on their Contact button each month. But, the company never received even a single call! I was shocked and the CEO of the security company was mad about the situation. When we started digging deeper to solve the riddle, we found out that the phone number on the website was forwarding all the calls to an outsourced call center. The problem was that during the process when we worked to increase the traffic to the website, the CEO of the company had decided to use the services of the call center, but didn't inform us or the website administrator! Due to a simple error (somebody just forgetting to change the phone number) the four months of work was wasted and hundreds of clients were lost!

In order to avoid such silly mistakes or even more significant errors, you should go through the whole process manually by yourself. Before investing money in a big launch or marketing communication, make sure all the processes are as smooth as they can be. Check it by yourself, ask your clients to share their experience, invite your colleagues or friends to imitate your clients, and go through the whole process from start to finish. If someone says that it looks silly, you have a chance to fix it rather than to risk a situation like the one I experienced!

 Recommended reading

1. Bernard Schroeder. *Fail Fast or Win Big*: *The Start-Up Plan for Starting Now*
2. Dan Olsen. *The Lean Product Playbook*: *How to Innovate with Minimum Viable Products and Rapid Customer Feedback*
3. Pat Flynn. *Will It Fly?*: *How to Test Your Next Business Idea So You Don't Waste Your Time and Money*

23. Foundations of building a strong brand

WHY IT IS NEEDED

According to the American Marketing Association, the brand is the "name, term, design, symbol, or any other feature that identifies one seller's goods or service as distinct from those of other sellers." Your brand identity is the representation of your company's reputation through various attributes and the more they are consistent, the stronger your brand impression is.

Brands are not built just so the owner can be proud of it. Strong brands help differentiate products and services and avoid competition on price. If you hold the monopoly in your industry or low cost-low price is your strategy, you can skip this chapter. But most startups face fearsome competition. Even high-end innovation-based businesses compete with the old ways of solving or simply ignoring the problem. A solid brand can transform your business from an unknown startup into a successful competitor and niche, or even market, leader. It is about the overall experience, not just the logo or a slogan. Yes, it takes time to build a great brand, so why don't you start it right now? Your customers will develop higher trust, lower resistance and price sensitivity, and will be more likely to purchase what you are selling.

 Prepare for brand development

The first and most important step in creating a brand is developing a complete understanding of the company and its position in the market. The good news is that you've already done the major part of this work:

- You know your target customers quite well and you know how they currently solve their needs (Chapter 3: Segmentation and potential market size, Chapter 2: Today solutions of customers' needs).

- You have a great and tested offer for them (Chapter 1: The Essence: Value Proposition, Chapter 10: Validating problem-solution-market fit).

- You have analyzed the market situation, and have evaluated competitors and possible trends for the future (Chapter 5: Busines environment and breakthrough innovations, Chapter 13: Evaluating profit and growth potential).

- You have even developed your positioning statement which briefly explains what you do, who your customer is, and why they should buy from you (Chapter 11: Create a strong positioning statement)

If you still have some doubts, do a SWOT analysis (Table 40) focusing on your most desired vision of your startup in the long run. Find out what the odds are for such vision, what may be an advantage for you, and what might cause your some extra problems.

Talk to your customers and distribution partners again to get a better understanding. Does their view of your company correspond to or contradicts with the vision you have?

Table 40. Summary of SWOT factor analysis

Strength	Weakness
Any characteristics, features, and resources that give you an advantage over others	Any characteristics, features, and resources that give you disadvantage relative to others
Opportunities	Threats
Any elements (not only in your startup but in the market on the whole) that could exploit to advantage for you	Any elements (not only in your startup but in the market on the whole) that could exploit to disadvantage for you

Proceed to the next task once you have a clear perception of your strength, weaknesses, opportunities, and threats. Don't try to build a brand randomly or just on emotions. The brand isn't just about what looks the prettiest and feels the most pleasant to the founders or anybody else. It should have a direct link with your business strategy. Your brand should drive your business forward, not just be visually appealing.

 Decide on the brand characteristics

Not all startups—or even mature companies—understand that a successful brand consists of a few harmonized components, including:

- Name and logo
- Product
- Customer touchpoints
- Personality and story
- Identity system

A great brand evokes certain feelings in your customers and a desire to talk about it. Therefore, before you can build a brand that your target customers trust, you need to know not only your positioning statement but also your vision and mission (if you have never defined them correctly, don't underestimate their importance). There are many different opinions of what characteristics should be included in the brand development. I prefer simple things because they are easier to implement and the expression "done is better than perfect" is almost a mantra for most startups. Look through this short Table 41 with examples of brand characteristics and complete it for your brand.

Table 41. Brand characteristics

Vision	What is happening in the world which makes your product necessary?
Mission	What is your startup's general purpose in this world?
Promise	What is your fundamental promise to your customers? Remember the main problems you are solving.
Attributes	What makes you different and valuable to customers? Remember your positioning statement and check if there is an answer as to how you are different and valuable for the customer.
Emotions	What do customers feel when they engage your brand (see it, buys, uses, talks about it, etc.)? It's very important to understand how they feel about themselves in context of your brand.
Personality	If your brand was a person, who would it be? Trust me, that's really important because you'll have to make many decisions related to your brand and if you have defined the brand personality, it will be much easier to make those decisions if you imagine that it is not you, but the brand personality who is making them.

 Create brand identity system: logo and brand book

The next step is to create the look, feel, and voice of the brand that will be carried through all your marketing channels, from the website to social media, advertisements, packaging, and everything else. Your brand identity is not just one single logo image. It needs to be able to change and adapt based on where it is used. Therefore, you must take into consideration all the different mediums across which the brand will exist, and design something that is flexible enough to remain identifiable across all channels. Assign this task to a professional; hire a graphic designer to create your logo and brand book (a guide to how your business cards, social media profiles, product packaging, and other visuals should look). If you are not a professional designer, it's better not to try and do a designer's job. Instead, prepare a creative brief, a comprehensive guideline for the designer about the brand identity you are building. That's why I suggested you fill the Table 41 in the previous task - it will help you greatly in explaining how your brand identity should be perceived. Most professional designers have their own creative brief, a set of questions you must answer in order for the designer to catch and visualize your idea correctly.

1. Find the designer. Ask your network for recommendations, check Freelancer.com, 99designs.com, Fiverr.com, or you can even talk to my designer Andrius at Greytastudio.com who designed the cover of this book and helped me in a number of other projects.

2. Provide a creative brief for the designer. If the designer doesn't ask you to complete his creative brief or send you his already prepared guidelines, don't hire this designer!

3. Validate the logo and overall feeling. The most important thing to check is not how much you like the whole brand visualization proposed by designer, but how your target customer views it and if they perceive the same idea that you wanted to communicate.

 Make your brand stay alive and consistent

Once you have confirmed your brand logo and other physical attributes (in some cases, even smell or taste can be branded physical attributes), make sure your website and online presence match the brand's identity according to the instruction in your brand book. Do the same for all other media (for example, packaging, business cards, promotional gifts, etc.). Following is a brief checklist of where your brand should be visible:

- Internet and online advertising
- Social media and content marketing
- Print, signage, packaging
- Physical environment (storefront or office)
- Sales and customer service
- All customer communications

Great brands always follow their values and stay reliable. Therefore you should consistently keep your brand promises. You can upload your newly created logo and corporate style overnight, but building a brand identity in your customers' minds requires far more time. Be patient and persistent following your brand identity guidelines. In the next chapter we'll talk about customer touchpoints, so make sure, you identify all of them and make sure your brand is expressed correctly.

 Recommended reading

1. Philip Kotler, Gary Armstrong. *Principles of Marketing*
2. Gregory Diehl. *Brand Identity Breakthrough: How to Craft Your Company's Unique Story to Make Your Products Irresistible*

24. Identify and seize customer touchpoints

WHY IT IS NEEDED

You should have already made at least a brief sketch of customer touchpoints during the feasibility study. Now it's time to take a deeper dive and to use this technique to prepare for the launch to the major market. Furthermore, after conducting a series of experiments, you've probably gained new insights about possible customer touchpoints: what actions customers take, how they choose their priorities, how they feel about one or another aspect of your product or service, which communication channels worked best and delivered your message most effectively, and so on. Let's not forget that your sales funnel/pipeline also is a bundle of customer touchpoints; you are taking customers from one stage to another, closer and closer to the purchase.

Identifying all possible touchpoints with the customer is very important when preparing for launch because it helps you better understand your customer's needs and behaviors, and helps you plan your marketing actions accordingly. If you do it right, you'll be able to:

- Create highly valuable and almost irresistible offers for your customers
- Communicate the message about your offers in a more efficient way
- Find and employ low-cost, high-efficiency communication and distribution channels
- Design an awesome brand experience and initiate word of mouth advertising

HOW TO DO IT

01

List Customer Touchpoints
Make a list of areas where customers can have a touchpoint with your brand

02

List Customer Contexts
Define possible contexts when customers can have a touchpoint with your brand

03

Map Out the Customer Journey
Map it out from the initial stage, through purchase, and then after using your solution

04

Identify Key Touchpoints
State and analyze the main issue, concern, or problem from customer's journey perspective.

Make a list of areas where customer can have a touchpoint with your brand

We've talked about service design and the customer journey map during the feasibility study. Later, you developed your sales funnel/pipeline based on a series of experiments. Now it's time to use both of them: customer journey map and sales funnel/pipeline. The task is very simple: write down all possible areas (exact touchpoints) where the customer can have an interaction with your brand. There are two popular ways to make such list:

1. *The sales funnel approach* lists every possible area of customer interaction according to the sales funnel stages and tasks.

2. *The POEMS method* lists every possible area of interaction with People, Objects, Environment, Messages, and Services that might be engaged by the customer.

Table 42. Possible touchstones with the brand

Sales funnel approach	POEMS method
✓ purchase channels	✓ People
✓ marketing channels	✓ Objects
✓ order fulfilment	✓ Environment
✓ research channels	✓ Messages
✓ feedback and relationship	✓ Services

Use the approach convenient for you. The goal here is not just to employ the use the methodology, but to write down all possible touchpoints with your customers. I've even met some startups who use both of those approaches: the first is to make a list and the other is to double check the list.

Figure 35. Example of customer touchpoint list

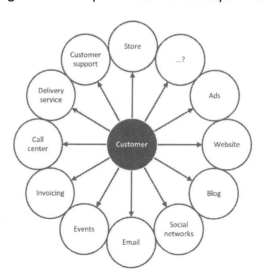

Make a list of possible contexts when the customer can have a touch with your brand

For each of the touchpoints which you have just outlined, the customer can complete several actions or activities. There is no one-size-fits-all scheme that defines when a customer can have a touch with the brand. It will be different for each industry and business. But generally, customer activities can be grouped into a few classic categories where the customer:

- Is yet not aware of a problem or need
- Understands that there is a problem or a need
- Is looking for and evaluating possible solutions,
- Is buying the solution
- Is using the solution
- Has already used the solution

This can be expanded to cover key areas for your startup. You should also include your findings from customer interviews and experiments. It may be that there are some specific situations which don't fall into one of the categories listed above.

Now that you have a list of the customer touchpoints and the context or activities when the customer can engage with those touchpoints, you should complete a simple table to map the customer journey through these checkpoints. Look at the example in Table 43 with activities listed across the top and the touchpoints down the left-hand side:

Table 43. Customer touchpoints and activity contexts

	Not aware of the problem	Knows about the problem	Look-ing for solution	Buying a solution	Using a solution	After using a solution
Events						
Online ads						
Social networks						
Website						
Emails						
Call center						
Store						
Customer support						

Map out the customer journey through touchpoints

Take each of your target customer personas and map their journey from the initial stage, through purchase, and then after using your solution. It's very important to stress that you don't have to do a customer touchpoint map for each individual customer. In most cases, that would be a terrible waste of time. You should have defined your target segment and customer profiles in Chapter 3: Segmentation and potential market size. So, create a customer touchpoint journey for each of your target customer segments. You should have at least two: new customers and existing customer (repeat sales).

Complete this task from the customer's viewpoint. Don't map out how you expect customers to act according to your sales funnel. It's much better to interview a few of your target customers and create the customer journey map accordingly. Try to keep it as simple as possible. The idea is to outline the context to help identify areas for possible improvement, whether it's improvement of your offer (value delivered to customers) or improvement of the method by which this value is delivered. Table 44 shows the basic example of new customer journey through the touchpoints with the brand.

Table 44. Example of customer journey through touchpoints

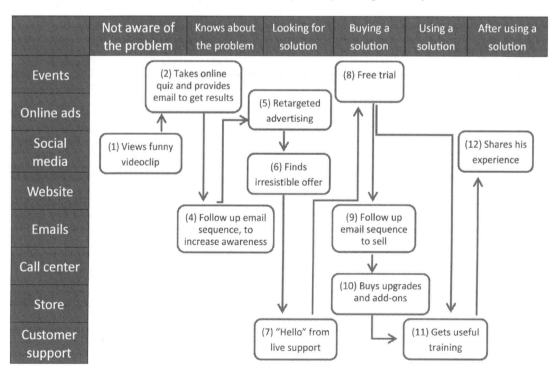

Identify key touchpoints and do in-depth analysis

Each startup can experience different issues such as low conversion, high customer acquisition costs, the fact that most customers are unaware of the problem they have, sales process taking too long, customers have doubts about the product, low customer retention and repeat order rate, and so on. You should have identified your main challenges during your experiments when you tried to sell your product to a limited market segment. Now it's time to look deeper into these challenges and eliminate the issues that are causing them.

State the main issue, concern, or problem from customer's journey perspective. If you don't see any problems or challenges, I'm a bit worried about you and your startup project! Every business at some time has at least something to solve or improve in order to grow and prosper. Once you have picked a certain problem, ask yourself why it is happening and how it could be eliminated. Look at your customer touchpoint journey map and identify the key touch points would seem most connected to the issue. Go through each key touchstone and complete the customer empathy card, as shown in (Table 45).

Table 45. Customer empathy card

	What does customer...
...see?	
...smell?	
...hear?	
...feel?	
...think?	
...tell?	
...do?	

Traditionally, you first notice what your customer does or does not do (for example, doesn't buy your product online), then you can listen to what your customer is telling you directly or indirectly. But this might not give you the complete picture. If you want to really understand why your customers behave in one way or another, you should get into their heads and try to figure out what they see, smell, and hear, and how they feel. Human emotions are unconscious and they are directly influenced by what we see, smell, and hear. A customer's perceptions, emotions, and thoughts are the result of what he saw, smelled, heard, and felt. And the customer actions are formed by those perceptions, emotions, and thoughts. So if you want to influence your customer's actions, see what you can change about what he sees, smells, hears and feels in each key touchpoint.

 Recommended reading

1. James Kalbach. *Mapping Experiences*: *A Complete Guide to Creating Value through Journeys, Blueprints, and Diagrams*

2. Yoram (Jerry) Wind, Catharine Findiesen *Hays. Beyond Advertising*: *Creating Value Through All Customer Touchpoints*

3. *Nicholas J. Webb. What Customers Crave*: *How to Create Relevant and Memorable Experiences at Every Touchpoint*

4. Jim Joseph. *The Experience Effect*: *Engage Your Customers with a Consistent and Memorable Brand Experience*

25. Craft an irresistible offer

WHY IT IS NEEDED

As defined by Mark Joyner (2005), the irresistible offer is "an identity-building offer central to a product, service, or company where the believable return on investment is communicated so clearly and efficiently that it's immediately apparent you'd have to be a fool to pass it up." Do I need to explain why each startup should have such offer? Actually, it's the very essence of the startup's success. Everything we have done up until now has been in preparation for creating your irresistible offer.

Figure 36.   Importance of irresistible offer

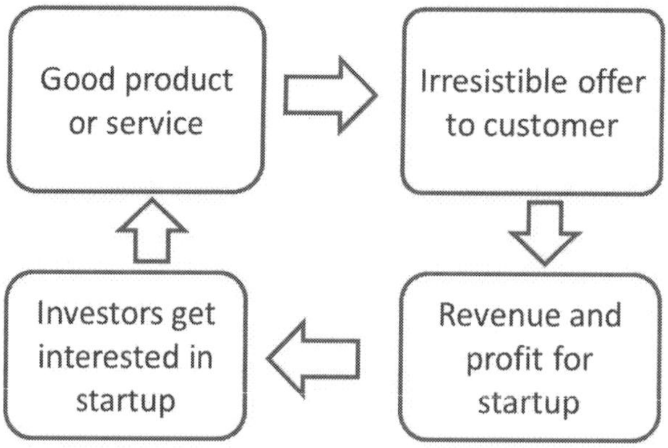

```
Good product          Irresistible offer
or service       ⟹    to customer
   ⇧                        ⇩
Investors get         Revenue and
interested in    ⟸    profit for
startup               startup
```

When you engage in any marketing activity, the irresistible offer must be your spearhead. If you have defined your customer's key touchpoints and have developed irresistible offers for certain touchpoints, your product launch will be far more successful. Even if you are not yet ready for to launch at large scale, and the irresistible offer will help you to gain significant traction, thus you'll become more interesting to other customers and potential investors.

Warning! An irresistible offer is not a magic bullet. You still need to have a good product or a service which will be the foundation of your offer. Otherwise, marketing simply won't work or it will be something like cheating on customers. As one man said, don't blame advertising if you are not successful selling a dead horse.

HOW TO DO IT

01 **Draft a High ROI Offer**
Create the best deal for your target customer and protect him from any risks in your offer

02 **Create Unique Selling Propositions**
Craft a unique selling proposition for each major touchpoint in your sales funnel

03 **Make Your Offer Believable**
Overcome customer skepticism by making your high ROI offers more believable

04 **Decide on Message Style**
Determine the style you'll communicate in your offer to be consistent with the brand

 Draft an offer with high ROI for your customer.

Everything is simple, especially if you continuously read this book and work on given tasks. Now your task is to create the best deal for your target customers and protect them from any risks in taking your offer. This is just a draft explaining the essential value you are delivering to your customers and how you secure them from any risks. Again, this is the moment of truth: if you came up to this stage hoping to provide just nice-to-have benefits for your customers, you won't be able to craft a high ROI offer for your customers and will have to go back to Stage 2: Hypotheses and Experiments.

Once you've clearly stated what great value you provide for your customers compared to their costs (not only price but time, needed efforts, convenience level, emotions, etc.), it's time to clarify and overcome possible objections and fears. If you were running your market experiments thoroughly, you should already have a slew of reasons why customers don't want to buy your product. If you did the tasks related to customer touchpoints, you should also have some ideas about how you could reduce the resistance. Here are most common solutions for how you can eliminate or at least reduce your customers' risks: money back guarantee, special payment plans (for example, take the product now and pay later if you are happy with the product), giving a free sample or freemium version, warranties, pay for results, free support, or extra help if something unexpected happens.

To tell the truth, it's amazing how *Hostaway* has crafted and communicated their offer (Figure 37). Actually, this is a great example of crafting an irresistible offer. The offer is crystal clear at soon as you hit their landing page: if you rent your property for vacations, you can get more bookings, save time (manage one platform instead of four), and avoid double bookings.

Figure 37. Hostaway landing page offer

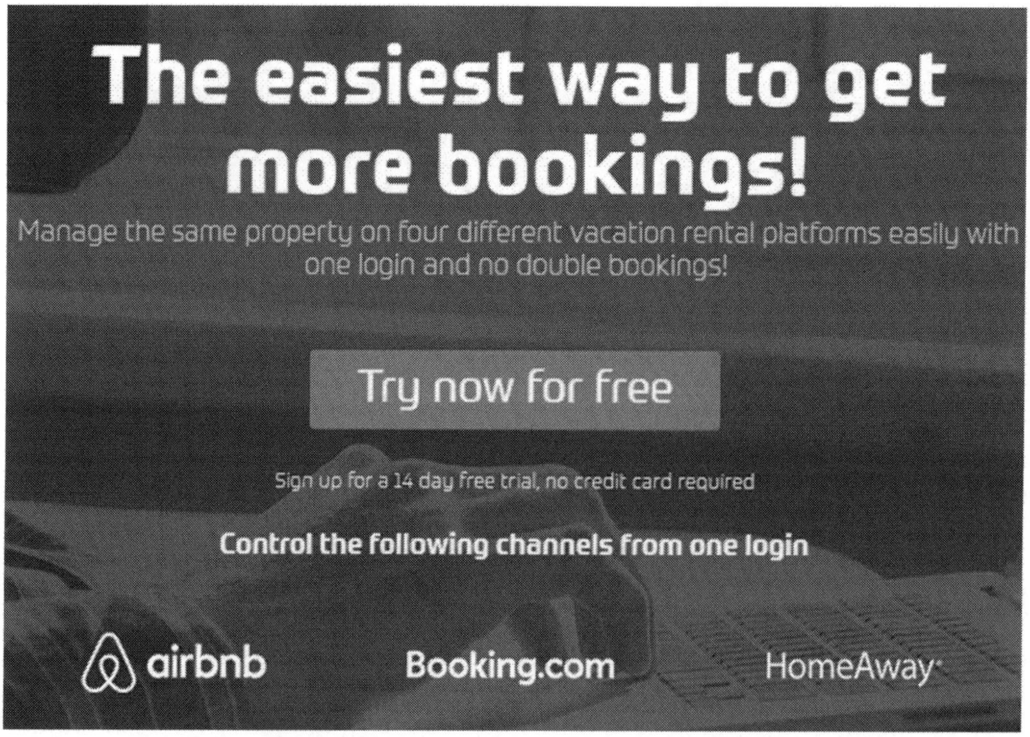

Source: Hostaway.com

The offer becomes even more appealing when you see such elements as:

- Starting with a free 14 days trial
- No credit card required
- Additional credibility built by showing "As featured in"

Another important aspect is that there is one clear call to action (button text "Try now for free") displayed at least three times on the landing page to increase the exposure of the main offer. Pro-active online support is another additional element that helps increase the conversion rate. If we check the pricing page (Figure 38), we'll see additional elements that make the offer even more irresistible:

- It has a clear and simple pricing,
- Explains benefits in details,
- Provides a guarantee - *"if you get a double booking while using Hostaway, the entire monthly fee is on us"*

Figure 38. Hostaway pricing page offer

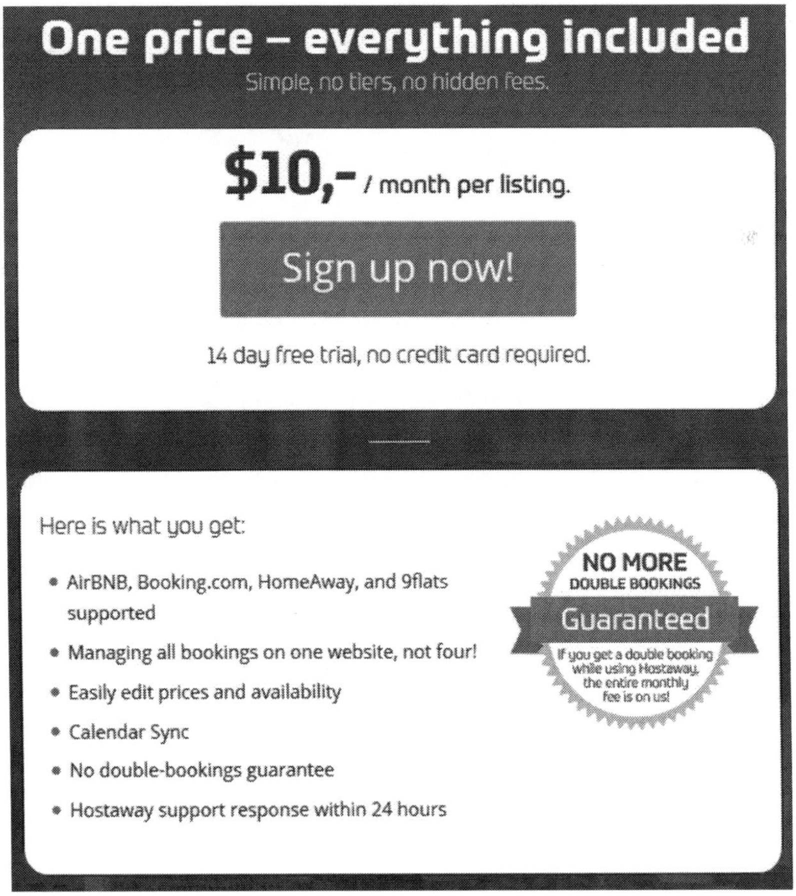

Source: Hostaway.com

Unique selling proposition (USP) for each key touchstone

As we've talked about Chapter 12: Testing Communication and Distribution Channels, you are building and improving a sales funnel/pipeline where the customer has to advance from one stage to another before they can finally purchase your product or service. Sometimes somebody gets lucky and sells their product without crafting a USP (or irresistible offer). But most of us are working in highly competitive markets, therefore, we have to put extra effort to sell our products and services.

If you develop your main USP for the final stage, that's Great. But if you were to craft a USP for each major touchpoint in your sales funnel/pipeline, it would encourage your customers to move faster towards the final stage of buying your product and maybe even becoming a repeat customer. It doesn't matter if you decide to craft only your main USP or a few USP for key touchpoints, it should be clear, simple, and brief. Your USP should be the message which answers these customer questions:

- Should I pay attention to this message?
- What are you trying to sell?
- How much will it cost for me?
- What's in for me? What value will I get?
- Why should I trust them at all?

If you want to make your USP even more appealing and effective, think about how you could make your offer meet the following characteristics:

- Easy to accept—Eliminate any obstacles for customers buying your product (for example, what should a customer do if he can't pay in the online shop because he doesn't have a credit card with him).
- Urgent or limited—If your offer is valid forever, customers will think they have unlimited time to think about it and there are fewer chances that they'll come back and purchase (for example, tell them that the offer is only valid until a certain date, or the exclusive price is valid only for the first 10 clients).
- With added value—Instead of a discount, you can add something on top of your main offer making it even more attractive.
- With no risk—Don't wait until the customer asks, tell him at once that this offer is risk-free (for example, Linkedin offers trial membership in premium account benefits for one month for free so you can see for yourself if you like the value).

Figure 39. B2B Prospex unique selling proposition

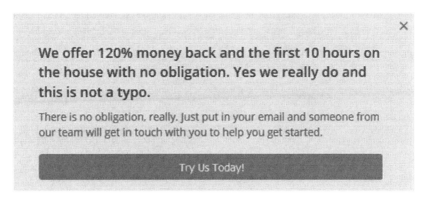

Source: B2BProspex (01.19.2017)

Even though we can't call B2BProspex a real startup as per the definition we agreed on, I think their value proposition might serve as a good illustration of an irresistible offer. This data entry outsourcing company is based in the USA, has been experimenting with quite a few things, and came up with the offer (Figure 39). It helped to build trust in front of the clients (removes risk) and to show that the company here is in it for the long run. As Murtaza Amin, the founder of *B2BProspex*, reported, more than 250 clients have been a part of this offer, and only twice have they had to give money back.

The second part of the offer makes it nearly irresistible: 10 hours per month for any back office work absolutely for free and with no obligation on the part of the client. *B2BProspex* does anything that the client might need (and that company offers), and even if it is a small project of only 10 hours, *B2BProspex* does it for free. This keeps clients from thinking of any other provider. Actually, two of their biggest clients who brought them tens of thousands of revenue over the years started with a small project ($200 - $300). Sometimes, this type of offer might be risky because it might attract non-paying clients, therefore I don't recommend using it blindly for everyone and in every case. But, for *B2Bprospe,x* it helped to get new leads faster than anyone else and also allowed them to maintain extremely high client retention rates.

Make your selling proposition believable

The bigger and bolder you make your USP (high value, no risk), the more difficult it is to prove and the harder you'll have to work to sell your believability and credibility. It's paradox: if you offer an average value, just a few potential customers will get interested and maybe somebody will buy. But if you provide a great offer, most of the potential customers will get interested, but they still won't buy it. That's because they will think the offer is too good to be true and there is a catch somewhere. Your task is to overcome their skepticism by making your USP more believable and eliminating any possible doubts. There are few things that can boost your credibility if provided in the right way and at the right time (remember customer touchpoints once again):

- ✓ *Social proof*—If customers see that many other people use your product or service, your offer becomes safer and not so risky.
- ✓ *Technical and factual proof*—This is very applicable for technology startups because sometimes it's very simple to prove that you'll be able to deliver the offer by showing technical data or facts.
- ✓ *Credibility and qualification*—Provide any pieces of evidence that prove your credibility and qualification. Even if it's not related directly to the product or service, showing yourself as credible person or company will make your offer much more believable.
- ✓ *High profile clients and endorsements*—If there are famous people among your clients or even if ordinary clients can give a positive testimonial about your product, this is worth its weight in gold to build your credibility and make your offer even more attractive. Showcase your high profile clients (with their permission, of course) using video and written testimonials.
- ✓ *Awards and recognition*—If you or your startup were awarded for some kind achievement at least partly related to the product or service you are selling, don't hide that. If a third party awarded and recognized you, it's a solid reason for customers to trust you more.
- ✓ *Logical*—If somebody thinks that your offer is too good to be true, show them why this offer is logical not only from customer's perspective but yours as well. If it's clear that this offer is also beneficial for you, there is no reason to be suspicious that you might be cheating and earning money by some other means.

Sintrafico, a startup based in Mexico City, creates smart mobility ecosystems that empower companies and governments to achieve a more efficient mobility, evolving traditional cities into Smart Cities. *Sintrafico* claims to have (and proves it) the largest real-time data network in Mexico which helps to monitor and analyze road speeds, congestion, traffic incidents, road safety, parking lots, road tolls, emergency systems, weather, public transport, carpooling, and bicycles, among others. It uses the data to create smart mobility solutions and analytics. *Sintrafico* serves different customer segments and helps them to:

- Reduce insurance claims and accident response times by up to 15% and keep them informed minute by minute of the adjuster's progress toward their care

- Identify the impact that mobility has on their current and potential real estate locations, more accurately valuing the potential of each location through smart areas of influence, traffic gauges, and more
- Quantify vehicle impacts, exposure times, and impact paths of their outdoor advertising and locations

Even though *Sintrafico* targets different customer segments with different value propositions, this startup did a good job strengthening the believability of all its offers. If you visit their website, you'll find many reasons to believe, including such fact statements as:

- more than 500,000 cars online
- 200 million speed reports per month
- 500,000 car incident report historical data
- 1 million locations analyzed and 10 billion reports processed
- and many more facts!

Decide which message style best fits your brand identity

If you remember when we talked about brand, we said that brand is not just a logo, but the overall experience for your customer. Therefore, it's very important to determine how you'll communicate your USP. Your messages should be aligned with your brand identity. There are few general rules to be followed when crafting the final message of your USP:

- Use the customers' vocabulary (not your professional jargon). Don't try to look smart, it's better to be similar to your customers.
- Speak about their problems and pains, especially those which they are facing at current touchpoint where your USP is being communicated.
- Show your solution as the perfect choice. Know what's most important for your target customers and address those aspects in your USP.
- Make the message personal as much as possible. The best message is one that makes each customer who reads or hears it feels like the message is addressed specifically to them.

If you want to go deeper and create your brand communication style, take a look at what Philip Kotler and Gary Armstrong (2003), indicated as possible styles for creating advertising messages. They are two of the marketing legends and thought leaders about brand messaging. Even though it was created a while ago, it's still valid and applicable today:

- *Slice of life*—The content of the message depicts real life situations regarding the use of the product. It is often the case that a life without the product and a life with the product are depicted, this way creating a contrast and emphasizing the benefits.

- *Lifestyle*—The content of the message demonstrates how the product creates a certain lifestyle. This method of content creation is very popular among manufacturers and sellers of luxury goods.
- *Fantasy*—The content of the message is presented as a dream or a fantasy about the product and its use. This style is often used to advertise products for women.
- *Mood or image*—The message content is formed to have a concrete mood, which reflects certain values, such as love, peace, happiness, joy.
- *Musical*—Proper use of music forms more interest in the product. Companies often use melodies for products so that the consumers would immediately understand what product is being advertised.
- *Personality symbol*—Advertisements depict a persona, who presents the product. Naturally, the persona has to be a significant figure and respected by the target audience. These can also include symbols, such as cartoon characters.
- *Technical expertise*—The product manufacturing process is shown and the aim is to emphasize the properties of the product.
- *Scientific evidence*—Scientific evidence is presented, thus proving that the product is better than other products in some regards.
- *Testimonial or endorsement*—With this style, respected personalities are hired to star in the advertisements, where they confirm the unique properties of the product.

Once you choose the style of your messaging, you should keep the same style in all your marketing communications, in order to build a consistent impression and make your brand becoming recognizable.

 Recommended reading

1. Mark Joyner. *The Irresistible Offer*: How to Sell Your Product or Service in 3 Seconds or Less
2. Cindy Barnes, Helen Blake, David Pinder. *Creating and Delivering Your Value Proposition*: Managing Customer Experience for Profit

26. Get ready to up-sell, cross-sell, and down-sell

WHY IT IS NEEDED

Selling one product and giving your customers one offer (even if it is irresistible offer) is not enough. At least it's not enough for smart entrepreneurs. Up-sells and cross-sells are one of the most cost-effective ways to add revenue to your startup and value for your customers. And the more revenue on average you get from your customers, the more you can spend to acquire new customers and grow your business much faster. Up-selling and cross-selling are mutually beneficial when done properly, providing maximum value to customers and increasing revenue without the recurring additional cost of most marketing channels. So, is there any reason why you should leave money on the table?

Would you like other people to sell your products without resulting up-front costs for you (just paying a commission from actual sales)? Or, if you have just one or two different products and have nothing to make up and up-sell or cross-sell offers, why not offer to sell other peoples' products and earn decent commission on that? Affiliate networks could help you in both cases.

HOW TO DO IT

01

Create Up-Selling Offers
Generate at least a few ideas to increase value and earn extra revenue per sale

02

Create Cross-Selling Offers
Think about how to encourage customers to purchase related or complementary items

03

Create Repeat Sales Business Model
Think about how you could sell once and get revenue multiple times

04

Consider Down-Sell Strategy
Be ready to downgrade your main offer if customers find it too expensive

05

Find Partners for Affiliate Sales
Find people who will sell your product and earn commissions per sale

Create at least three up-sell offers and test them

Up-selling is the practice of encouraging customers to purchase a comparable, higher-end, and more expensive product than the one offered initially. It means you can increase your revenue per sale by selling more to the same customer during the same purchase (this includes various upgrades in quality and quantity). Up-selling often employs comparisons of different offers in order to market higher-end products to customers. Showing potential customers that other versions or packages may better fulfill their needs can increase average order volume and make users even more satisfied with their purchase. If you want to succeed in up-selling, you should help your customers to visualize the value they will get by ordering a higher-priced item.

So, now it's your task to create at least three ideas for how you could increase the value for your customers and earn extra revenue per sales. Think about how you could upgrade your main offer to a higher-end offer. It might be a good idea to review your data from the hypothesis verification and customer interviews. Maybe there is something that was desired by certain customers? Even if this target segment is small, why not try to test this offer as an up-sell. If done correctly, your mainstream customers will stick to the main offer, while this particular segment would have a chance to upgrade their offer and get more value out of it.

Most startups wonder how much they should discount the up-selling offer. The answer is that you should test it. There is no stock answer because your industry, your product, and your customers are all variables. Most empirical research shows that the bigger the discount, the higher conversion of the up-sells. Some e-commerce experts recommend offering at least a 25% discount, while others say that the emotion of the special offer and how the additional value is communicated is a far more important factor for successful up-selling compared to the size of discount (which can be just 10% or even less).

By the way, it's not a big technical issue to implement the up-sell on your website. There are many third party solutions that can help implement up-sell strategies, even for those entrepreneurs who have no coding skills. As an example, OneClickUpsell is just one of great apps for up-selling if you have your products on Shopify. If you have your website built on WordPress, you can use the WooCommerce plugin with built-in functionalities for up-selling and cross-selling.

 Choose at least three different cross-selling strategies and test them

Cross-selling is the practice of encouraging customers to purchase related or complementary items. Generally, you identify products that satisfy additional, complementary needs that are unfulfilled by the original item. Usually, cross-selling proposes products users would have purchased anyway, but cross-selling can also encourage users to take a look at products they didn't previously know you offered. Cross-sell helps to increase the average customer lifetime value by selling more to the same customer over the time. In e-commerce, cross-selling is often used on product pages and during the checkout process. It is similar in physical stores—when the customer is ready to pay, the seller politely asks if the customer would like to add a particular product, and explains how great this offer is for the customer.

Think about your own or third party products you could cross-sell. If needed, find partners whose products you could cross-sell and earn additional revenue through decent commissions. Once you have a list of products available for cross-selling, choose at least three cross-selling strategies and test them in practice:

1. *Complementary or similar product*—Propose complementary or similar products to the one the customer has chosen.

2. *Complementary service*—It's not just an opportunity for additional revenue, but a good way to overcome the client's objections against a product which requires an installation or advanced maintenance that the customer might not be able to manage alone.

3. *Automatic cross-selling*—This is generally the idea of "Customers who bought this product also bought…." This feature automatically selects matching products based on the order history and buying habits of your customers. This method has become an essential tool for online shops and there are no reasons why startups who sell their products online should not use it.

4. *Incentivize*—This includes tempting offers such as "free delivery on orders more than $20." The call to action is designed to encourage customers to just buy that little bit more. You might also try a discount or gift voucher for orders over a certain amount.

5. *Sold separately*—this concept is based on the fact that if customer wants to get a complete product A, he has also to purchase product B and product C. You must be absolutely clear about this in all your communications, because otherwise, some customers might feel that you have cheated them by offering a great price deal, but the product is not really complete.

6. *Sell the look*—Offer your customers an idea of how his product will look in combination with others. If they like the overall look, there is a possibility that they will buy all the products at once or at least few of them. It's different from "Sold separately" strategy because it's not necessary to buy products B and C to successfully use the product A.

7. *Bet on customer's taste*—Once the customer has found what he is looking for, you can manually or automatically suggest products of the same style, color, or

material. Showing additional products that customer yet has not seen but might like is a common strategy. It's different from automatic cross-selling because in this case, you have to propose individually selected products that match the estimated style and interest of the particular customer.

8. *Expert recommendations*—Using quotes from industry experts, thought leaders, or famous people, who are already your clients, can usually help to drive customer's attention to certain products, especially if these products are highly sensitive to perceived value and it's hard to measure the objective value.

9. *Discounted second buy*—Usually a discount is offered for the next item or next purchase. The most basic example: "buy two, get third for free" or "Thank you for buying! Here is a 20% discount coupon for any products you like (coupon valid until...)."

10. *Exclusive chance*—Special offer for a limited time or selling-out a limited number of items. This offer is available only for those customers who already bought something related to these products. This cross-sells strategy is based on scarcity, meaning there is a limited possibility to get something exclusive. Be sure to act honestly.

Up-selling and cross-selling are not just about gaining extra revenue, it's an opportunity to engage with your customer and grow a relationship. Don't brag and, by all means, don't push unwanted products! You should offer something that brings higher value to the customer. The goal here is to make customers feel like you are trying to help them to get the most out of their purchase. This is a different mindset: instead of concentrating your thinking about your wish to maximize your revenue and profit, you should think and act in the way that the customer would benefit from the deal as much as possible. This is the key to successful and long-term business.

No matter how small you are and at how early the stage of your business, think about up-selling and cross-selling from day one. ZaliZali could barely be called a true startup per definition we have discussed, but this small raw food company makes a great example for cross-selling and up-selling at an early stage. ZaliZali makes different sprouts and greens (like sunflower, alfalfa, peas, wheat grass, barley greens, mung, adzuki, garbanzo, green lentils, etc.) and sells them directly to the customer. Even though ZaliZali is working in a small market (Lithuania), they have already learned and implemented cross-selling by providing an additional service (healthy food educational programs for children) and new side products. They also did a great job in up-selling. They introduced a discount program and free delivery to encourage larger orders, as well as adopted a simple strategy based on the concept of multi-level marketing: certain customers became sales agents who distribute products among their friends. If the company continues to validate their learning at this rapid pace, their experience could become a strong foundation for a business franchise model.

 Create a repeat or subscription-based sales model

Selling Products and services to the customer is what we are working towards and what we expect to happen. Selling to the customer as often as possible is what we wish for. Selling to the customer just once and getting revenue multiple times is what dream about. We've talked about subscription and membership revenue models in Chapter 7: Financial assessments. Now it's time to look at this revenue model again. It is likely that not all businesses are equally suitable for subscription or membership revenue models, but you can at least consider it at least for few minutes. If you had to implement this type of revenue model, what would it look like?

I had a client in my practice that was selling fruits in the local market and on a wholesale basis to retailers in other towns. He wanted to expand sales and get more stable revenue. Nothing fancy, nothing related to startups. But after a while, we came to a new solution, the "fruit subscription!" The fruit seller offered to deliver fresh fruits to local companies 2 to 5 times a week for a regular monthly fee. Most of the companies were used to spending money for coffee anyway. Fruits are more healthy (contain vitamins, fiber, "good" carbohydrates, etc), but companies never thought to offer them for office employees like an alternative for a coffee break because it was too much trouble to buy the fruit, deliver them to the office, wash them, and serve them on the table. The fruit seller offered a one-week free trial and delivered seasonal fruits to offices and took care of all the details. The result was fascinating! Nearly 70% of his customers signed a "fruit subscription" agreement after the free trial. The new approach, even in such traditional industry, created a stable and meaningful revenue stream. In addition, the fruit seller got meaningful word of mouth advertising, became better known, and attracted new retail clients (the same people from offices came to his local market and bought fruit for home). If the fruit seller could imagine a subscription business, I'm sure that you also could come up with and interesting idea for how to create a stable, ongoing revenue stream.

If your business is quite specific or you simply can't come up with a subscription or membership revenue model, focus your attention on repeat purchases. Even if you are selling one-time sell products (which are sold only once and there are no related additional products or services), take some time to give it some thought. But if you are like most businesses, there are two ways to increase repeat purchases or continued use of your products or services:

1. *Loyalty programs* that help to retain customers and even to encourage them to recommend you to their friends. This could include providing exclusive discounts or special access for loyal customers, retargeting customers with abandoned carts, emails and promotions for a repeat purchase, using email to send

personalized offers and suggesting products, surprising and delighting your customers by giving a small unexpected gift, etc.

2. *Customer lock-in* or *high switching costs*. If it's relatively easy for your customer to switch from your products to your competitors', customers will be more price-sensitive and you'll probably have a higher churn rate. You may want to consider tactics for locking in customers to your product or solution (through long-term contracts, unique technology, or data that can't be easily transferred).

Consider your down-sell strategy

If your customer declines an upsell offer or even quits your sales page or physical store, you can offer them a lower-priced offer called a down-sell. You can downgrade main offer if you feel that it's too expensive for the customer. It doesn't mean that you should have to apply just a plain discount and keep everything else the same as your regular offer. Maybe there are some unnecessary features that could be excluded from the offer and this way, the final price of the offer could be lower. You still want to keep an attractive profit margin for you and leave an incentive for the customer to buy a regular offer later when he needs additional features and benefits.

Up-selling and cross-selling are great strategies, but only when your customers are getting more value. But sometimes customers don't want additional value. To the contrary, maybe they need just a few features or benefits, but your main offer forces them to buy a whole bundle at relatively high price. When you down-sell you build trust and demonstrate you are acting in your customers best interests. Be aware of how many customers view your offer but don't buy. That is your potential for down-sell. Sure, not all of them will become your buyers, but at least some of them could. Your task is to figure out how you could downgrade your main offer and test these solutions in the market.

Find partners for affiliate sales

It would be foolish not to try to employ affiliate sales in your marketing strategy. Whether you want to find people who would sell your product or to find products which you could add to your cross-sell strategy and earn commission, affiliate networks might be very valuable. The best thing is that if you want other people to sell your product, you pay nothing for advertising until particular results are achieved (for example, you get visitors to your site, signups to the product trial, or even sales). If you already have a good traction and would like to add a few additional products to your cross-sell strategy, affiliate networks can help you find such products and secure your commissions. The affiliate network operators act as a third party guarantee (if you generate sales, commissions will be guaranteed to be paid by an affiliate network operator). Affiliate programs may follow different models and you need to decide what fits you best:

- *Cost Per Click (CPC)* model pays for "clicks" no matter whether if the referral traffic helped to generate a sale or not (similar approach as Google AdWords).
- *Cost Per Action (CPA)* model pays for specific actions including simple form submissions, downloads, surveys, sharing on social networks, etc.
- *Cost Per Lead (CPL)* model pays for leads (usually a "signup" that involves email or credit card verification as it makes the lead more valuable).
- *Cost Per Sale (CPS)* model pays for actual sales and it means that product seller shares a percentage of sale value with the advertiser.

If you'd like to try an affiliate sales model, I'd recommend starting with CJ Affiliate. It was formerly known as Commission Junction and it's one of the oldest and most popular affiliate networks. This affiliate network is preferred even by some of Fortune 500 companies and major online retailers, so it's well trusted and tested network. You could also check other affiliate networks like ShareASale, Rakuten Affiliate Network, Affiliate Window, Tradedoubler, Zanox, Max Bounty, PeerFly, FlexOffers, ClickBoth and etc.

 Recommended reading

1. Mark Joyner. *The Irresistible Offer*: *How to Sell Your Product or Service in 3 Seconds or Less*
2. Steven Daar. *Profit Hacking*: *The Web Entrepreneur's 3 Part Formula For Maximizing Success*

27. Marketing plan on one page

WHY IT IS NEEDED

Throughout my practice, I've seen many different approaches to developing marketing plans. A clear and actionable marketing plan helps you to stay focused on the main activities that bring you closer to your main marketing goal, which is to create profit. Big companies prepare their annual, quarterly, and monthly marketing plans covering all their business activities in general and each of their activities or product groups separately and in great detail. These marketing plans can consist of 30 or even 100 pages. But the bigger the volume of any plan, the harder it is to implement it and the more effort that is needed. Therefore, the classical approach to creating a marketing plan might not be the most effective way for startups. In addition, during my global research on startups, I found that most startups have the wrong ideas about how to create their marketing plans. We discussed some of those major mistakes at the beginning of the book.

So, we have a dilemma: every startup needs a marketing plan to stay focused on the main activities that help to create a profitable and scalable business, but startups are not big companies and therefore, the classical approach to marketing plan might be a little bit frustrating for them. This chapter shows a simple method for creating your marketing plan literary on a single page. It's not done in a conventional way and it doesn't include as many details as a traditional plan. But, a marketing plan in this form will give you a clear view of your main marketing goal, what intermediate objectives you are seeking, and what tasks you should do to achieve the goal. For most investors and entrepreneurs, it's just enough. What I like most about it is that the marketing plan is very actionable.

HOW TO DO IT

01 Define the Main Goal
Use the SMART methodology to define your main marketing goal

02 Outline the Objectives
Figure out what generally needs to be done to achieve the goal

03 Break Out Objectives Into Tasks
List all tasks that must be done to complete each of the objectives

04 Tie Tasks to Dates
Make your marketing plan more actionable and trackable by setting due dates and budget

 Define the main goal of your marketing

What is your main marketing goal? Goals such as more paying customers, increased sales, and higher profit are too generic to be included as your main marketing goals. We have talked about different marketing goals in Chapter 12: Testing communication and distribution channels. Each marketing plan is prepared for a certain period (for example, for 12 months), for high season, for a special event, and for a certain goal. The most common case is to prepare an annual marketing plan and set a goal to increase net profit, sales revenue, or any other metrics during the period. Therefore, your main marketing goal should be oriented towards the same period (in most cases - one year). Use the SMART methodology to define your main marketing goal:

- **S** (specific)— The goal is clear to anyone that has a basic knowledge of the project.
- **M** (measurable)—It's easy to find out when you have achieved the goal.
- **A** (action-oriented)—Sounds not like a dream, but as task or job to be done.
- **R** (realistic)—Is possible to achieve given the availability of resources, knowledge, and time
- **T** (time-based)—There is a defined time when the goal should be achieved.

Let's talk about an example. To tell you the truth, not many startups agreed to share their full marketing plans with me and I understand their reasons. I'm very thankful for all startups that took part in the research and took the time to have an in-depth interview with me and provide additional answers by email. So, in this case, let's take my personal example. While writing this book and having so many personal interviews with startups, I was suggested to create online video courses for startups. These courses would help startups founders to build their profitable and scalable business faster by effectively aligning marketing activities. The main goal of my marketing plan could look like in Figure 40.

Figure 40.   Example of the main marketing goal

> To sell at least 1,000 startup marketing courses online at average price of $239 in 12 months after the book launch

It is specific, measurable, action and time-based, and because it indicates the action "to sell," explains what should be sold, how many, at what price, and when this goal should be achieved. Is it realistic? It depends on the resources I currently have or can acquire. When I shared this goal with one of my friends, he said, "Great goal, but a tough one." I agree it's not easy, but maybe it's possible because by then, I'll be a published author and will have readers all around the world. We should proceed to next step to assess if the goal is realistic.

 What objectives must be completed to achieve the goal?

Once you have a clear and measurable goal, try to figure out what generally needs to be done to achieve the goal. Make a list of three to six intermediate objectives which if achieved, would also help you achieve your goal. Remember that you are creating a marketing plan on one page, so don't get too deep into the details. Focus on your strategy (which you should have developed in chapter 14), and plan this objective at a tactical level. Some marketing specialists would rather call it an outline or a roadmap rather than a plan, but don't worry about the name at the moment. You need to create clear and actionable instructions for yourself on how to boost your startup business.

Let's continue with the example. If I want to sell my online courses, there are five intermediate objectives to achieving the main goal (Figure 41). It's obvious that first of all, I have to create the online course, which will involve market research and other tasks, but we'll talk about them in the next step. As you see, I've set a qualification criterion for my courses: they must be really worth at least $500. This is double compared to the price I plan to sell at. Why have I made such a criterion? Before investing time and money in larger scale marketing I want to get market verification that target customers find this product at least two times more valuable than the price at which I plan to sell it at large scale. Imagine how much easier it will be to sell if people see, feel, and understand that it is much more valuable than the price it is sold at.

Figure 41.   Main goal broken down into objectives

Courses will be sold online, so driving targeted traffic will be one of my main objectives. But how much traffic should I plan to reach, if I want to make 1000 sales? I came to these measurable objectives by thinking backward from my goal. I want to make at least 1000 sales and expected average conversion rate is about 7%. This is a hypothesis based on industry average conversion of similar tools and tactics I plan to use, so my final objective is to at least meet the industry average of 7% conversion rate on the course sales page. This page will be shown not to random visitors, but to engage potential customers. If I succeed in achieving such conversion, it means I'll need roughly 15,000 activated, engaged target customers (for example, they should see my free online seminar series before they visit the course sales page). I think (this is another hypothesis that must be tested) that email marketing automation would be the most effective channel to reach potential customers and activate them. But I need to collect email addresses first to implement email marketing automation later. In order to acquire email addresses for potential customers, the landing page will offer one to three lead magnets (something valuable for startups absolutely for free and with no obligation, just in exchange for the email address). So here comes another measurable objective: acquire 50,000 email addresses. Why

50,000? Because for the next objective (activation) we've set a 30% conversion rate, based again on the industry average. Finally, we can calculate how much traffic we need to drive to our landing page if we want to collect 50,000 email addresses and the landing page conversion rate is expected to be 25%. The right answer is 200,000 targeted visitors.

Remember that we also have to check if those intermediate objectives inevitably lead us to the main goal. If we drive 200,000 visitors to an initial landing page which has 25% conversion rate, we'll collect 50,000 email addresses. If email marketing automation campaign achieves a 30% conversion rate, we'll get 15,000 engaged potential customers. And finally, if we have a sales page with an average 7% conversion rate and we offer a really valuable product, we'll have 1,050 sales. The goal would be reached!

 Tasks to be done, to complete each objective

The next task is to break out each of the objectives into smaller more detailed tasks. Yes, it's easy to say "drive at least 200,000 targeted visitors," "achieve at least 25% conversion," but when it comes to the implementation of these objectives, you might get stuck. In order to avoid getting stuck, ask yourself one simple question: "what needs to be done to achieve this objective?" Apply the same principle as in the previous tasks when you were breaking out the main goal. Also, always double check if the objective will be achieved if you successfully complete those tasks.

The serious project manager would say that each of those tasks should be made according to the SMART methodology. But, actually, it's up to you to decide if you want those tasks to be highly specific or more like major guidelines. The more specific you make the tasks, the easier it will be for you to implement the plan, because you'll already know precisely what has to be done and that it is more or less realistic. But in some cases, startups always face a lot of uncertainty and it's really difficult to set highly specific, lower level tasks because so many things can change very quickly. As far as I've found out during the startup case studies, the best practice for most startups is to set general tasks to be done to achieve the particular objective and to figure out along the way how to test it.

Here is an example what the marketing tasks could look like for each of objectives (Figure 42). It doesn't require much explanation. If you are preparing a marketing plan not only for yourself but for a team, it might be wise to at least explain each task in a couple of sentences. By the way, you are welcome to download this template from www.evolutioncurve.com and use it for outlining your marketing plan. Print it out on a single page and keep it in front of you in your workspace. This doesn't require much of your time and effort but will help you not to lose track of your progress.

Figure 42. Objectives broken down into tasks

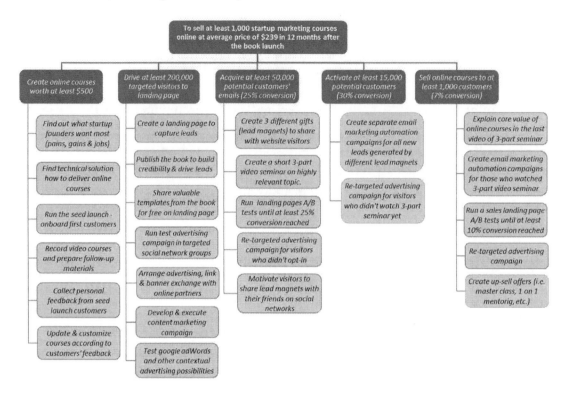

Tie tasks to dates in a simple Gantt diagram or Excel

Now, it's about time to make your marketing plan more actionable and trackable (Figure 43). Having a marketing plan is good and helps a lot, but if you want to achieve even greater results you must plan your marketing actions based on time and money. Basically, you must decide when each of your tasks will be done and how much money it will cost. There is no one-size-fits-all solution

You can put your tasks in your personal calendar (online or offline), time planning app or software, or your company CRM if it has objective and task functionality. There are many specialized free and fee-based software solutions for drawing Gantt diagrams for your projects, including your marketing plan. Using a Gantt diagram for planning and managing tasks allows opportunities to join, combine, or even do some tasks simultaneously (even from different stages) which might save you time.

The example shows the main principles of putting your marketing plan in Excel spreadsheet. Most startups find this solution for marketing planning easy applicable and very helpful because it allows them to:

- Create tasks for objectives, subtasks for tasks, and so on and put comments on each of them. So you can go as deep into details as you want and everything will be on track. If you want to see the general, strategic view, you can hide grouped rows with sub-tasks and tasks.

- The top row of the table shows the timeline (usually months or weeks). Marking certain cells with your chosen color allows you to easy to see the tasks you should be focusing your time on.
- The bottom row of the table shows the sum of money required for all marketing tasks each month. All you need to is to add the amount of money required for each task in already colored cells.

You can find this spreadsheet in the set of templates for download at www.evolutioncurve.com/templates. I hope you'll find it useful, too.

Figure 43. Marketing plan with budget, timing, and responsibilities

	No	Tasks	Priority	Budget	Responsible person	January	February	March	April	May	June	July	August
66	**4.1**	**1 task necessary to complete the objective**	1	**0**									
67	4.1.1	Sub-task		0									
68	4.1.2	Sub-task		0									
69	4.1.3	Sub-task		0									
70	**4.2**	**2 task necessary to complete the objective**	2	**7.220**									
71	4.2.1	Sub-task	1	2.610									
72	4.2.2	Sub-task	2	750									
73	4.2.3	Sub-task	3	3.400									
74	4.2.4	Sub-task	1	460									
75	**4.3**	**3 task necessary to complete the objective**	1	**15.675**									
76	4.3.1	Sub-task		0									
77	4.3.2	Sub-task		3.745									
78	4.3.3	Sub-task		5.830									
79	4.3.4	Sub-task		6.100									
80	**4.4**	**4 task necessary to complete the objective**	1	**2.150**									
81	**4.5**	**5 task necessary to complete the objective**	2	**1.000**									
82	5	Objective No.5: ____________		5.920									
83	5.1	**1 task necessary to complete the objective**	2	**2.500**									
84	5.2	**2 task necessary to complete the objective**	3	**460**									
85	5.3	**3 task necessary to complete the objective**	2	**0**									
86	5.3.1	Sub-task	2	0									
87	5.3.2	Sub-task	2	0									
88	5.3.3	Sub-task	2	0									
89	5.4	**4 task necessary to complete the objective**	3	**2.500**									
90	5.5	**5 task necessary to complete the objective**	3	**460**									
91		Total budget		68.220		12.710	27.160	3.160	7.680	1.300	5.700	3.800	0

Recommended reading

1. Allan Dib. *The 1-Page Marketing Plan: Get New Customers, Make More Money, And Stand out From The Crowd*
2. Alexander Chernev. *The Marketing Plan Handbook, 4th Edition*
3. Philip Kotler, Gary Armstrong. *Principles of Marketing*

28. Execute-Measure-Learn

WHY IT IS NEEDED

The learning process never stops, especially after the product launch. Marketing metrics help to measure the output of your efforts and make more effective decisions. Your product might be awesome, your marketing plan might be very original with effective growth hacking solutions built-in, but with poor execution and no measurement, you won't get great results. If you don't measure, you can't learn. This is extremely important in marketing. I've prepared and helped to implement marketing plans for more than 50 companies in different industries and have never seen a case where the marketing plan could have been implemented without any changes. As one professor said, "It's a bad plan if it was not changed during the implementation." So, without measuring, how you will learn what changes are needed?

The execute-measure-learn process in marketing saves you from wasting your time and resources for things and activities which are not important, helps avoid similar mistakes in the future, and allows you to achieve your goals faster.

You have to stay persistent, but not stubborn, and miracles can happen. As Rennie Popcheva-Capri, the co-founder of *Embrioo*, remembered, they started just with a laptop, $1,000, and not more than 100 people in the neighborhood as their network, and without having an investor. Today *Embrioo* is an open innovation platform that disrupts the existing model of how new ideas, concepts, and inventions are shared and commercialized. *Embrioo* is an award winner at Creative Business Cup, Copenhagen; award winner at Sheffield University Innovation Challenge; 2015 Forbes Annual Awards, Best Startup; featured at TEDx and at Forbes in 2014; recently announced as one of the best ideas coming from Europe; and Winner Ideas from Europe Challenge, 2016-2017.

HOW TO DO IT

01 Define Tasks for Each Week
Track your marketing plan calendar and update it accordingly

02 Measure and Report at Checkpoints
Do a brief report on your weekly goals and which ones you've achieved

03 Learn What Didn't Work Out
Identify the cause of failure and determine what has to be changed for the future

Execute: define marketing tasks for each week

Track your marketing plan calendar and update it accordingly (personally, I use an Excel spreadsheet for this purpose). If you are good at time planning, I'm sincerely happy for you. But for most startup founders, time planning is a very hectic issue, because so much has to be done and there is so little time. Review your marketing plan and pick up to three marketing goals you want to achieve within a week. Yes, pick only three goals at maximum you want to achieve within the upcoming week. There are four main options that you can do with all your tasks concerning the implementation of marketing plan or in any other area of your startup development:

- *Do it by yourself*—Pick the most important tasks that you can do the best, and do them. Focus not only on your weekly marketing goals but also on the bigger picture. Having a one-page marketing plan would help a lot.

- *Delegate it to somebody*—Our opportunity to do certain tasks is mainly limited by the time and skills we have. Decide which tasks should be delegated to your colleagues, partners, freelancers, or maybe somebody else (for example, maybe your family members or friend could give you a hand in certain moments).

- *Schedule it for later*—Don't worry that not all tasks will be finished as planned. We are just humans after all. If you are not able to complete some tasks as planned, re-schedule them.

- *Cancel and forget it*—Circumstances may change and you shouldn't stay blindly connected to your initial marketing plan. If some tasks or measure which you planned a while ago lose their priority, don't bother with them. Delete and forget! Replace them with more efficient marketing solutions.

 Measure: weekly checkpoints and reports

Even if you are the only founder, do a report for yourself. At least a brief report, including what were your weekly marketing goals and which ones you've achieved. Take a few minutes to think about obstacles you've faced and opportunities you might have found or still need to discover. Having periodic checkpoints helps you progress much faster and sometimes avoid painful mistakes. The in-depth interviews with successful startups revealed that there are three main types of checkpoints:

- Weekly checkpoints
- Monthly checkpoints
- Milestone checkpoints

Milestone checkpoints are related to specific intermediate goals and achievements which we've talked about in Chapter 16: Setting up fundraising milestones. I highly recommend that you start using all of these checkpoints and review your startup's situation through specific metrics (which are explained in Chapter 30: Viral loop and key metrics).

 Learn: what didn't work as expected and what to do next

When achieving marketing objectives, the flow of events may turn in another direction and the actual results may not match the expected results. If the end-result is worse than was expected, you need to identify the cause of failure and determine what has to be changed.

1. Determine the reasons behind the failure
   - In which stage did the failure occur: in the strategic decision or tactical implementation?
   - What has been proven ineffective: just a certain marketing measure or the entire concept?
2. If there is no basis for thinking that failure was brought about by a certain strategic decision (all your hypotheses still remains confirmed), then you need to change the tactical measures. It is cheaper and easier to switch tactics than to change the entire marketing strategy or even the whole business model.
3. If tactical measures have proven effective (generally meaning that the offers are presented to clients on time and on the spot), but the end-result is not what was expected, then you need to conduct further analysis.
   - Internal analysis: Did you really present an irresistible offer to your target customers? Is your company and are your partners actually doing what you've promised to do? Can the client doubt anything?
   - Market demand analysis: Did the market itself shrink or change? What trends are currently dominating the market? Do they differ from those that served as a basis for the prepared strategy and business model?
   - Competitor analysis, both quantitative and qualitative: How many competitors are there in the market? What do they offer? How actively or aggressively are they executing their marketing strategy? In which areas do you face competition and why are you losing?

SlideModel provides their customers with more than 12,000 PowerPoint templates and designs. The business is built on a subscription-based revenue model, and the templates are downloaded directly from the website. The founders of *SlideModel* thought the main marketing strategy would be based on online advertising like Google AdWords and so on. They spent money on online ads for several years until they figured out that there were other channels with a higher ROI. Due to increased competition, online advertising became much more expensive, and the lack of ad campaign optimization didn't allow them to achieve higher ROI. So, once you implement any marketing decisions, measure the results and don't wait years to do so.

 Recommended reading

1. Philip Kotler, Gary Armstrong. *Principles of Marketing*
2. Jim Joseph. *The Experience Effect*: *Engage Your Customers with a Consistent and Memorable Brand Experience*

If you have planned and set up your marketing system, have significant traction, and see a profit, now it's time to focus on implementing one or more growth engines, automating your marketing, and undertaking and many other tasks designed to scale your business.

If you are not yet profitable, maybe there is no sense of urgency to implement the tasks included in the next chapter. Have you already crafted and tested your irresistible offer with up-sell, cross-sell and down-sell strategies? Have you prepared a consistent marketing plan? Are your variable costs per customer low enough compared to average customer lifetime value? Is the overall conversion rate of your sales funnel/pipeline high (that is, do newer marketing communication costs pay off well)? If all those parameters are good enough, you just need to increase sales volume. Adding more potential customers to your sales funnel/pipeline should give you an opportunity to scale your business and get your well-deserved profit.

Stage 5: Growth Hacking

Finally, we come to the topic that interests startups the most. Growth hacking for many startups seems like a magic wand that can solve all of their problems. But, as we have already discussed, this kind of thinking is one of the most dangerous mistakes in startup marketing. If you don't have the appropriate marketing foundations for your startup (that is, market fit, positioning, sales funnel, etc.), premature growth will ruin your business and waste your resources.

The secret behind effective growth hacking is to follow a proven framework and to implement the right strategy at the right time. Every decision that a growth hacker makes is driven by seeking measurable growth. All strategies, tactics, and tools are used in order to grow the business. But if growth is measured just by vanity metrics, these efforts are meaningless. Therefore, not every successful growth hack brings real growth.

Some of the growth hacking principles should be built into your product or your sales funnel, but some of them can be effectively used only when you have launched your product into the market. In this stage, we'll talk about measuring your startup's business growth, what is a viral loop and how to create it, how to choose the right engine of growth, and how to increase your profit and automate your marketing.

The main goals of this stage are to:

- Create a viral loop
- Choose the right growth engine
- Use leverages everywhere including marketing

29. Viral loop and key metrics

WHY IT IS NEEDED

Would you like your clients to be an advertisement for you and make their friends become your new clients? If yes, create a viral loop! It might sound a bit complicated but, actually, there is nothing mystical. You just need to slightly upgrade your sales funnel, which we'll talk about it in this chapter. If there is no such viral loop created, you shouldn't expect much word-of-mouth advertising or referrals from your customers. You will have to attract each new potential customer on your own without expecting miracles to happen. It's much easier to scale a startup business if you have a viral loop and focus on the key metrics of your growth.

There are many metrics used by startups and even VC investors, but most of those metrics are vain. They are also known as vanity metrics and include registered users, downloads, raw page views, tweets, etc. Most of them look elaborate and logical and provide satisfaction to the founders as well as the investors about the progress of the startup's development. But, indeed they tell nothing about your real growth. Most startups die because they try to do too many things at once. The same could be said about the vanity metrics that too many startups use to measure their progress. When things don't work out, they can't figure out why the strategy failed, even when their chosen metrics might have shown progress and a promising future. We'll focus on the key metrics related to startup marketing which show you how well your startup is progressing towards achieving a profitable and scalable business.

 Upgrade your sales funnel into a viral loop

The first thing you should is to review and upgrade your sales funnel which we talked about in Chapter 12: Testing communication and distribution channels. If your initial sales funnel ends up with a successful sale or additional up-selling and cross-selling, you should add an additional phase in your sales funnel where your current customers recommend your product or service and attract new targeted customers into your sales funnel (Figure 44).

Of course, we have to admit that not all products are viral and a viral loop for some of them would be difficult to create. For example, social media and multi-player games are highly viral because users naturally invite their friends to join. But consider, for example, medicine to cure hemorrhoids. Not many customers will be joyfully sharing their experience of such a personal matter with their friends or colleagues!

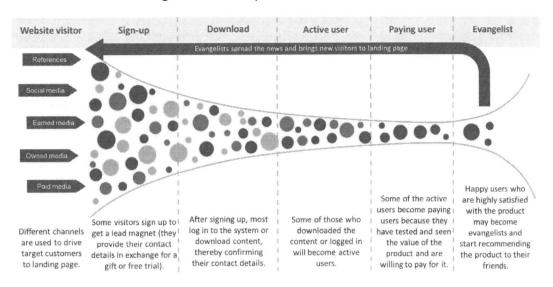

Figure 44. Example of sales funnel scheme

Website visitor	Sign-up	Download	Active user	Paying user	Evangelist

Evangelists spread the news and brings new visitors to landing page

References
Social media
Earned media
Owned media
Paid media

Different channels are used to drive target customers to landing page.

Some visitors sign up to get a lead magnet (they provide their contact details in exchange for a gift or free trial).

After signing up, most log in to the system or download content, thereby confirming their contact details.

Some of those who downloaded the content or logged in will become active users.

Some of the active users become paying users because they have tested and seen the value of the product and are willing to pay for it.

Happy users who are highly satisfied with the product may become evangelists and start recommending the product to their friends.

I truly hope you'll find at least one or more aspects of how your product or service might be interesting for your customers to share. In some cases, it is wise to detach personal experience from your product to make customers more inclined to share the story. Another important condition for viral marketing is that you can start a viral loop working only when there is a customer base that can go viral. If you have at least the initial base of happy customers, plan exactly how you will create your viral loop/referral generation mechanism. Here are the top 10 recommendations from successful startups who managed to create effective viral loops:

1. *Make it simple to recommend you.* This is probably the best advice for creating a viral loop. If you make your customers happy by over-delivering additional value and it is easy to recommend you, at least some of your customers will do that even without any effort on your part. Just make it simple to recommend you!

2. *Surprise your customers by focusing on pleasant experience.* Creating a customer experience that pleasantly surprises your customers is something money can't buy. People love when they get more than expected and they tell others about those experiences.

3. *Ask for a recommendation at the right time.* There's no ideal time to ask. Instead, you should integrate a soft ask into your sales process from the very beginning and remind them throughout. Politely for referrals after you know that they are fully satisfied with your product or service.

4. *Create different levels of recommendations.* It is tempting to think of recommendations and referrals in strict and categorized terms. There are many different levels

of engagement when it comes to personal and online reviews. Recommendations that require customers to think and write something are the most extreme and quite a few customers will agree to do that. A much simpler recommendations options could be a simple thumbs up or thumbs down, star ratings, or at least integration of social network sharing buttons.

5. *Offer a benefit in exchange for a recommendation.* It could be a discount, service credits, an upgrade, a free item, or some other trigger that will entice clients to provide referrals. But avoid giving money in exchange for a recommendation. Offering a double benefit is one of the most common solutions to encourage recommendations. Give a benefit to both the new customer and the one that referred him.

6. *Personally, reach out to your most influential customers.* Seek referrals first from your most influential customers, especially if your resources are limited or you lack official testimonials. Even if they are not your best customers, their opinion might be important for many other potential customers.

7. *Use customer satisfaction surveys to identify potential advocates.* This gives you the opportunity to ask customers what they really think of your service. We'll talk about NPS (Net Promoters Score) in the next task. If you would ask your customers "How likely from 1 to 10 would you be to recommend us?" you could identify your most passionate advocates and evaluate the overall satisfaction of your customers.

8. *Remember special occasions.* Sending your customers a card or gift at Christmas or on their birthday builds stronger personal relationships with your brand. This doesn't have to cost very much (an ecard is better than no card), but a handwritten card or a small symbolic gift will create a stronger *Wow!* effect. Everything depends on your business economy, customer lifetime value, and new customer acquisition costs.

9. *Solve all problems quickly.* If anything goes wrong, put all of your efforts into fixing the problem and then send regular notices regarding your progress to keep the customer updated and in contact with you. If you counter your client's disappointment with a personal approach and exclusive service, most likely you'll be referred as a positive example of how problems should be solved and that your company takes care of its customers.

10. *Remember to say thank you for every referral.* Always express your gratitude when a customer refers you. Most clients who refer you aren't doing this to get a reward (unless you implemented a program that offers special benefit), but everyone likes to feel appreciated. A basic thank you email or a phone call can be an additional encouragement to keep your clients spreading the good word about your business.

Loyal customers who are also your advocates promote your brand, product, or service to other potential clients. Think about how you could help them to do it and express your gratitude in a respectful way.

Forget about vanity metrics and focus on traction

Many startups think that more metrics is better because it is smart to track and measure everything. Therefore, too many startups focus on vanity metrics: numbers that look good in the report and can make the founder feel awesome, but they don't really mean anything important. Vanity metrics (for example, registered users, downloads, raw page views, tweets, etc.) can be easily manipulated and do not necessarily correlate to the numbers that really show the progress of your startup development towards becoming a profitable and scalable business. You should avoid vanity metrics and focus on measuring what really matters.

Ash Maurya (2015) suggests that instead of aiming for too many goals, to define and aim for a single traction metric. Traction is the rate at which a business model captures monetizable value from its customers. It indicates the output of your business model and serves as a clear measure of progress for startup founders and investors.

Generally, metrics can be of four types and are used for different purposes:

1. *Qualitative*—Mainly focuses on usability and customer's satisfaction (for example, what visitors do on the website, what problems are most frustrating in their life, and which of your proposed solutions seems to work best).

2. *Quantitative*—Is mostly used to measure the engagement of target customers (for example, to evaluate visitors' behavior on the website, track conversion and bounce rates).

3. *Comparative*—Helps to find improvements because it is used to compare the behavior of target customers in different scenarios (for example, website A/B testing, email campaign A/B testing).

4. *Competitive*—Allows evaluation of how you rank in different aspects compared to your competitors (for example, pricing comparison, distribution channel comparison, and revenue and growth comparison).

Whichever type of metrics we are talking about, it should meet the criteria known as 3A:

✓ *Actionable*—Each metric should help you make a decision. If you can't make a decision based on the metric, why should you waste your time collecting the data? Feeling awesome about great numbers and having the illusion of progress doesn't count. For example, what decision you can make if you know that the number of your website visitors has changed from 10,000 last month to 20,000 this month? You could say, "That's awesome! We have two times more potential customers coming to us!" But the truth is that this metric doesn't allow you to make any decisions, because you don't know what made those additional visitors come to your website or who those visitors are (for example, it's easy to buy fake traffic like 1000 visits for just $5, so the increase of 10,000 visitors might be worth just $50 but will bring you no value at all). Instead, if you run an A/B test of the landing page, track how many visitors are activated (for example, sign-ups, downloads, registers to a free trial, etc.). Knowing that landing page A had 17% conversion and landing page B had 22% conversions, you can set B as your default landing page and you'll increase your conversion.

✓ *Accessible*—It's obvious that you must have the opportunity to access all the data needed to calculate the metric. Let's say a book is put on Amazon.com for free or heavy discounted download for a limited time. Amazon provides extensive data how many users have downloaded or ordered the printed book. But that's just another vanity metric. Why? Because we don't know how many of those people read the book or even opened it. So far, it's impossible to get that kind of data from Amazon. We can't measure how many actual readers the book had, especially because it was given for free or as a heavy discounted download. Anybody—even those without any interest in the topic of the book—might have downloaded it just because it was listed for free. Instead, if there is an invitation and special link at the beginning of the book to visit a particular website and download additional bonuses, it becomes very easy to calculate how many people have opened the book, read at least the first few pages and become interested, because they've downloaded the bonuses. (By the way, if you noticed, I'm doing the same with this book!)

✓ *Auditable*—You must be able to validate the data any time you have the need. If you get data only once and have no repeat access to double-check it, the reliability of the metric might come under scrutiny. This is extremely important if you go for fundraising and have to prove to potential investors the traction you have at the moment. Therefore, use web site traffic analysis tools (for example, Google Analytics), URL shortener and link management platforms (like bitly.com or goo.gl) for all links you share during your experiments. These platforms will show you how many times each link was clicked. You might also consider different phone numbers to track the amount, duration, and qualified leads if you receive most of the inquiries via phone. Just think a bit broader than the most obvious metrics.

As an example, consider *Mercadoni*, probably the fastest growing e-commerce startup in Latin America. This hyper delivery company (currently focusing on groceries) is often compared to Uber since they are a social, third party logistic with a similar growth and business model. Founded in April 2015, *Mercadoni* is now established in three countries (Colombia, Mexico, and Argentina) and prepared to expand to two additional countries by the end of 2016. Five months after their launch, the company received $2 million in funding from the group Axon Partners and 14 months after their launch, they started preparing for the second round (series A). Using just those figures alone would be a vanity metric because investment is not your income and it doesn't give any idea about your real traction, revenue, and profit. But once we add the fact that *Mercadoni* already has more than 300,000 registered users with a repurchase rate of more than 60% in a two-week time span, that provides us with quite a good indication of their real traction. I'm sure Francesco Lanzi and the other co-founders of *Mercadoni* track additional metrics that help to calculate the monetizable value of customer traction, but I am not in a position to share these details publically.

 Define your sales funnel performance metrics

Dave McClure (2007) introduced five pirate metrics under the acronym AARRR.

1. *Acquisition*—Users come to the website or physical store from various channels.
2. *Activation*— Users enjoy their first visit and have a happy experience.
3. *Retention*— Users come back, visit the website or store multiple times, and open emails, etc.
4. *Referral*— Users like the product or service and refer others.
5. *Revenue*— Users conduct some monetization behavior.

These are very good for understanding the main idea of important metrics, but you should focus on more detailed metrics specific to your sales funnel. Pay attention to how effectively you generate leads and convert them into paying customers.

Figure 45. AARRR metrics in a sales funnel

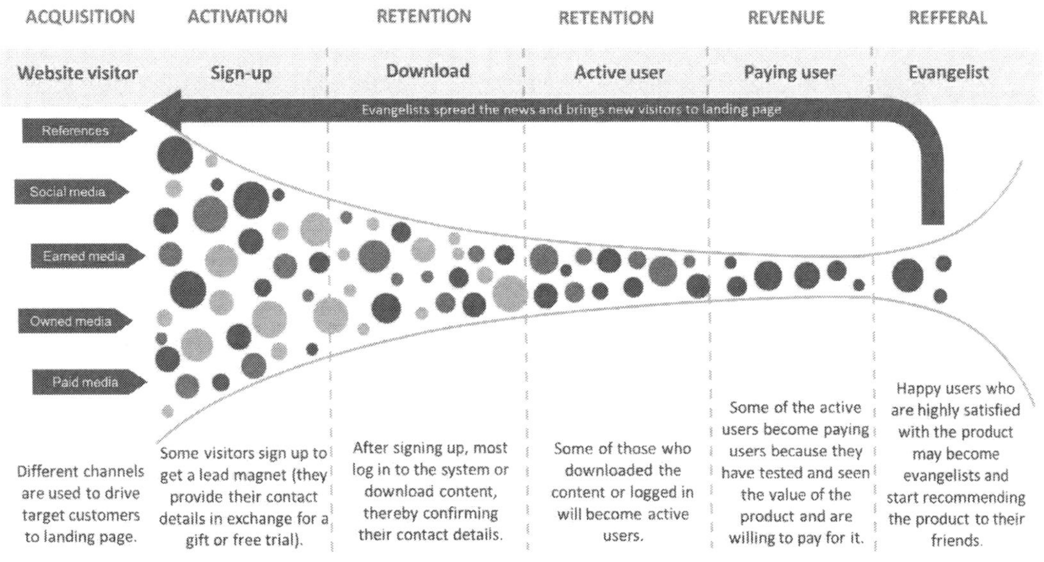

Basically, the three most important metrics that are the same to all startups include: customer lifetime value, customer acquisition costs, and duration of the sales funnel cycle. And, a number of specific metrics are related to each startup's sales funnel which might not be equally important from startup to startup.

- *Customer Lifetime Value* shows the revenues generated by customers compared to the costs associated with acquiring them. Basically, it means how much you will earn per customer on average during the whole time they remain a customer.

- *Customer Acquisition Costs* shows how much it costs on average for you to get a new client. All costs to acquire customers over a given time are divided by the number of customers you acquire in that given time. Complexities arise when you take into account different variables that may be included in the formula, such as sales, support, and marketing staff compensation.

- *Duration of Sales Funnel* Cycle is the average time (usually in days) needed to transform a lead into a paying customer. The shorter the cycle, the faster you create new paying customers.

- Metrics related to sales funnel specifics:

  - *Click Through Rate and Website visitors* shows how many times the content or a link was displayed and how many times the link was clicked and you received a visitor. Without additional context, this might become one of the vanity metrics that we talked about earlier. By running A/B experiments with different channels, messages, and visuals, this metric allows you to easily evaluate which one was more effective.

  - *Social Media Engagement* estimates not just how much time the content was displayed, but also what actions it provoked (for example, clicked Like, click on the link, comment, re-share). You might have a great reach on social networks, but that's just another one of the vanity metrics if there is no engagement.

  - *Content Downloads* should be measured if you are driving leads to your website with lead magnets (apps, videos, articles, e-books, templates, if and resources available for download in exchange for a particular action, for example, sign up or sharing on social networks). Comparing which lead magnet generates more downloads (higher rate of lead activation) helps to improve the conversion of your landing page.

  - *Subscribers* (to your blog, newsletter, discount program, etc.) indicates how many people have opted in to receive communication directly from you. Is your list of subscribers growing? Are you actively engaging your subscribers (most interested audiences) with relevant content?

  - *Sales conversion rate* shows how many leads became paying customers after they were exposed to your sales offer. If you gave an offer to 1000 potential clients and only 20 of them bought from you, your conversion rate is 2%.

- *Revenue per sale (average order size)* shows how much revenue on average your one sale generates. This metric is highly important for companies with many products that might be sold to the same customer (for example, e-commerce business with multiple products) and almost useless for single-product companies, especially if they are only sold to the same customer a single time.

- *Up-sell and cross-sell conversion rate* is a similar metric to sales conversion rate. It shows what percentage of customers to whom you proposed additional offers (up-sell or cross-sell) took that order and bought from you. Let's say you decide to offer something additionally to those 20 customers who already purchased your product. If 5 of them take the deal, you'll have a 25% Up-sell conversion rate. Not bad!

- *Revenue per up-sale and cross-sale* show how much revenue is generated due to up-sell and cross-sell offers. It is the same as average order size but calculated just for up-sales and cross-sales. This metric together with the up-sell conversion rate tells you how well the upsell strategy is working. Experimenting with different offers and different ways of communicating them can help increase one or even both metrics and bring you significant additional revenue.

- *Customer Retention Rate* (CRR) indicates how effectively your efforts are aimed to engage and nurture existing customers to start the sales cycle over again. Tracking this metric could help you to make decisions on how to improve customer loyalty, marketing communication, sales and customer service.

$$Customer\ Retention\ Rate = \frac{Original\ Number\ of\ Customers - Lost\ Customers}{Original\ number\ of\ customers}$$

- *Number of Opt-Outs* shows the number of people who elected to opt-out of your communications or closed their accounts for any reason. If you notice an increase in the opt-out, it might be a signal that your marketing communication is too pushy or you are targeting wrong leads and your offers are not relevant to them.

- Referral *Metrics* are important because recommendations from existing customers are the most cost-effective source of new customers. Therefore it might be wise to track the number and percentage of users referred, referral acceptance rate, and etc.

Steve Blank and Bob Dorf (2014) have put some thought into the four main questions to ask when trying to identify the most important metrics for startups: how many, how fast, how much, and how good? You have to decide on your own what metrics to use, but these questions are a good guideline to determine if you are tracking the right set of metrics:

- How many leads do you acquire and from what channels? How many of those leads become paying customers? How many of those leads and customers are lost and why?
- How fast do you generate new leads? How fast do these leads travel through your sales funnel and become your paying customers? How fast is your viral message spread?
- How much does each lead, conversion, and paying customer cost?

How good are leads that you acquire and from what sources they are better? How good are your customers in terms of their average order size, repeat purchase, and references?

 Estimate possible virality effect with three key metrics

Once you've established what's to be measured in your sales funnel, it's time to measure virality if you want to achieve really good growth. Viral loop, viral effect, virality...let's keep it simple. If you want to estimate how widely your marketing message could be spread through the word of mouth or user references (virality effect) there are three main metrics you should know and use in practice:

- ✓ *Net Promoter Score*—Reflects customer's satisfaction and the likelihood that they will recommend you to someone. This does not indicate any actions but just the customers' satisfaction with your product or service at the moment.
- ✓ *Copulation Rate*—Indicates how actively customers are spreading your message. It takes into account just spreading the message or sharing your content, but doesn't estimate whether the message is forwarded to your target customers or not, nor the effect on sales or conversions.
- ✓ *Viral Coefficient*—Shows how many new active users your current customers bring. It is you who define who should be counted as a user (for example, trial user, free account user, paid user) because you decide at which stage of the sales funnel you will measure the conversion.

Net Promoter Score (NPS) is based on one simple question: "How likely from 0 to 10 is it that you would recommend us to your friends or colleagues?." The NPS is a simple and effective alternative to traditional customer satisfaction research to measure customers' loyalty to a brand. Users answer by scoring on a 0 to 10 scale and are divided into three groups:

- *Promoters* (scores 9 to 10) are likely to buy more, remain as customers longer, and make positive referrals
- *Passives* (scores 7 to 8) behavior falls between Promoters and Detractors, therefore, their answers are excluded from further analysis
- *Detractors* (scores 0 to 6) are less likely to exhibit value-creating behaviors and they will probably express their dissatisfaction with the brand

Figure 46. Calculation of Net Promoter Score

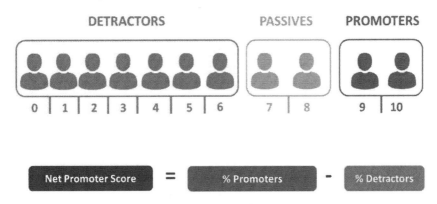

Which NPS rating is good depends on the industry and other factors. But one thing is clear: it's not enough to have just a positive NPS. Several agencies publish annual industry NPS benchmarks. Customers in some industries are more likely to recommend companies due to industry specifics. Therefore, if your NPS is lower than 60, in certain industries it might be a warning sign that you are doing something wrong. On the other hand, customers in other industries by nature are more reserved and don't like sharing recommendations. Therefore having the NPS score be higher than 30 might be a great achievement in these types of industries.

Take your customer touchpoint scheme (Chapter 24: Identify and seize customer touchpoints) and find those touchpoints where you could ask your customer how likely they are to recommend you. It would be even better if you could combine this one-question survey with asking them to provide an actual recommendation via social networks or even to give a personal testimonial or endorsement.

Copulation Rate was introduced by Mark Joyner (2005) as a measure of the virulence of marketing campaigns. Actually, Mark Joyner started using this metric in 1995 and it still remains a tremendously powerful measurement to predict the viral success of your campaigns. It allows you to put a number on your campaign and know instantly how well it would perform thanks to the viral effect.

Copulation is measured in periods of time. For example, it can be a 10-day Copulation Rate or a 30-day Copulation Rate. This metric shows for each person who sees your message, how many people they will refer it to. Basically, if your Copulation Rate is higher than 1.0, it meant that your marketing message has a built-in virus and the pool of people talking about your business and carrying your message would progressively get larger and larger. If your 10-Day Copulation Rate is 1.1, it means that at the end of 10 days, 100 people who saw your message would spread the word to 110 new people, and these will share your messages with additional 121 people within 10 days, and so on. By contrast, if your Copulation rate is lower than 1.0, you'll still have a viral effect, but it will get less and less powerful (it won't spread like a virus). As for example, if your 10-day Copulation rate is 0.8, it means, that 100 people who saw your message will share it with 80 people, and those within 10 days will share this message just with 64 people. So, you will constantly have to boost your marketing campaign with other communication channels. If your Copulation Rate is 0, nobody is sharing and forwarding your message and you have to reach each new potential customer by putting forth your own efforts.

If you want to measure your marketing message's Copulation Rate, you already know what to do: run an experiment! Create a message and spread it to a certain number of people. Do nothing more except counting how many additional people were reached (social networks are probably the easiest way to test your messages because you can see the statistics of how many times your messages were viewed). Once you have your 10-day Copulation Rate, you can estimate the viral effect of your message and how many people potentially could be reached (Table 46). You can make some automated calculations in this online worksheet.

But, take note. Copulation Rate is not permanent and depends on a number of variables. First of all, the initial calculation is based on your short term estimation, therefore, it might change dramatically later. Even though the message is being shared by other people, the newly reached people might not be your targeted customers and the communication effectiveness might decrease. Furthermore, messages get old and become less relevant (for example, even an incredibly funny video becomes less interesting after viewing it a number of times).

Viral Coefficient, suggested by Steve Blank and Bob Dorf (2014), helps to measure the number of activated users referred by your current customers. If a customer invites ten friends (copulation rate is 10.0) but only one of them actually activates and buys from you, your viral coefficient is 1.0. It doesn't matter how many visitors were generated by

Table 46. Examples of copulation rate influence on viral reach

10-day Copulation Rate		10-day Copulation Rate		10-day Copulation Rate	
0.5		1.01		1.21	
Days	Viral reach	Days	Viral reach	Days	Viral reach
1	1,000	1	10,000	1	10,000
10	500	10	10,100	10	12,100
20	250	20	10,201	20	14,641
30	125	30	10,303	30	17,716
40	63	40	10,406	40	21,436
50	31	50	10,510	50	25,937
60	16	60	10,615	60	31,384
70	8	70	10,721	70	37,975
80	4	80	10,829	80	45,950
90	2	90	10,937	90	55,599
100	1	100	11,046	100	67,275
200	0	200	12,202	200	452,593
300	0	300	13,478	300	3,044,816

the reference. One customer generated only one activated new customer. This is the minimum for real viral growth. If at least two people who were invited by one customer would signup and become your new active customers, the viral coefficient would be 2.0. That would give you an opportunity for exponential growth: every customer gets two new customers! Just imagine the growth speed! In just ten referrals cycles, your first 10 customers would become more than 5,000 customers (10 → 20 → 40 → 80 → 160 → 320 → 640 → 1,280 → 2,560 → 5,120). That would be an amazing viral loop and a great growth hack.

The formula for the Viral Coefficient is shown below:

Viral Coefficient = Invitation Rate x Conversion Rate

Invitation Rate — invites sent per user

Conversion Rate — % invited users who take the action

Cycle time is also important to keep in mind because it shows how long it takes long from sending an invite to taking action. The shorter the cycle time, the faster your message is spread. Steve Blank and Bob Dorf (2014), recommend trying to achieve a viral coefficient greater than 1.2 or 1.3, which is closer to linear or modest growth. If the viral coefficient is below 1.0, there won't be any viral growth (cycle time become meaningless) and you'll definitely have to find additional channels to get more new clients.

Update your marketing plan

Be sure you've identified the key metrics for your business model success. Prioritize your metrics and limit the number to no more than 10. You could do more, but in most cases, 10 key metrics is far more than enough to monitor your startup's true progress, make decisions, and take targeted actions instead of getting lost in numbers. Update your marketing plan with those tasks needed to track the necessary data and monitor key metrics. Don't expect that measuring the progress of your startup will happen on its own. At the very least, you will have to set up your marketing information system: what data, when and how should it be collected, how it should it be treated, how often should it be reviewed, and what decisions can we make based on these key metrics.

Recommended reading

1. *Ash Maurya. Scaling Lean*: *Mastering the Key Metrics for Startup Growth*
2. Jessica Donlon. *The Marketing Score Blog. 18 Marketing Performance Metrics that Matter*
3. Ryan Holiday. *Growth Hacker Marketing*: *A Primer on the Future of PR, Marketing, and Advertising*
4. Alistair Croll, Benjamin Yoskovitz. *Lean Analytics*: *Use Data to Build a Better Startup Faster*

30. Growth engines: sticky, viral, paid

WHY IT IS NEEDED

Now that you know what metrics you should use to measure your growth, it's time to decide which growth engine you'll use for scaling your startup. Without choosing your growth engine, you are leaving your startup's growth to chance. My global research on startups in 2016 revealed that more than a third (34.2%) of startups, that already have found product-market fit, don't know what growth engines are or how to employ them, even though they were introduced by Eric Ries in 2011.

Before spending your major budget on promotions, it would be wise to focus on one or more of these growth engines. When you do, you'll build sustainable growth that will drive your business forward. And, when you tie those growth engines to the metrics we just discussed, you'll always be aware of how your startup is growing and will have clear insights on how you might even accelerate its growth.

HOW TO DO IT

01
Audit Your Efforts to Grow
Assess everything you currently do to accelerate your startup's growth

02
Consider the Sticky Engine of Growth
Keep growing while focusing your marketing on retaining customers for the long term

03
Consider the Viral Engine of Growth
Implement a viral loop to get a significant portion of new customers through referrals

04
Consider the Paid Engine of Growth
Track how much you spend to acquire new customers and how much you earn from them

05
Look for Possible Optimizations
Focus on increasing customer lifetime value and conversions in all sales funnel stages

06
Decide Which Engine to Use
Focus on one engine at first and after it is implemented, proceed with another

 Audit how well your marketing is targeted towards business growth

The first step that I would suggest is to assess everything you currently do to accelerate your startup's growth:

- Is your main marketing goal related to growth? Is it tied to at least one of your key metrics?

- Do you have some features in your product that nearly effortlessly drive new customers to you?
- Is there a direct network effect of customers who want their friends to use your product or service too and they are willingly inviting them to join?
- Do you encourage your happy customers to spread the news of their new-found product? How do you do that and what is the most effective way?
- Are you running a highly-effective marketing campaign? What are your average customer acquisition cost and average customer lifetime value?
- Do you have any partnerships that bring or could bring you new leads to your sales funnel/pipeline?

Examine your sales funnel or viral loop and identify the main constraints that limit your growth. What can you do to remove these limitations? If you have conversion problems within your sales funnel, solve them first and only then spend your time and money to employ a growth engine. Otherwise, you'll just waste your resources to drive potential customers to your sales funnel/pipeline but will lose most of them somewhere along the way.

Consider the sticky engine of growth

A sticky growth engine happens when you have the opportunity to keep growing while focusing your marketing on retaining customers for the long term. It works especially well for products that need to be purchased repeatedly in order to continue to use them (for example, home cleaning products, access to online music, or access to a pool of qualified candidates to hire for your business). Most sticky growth engines use a subscription revenue model or loyalty programs for repeated purchases. When you have a product that is built on repeat purchases or subscription and you have an exceptionally low attrition rate, you only have to acquire a small number of new customers to keep growing. So, depending on the specifics of your business, before focusing on finding new customers, pay your attention to current ones.

Not every business can employ a sticky growth engine by default. But the main limitations is usually just in your head (remember the vendor who offered the fruit subscription service). Maintaining low customer attrition is vital. Therefore, if you choose to employ this growth engine, you need to do everything you can to keep your customers coming back on a regular basis. Here are few pieces of advice from startups that have achieved significant growth by keeping their customer attrition rate very low:

1. *Do more than promised. During my interviews, all of the startups that employed a sticky growth engine acknowledged that this was probably the main success*

factor. It's not easy to surprise your customers every time, but try to go extra mile for them.

2. *Collect quantitative and qualitative data.* It's not enough to know how many customers you lose over time, you have to figure out why you are losing them. *Doing customer surveys can help a lot, especially if you can do it* in person. This would give you in-depth feedback from your most trusted customers. If you have thousands of clients, think about implementing an automated survey solution at particular touch points (for example, if customers cancel a subscription, you should definitely ask why they made their decision).

3. *Keep building new value and running experiments. This is directly related to* the first point of doing more than promised. If there is no innovation or added value proposed to loyal customers, churn rates tend to increase. Regularly ask yourself how could you improve the solution to the customer's problem, could you solve another problem for them, or could you give them any extra benefit?

When Ventafun developed their first MVP, it was basically an affiliate marketing platform where influencers got a commission from their recommended product sales. Ventafun released that MVP platform to some early adopters and faced many challenges acquiring companies to add products to the platform. If there are no products, it's not interesting for influencers to join the platform, therefore there are no actual sales, and there is no revenue. Manual efforts to onboard companies that would provide products took a couple of months until the founders realized it was impossible to compete with Groupon's platforms and sales executives. Even though it's not yet at a stage when the startup should think about growth hacking, Ventafun has changed their approach towards a smarter way of working. They got in touch with a few wholesalers that provided drop-shipping services in Spain and signed a couple of strategic contracts with them. That move allowed Ventafun to add hundreds of products to their platform without additional manual sales efforts. This strategic move was a sticky engine of growth. Once the contract was signed, it allowed them to continuously add new products (the more products those wholesalers produce, the more products are uploaded on Ventafun platform). Even though Ventafun later has pivoted their general strategy and value proposition, this move alone has reduced products acquisition cost by 80% and assured significant growth of product variety.

 Consider the viral engine of growth

This growth engine basically means that you have successfully implemented a viral loop and a significant portion of your new customers are coming through references. It may happen by different scenarios: customers may tell their friends, they may share a link to your product, or they may simply use your product and people around them take notice (Think about what happened when the iPhone was first released. If somebody showed up with an iPhone, almost everyone else wanted to get it, too).

There is one highly important aspect to consider: How many new clients should your current clients refer to keep your business growing. If you have a sticky product and a low churn rate, even just a few references might keep you growing. But what if you have a one-time sell product? If a customer buys your products and he won't need another one for a long time (for example, how many electric cars you can sell to one customer?). If this is your situation, the most critical element here is to make sure that every customer brings more than one friend to your business. If you sold your first product release to just five customers and you put all your bets on the viral engine of growth, these customers should refer at least six new customers. Later these six customers should refer at least seven other new customers. Otherwise, your business won't be growing.

The viral engine of growth for most startups looks very simple to build. But that's not the case in reality. It's incredibly difficult to build intentionally, especially if your product doesn't have a built-in *Wow!* factor. People don't advertise brands and don't promote products unless they are incredibly happy about them. Marketing material for viral growth and viral marketing tools like MaitreApp help a lot and we'll talk about them in one of the up-coming chapters. But, in order to rely on viral growth, your product needs to be awesome (not for you, but for your customers) and fit your target market perfectly. If something isn't perfect, the viral loop most likely will hit a dead end.

Futstat from Brazil aims to register the achievements of amateur and professional athletes and help to share their story with others. Generally, the concept of this startup is favorable for employing a viral engine of growth because each user of this platform will be coming back to check his data and will share it with others, thus bringing new visitors and users to the platform. With a bit of marketing effort, this startup could achieve significant growth by exploiting the viral engine of growth. The same could be said about *Arbunize*, the platform for creating outstanding resumes online. Even though it originated from India, it has now expanded to Spain, Argentina, Brazil, and other countries. Part of their success was a viral engine of growth: resumes have a viral effect when published publically, also by doing the personality assessments, users are encouraged to invite friends and peers to provide endorsements. That allows news about *Arbunize* to spread virally without using paid advertising.

Consider the paid engine of growth

Paid growth is the most common engine of growth. It literally means you pay to get new customers. You buy advertising to drive traffic to your sales funnel, you pay commissions to affiliate partners for certain actions of your target customers, you hire a PR agency and invest in public relations that doesn't look like direct advertising, and you employ sales teams and real estate to attract foot traffic. There are two main aspects to keep in mind:

1. Your customer acquisition costs always should be lower than your customer lifetime value. Otherwise, there is no sense in trying to grow because instead of earning a profit, you'll be losing money.

2. As long as you're making a profit on each customer, you can re-invest your profits into more advertising to accelerate growth. But unfortunately, the marginal costs of additional advertising are getting higher unless you find new alternatives. It means that you typically start advertising on most cost-effective communication channels, but when you want to grow, you have no choice but to buy more expensive advertising.

The main lesson with the paid engine of growth is to always track how much you are spending to acquire new customers and how much marginal revenue you'll get from it. Most startups run into problems when they don't control their advertising costs. Make sure you have a system how to track the effectiveness of your advertising in different communication channels and conversion rates in the separate stages of your sales funnel.

 ## Look for possible optimizations

In order to get better financial and business growth results, you should know where to optimize your sales funnel and customer journey. This is achieved by regularly checking metrics and analyzing how they affect one another. Once you have at least few hundred active users and paying customers, it would be reasonable to do at least a simple cohort analysis. Even though it may sound difficult, it is not difficult in practice. If you want to optimize your advertising campaign, you should group your actual customers and active users (who yet haven't converted to paying customers), into cohorts by how they were attracted to your sales funnel (for example, Facebook advertising using different campaigns, content sharing through various sources, affiliate programs, and so on). The main goal is to draw the most common customer journey maps from different cohorts, compare them, and find possibilities to optimize your sales funnel and customer journey. For example, maybe customers who first accept a free trial have higher retention rate and more often become your loyal customers? If so, which advertising channels and messages bring higher conversion rate for signing up for a free trial?

Usually, the optimization is focused on increasing conversion in different stages of the sales funnel and customer lifetime value (we'll talk about it more in the next chapter Profit hacking: economics, conversions, and traffic). But most startups neglected to use two important types of optimization:

1. *Strategic optimization* focuses on aspects that will have major and permanent (or at least long-term) effect, like:

   - How to create a network effect, such that each customer would invite new customers to create a network (for example, what's the purpose of using Facebook or any other social network if they are not your friends)?

   - How to create a constant revenue stream and keep low customer attrition rate? Is it possible to create customer lock-in or high switching costs?

   - How to increase profit margins per average order, per customer? Which additional products and services could you offer to increase cross-sell revenue and profit margins?

2. *Velocity optimization* focuses on speed and how quickly your sales funnel transforms leads into paying customers. Velocity optimizations might require taking into account such aspects as:

   - How many times have the potential customers been to visit a website or physical store before making a purchase or any other conversion throughout the sales funnel? What could you do to shorten this cycle?

   - How many customers tell their friends about the product and in which sales funnel stage do they do that? To how many friends do they refer the product? What could you do to initiate those recommendations faster, stronger, and with larger coverage?

   - How fast are referred leads activated in the various stages of the sales funnel? How fast are they become paying customers?

You can draft your initial plan of possible optimizations, but it will change often, maybe even every time you get updated metrics. Focusing your attention on one or couple of key metrics to optimize seems to be the most proven tactic for most successful startups. Don't spread yourself too thin, but look for bottlenecks and sales funnel stages where the optimization could create the highest impact to your profit and business growth. Optimization is a never-ending process vital to a startup's efficiency, scalability, and future.

 Decide which engine of growth to use and update your marketing plan

Actually, you use more than one engine of growth. But the more techniques and tools you try to combine, the harder it will be to implement. Just imagine the situation if you've developed a "sticky" product (repeated sales, low attrition) and you're also working to initiate a viral effect by paying or giving some type of bonus to your customers to spread the word about your product. It would be very difficult to figure out what is working and what is not. If you are a large company and have the resources to coordinate and implement a few engines of growth (along with the rest of your marketing activity), that's great. But most early stage startups have very limited resources and lack the time to implement multiple growth engines. Therefore, small companies should first focus on one engine and when it is implemented, proceed with another engine of growth.

Whichever engine of growth you've chosen, review your marketing plan and update it accordingly. What needs to be done by when in order to implement the chosen growth engine? Will related tasks and measures require additional budget? Who will do all those new tasks? Will there be any changes in your time scheduling for old tasks?

 Recommended reading

1. Eric Ries. *The Lean Startup*: *How Today's Entrepreneurs Use Continuous Innovation to Create Radically Successful Businesses*
2. Neil Patel, Bronson Taylor. *The definitive guide to growth hacking*
3. Ryan Holiday. *Growth Hacker Marketing*: *A Primer on the Future of PR, Marketing, and Advertising*

31. Profit hacking: leads, conversion, and economics

WHY IT IS NEEDED

Most startups focus on product development, fundraising, and achieving another product development milestone. Profit mostly takes on a lower priority and becomes something to be taken care of later when significant growth is achieved. But this is a very irresponsible attitude! More than 53.1% of the startups I surveyed in 2016 didn't focus on profit at all: 16.1% didn't know anything about profit hacking or how to do it and another 37% didn't think it was important for them. Only 34.7% of startups have adopted and were constantly working on solutions to improve their profit. By contrast, those startups that were focused on profit from the very beginning have achieved much greater success in the market by every measure (accumulated investments, business growth, and profit).

Your resources (marketing budget and time) are limited. In order to achieve the best results, you must focus your efforts on the right issues and allocate your resources accordingly. We've already talked about the main principles of optimizing your growth engines, now it's time to dive deeper into how to optimize or hack (if you prefer) your profit.

Phil Frost (2012) in one of his blog posts named three buckets of online marketing for pursuing profit: traffic, conversion, and lifetime value. Steven Daar (2014) indicated three similar pillars (traffic, conversion, economics) while talking about profit hacking techniques. So, to keep things simple, there are three main assets from a marketing perspective that create your profit. Increase any of them, and you'll get better profit. If you keep increasing them one at a time by taking small, consistent steps, you'll hack your profit potential.

HOW TO DO IT

01 Learn the Sequence of Profit Hacking
Focus on business economics and conversion first, and traffic last

02 Increase Customer Lifetime Value
Find ways to increase your average profit-per-sale, even if it's just a few percent

03 Increase Conversion Rate
Analyze your key metrics and focus on tests that have the greatest potential impact

04 Find Your Next Alteration
Work with all three domains: leads, sales conversion, and customer lifetime value

Check the initial sequence of profit hacking

Steven Daar (2014) says traffic is a commodity, but conversion and economics are assets. It's hard to disagree with him! When you master conversion and economics (revenue stream), it will be significantly easier to buy targeted advertising and get traffic, which will result in qualified leads. The higher your customer lifetime value, the easier it is to get traffic and leads because you can afford to spend more on advertising. This is especially true for startups because there is no reason for early stage startups to waste their budget on driving traffic until the product-market fit is found (economics) and an effective sales funnel is built (conversion rate). So the initial sequence for profit-hacking for startups should be (1) Economics → (2) Conversion → (3) Traffic.

Profit is defined by the formula:

Profit = Leads x Conversion Rate x Customer Life time Value

It's obvious if any of those variables is equal to zero, your profit is zero. But even making just a slight increase in each of them could result in a multiplier effect on your profit. Would it be difficult to increase traffic, conversion rate, and average customer lifetime value each of them just by 2%? How much do you think your profit would increase?

$$1.02 \times 1.02 \times 1.02\% = ?$$

Thanks to the multiplier effect, your profit would increase not by 6%, but 6,12%. And, there is something even more interesting. Increasing traffic, conversion, and customer lifetime value each by 20%, would result in you having a 72.8% higher profit! Not bad.

$$1.2 \times 1.2 \times 1.2 = 1.728$$

By doubling your traffic, conversion and customer lifetime value (increase each by 100%) you'll get 8 times higher profit (800% increase). That's what I call profit hacking! Don't you think it is worth trying? Just think what results you could achieve if you continuously look for additional ways to increase your traffic, conversion, and customer lifetime value.

 Find the ways to increase customer lifetime value

Economics is the core component of all marketing. As you already know, customer lifetime value is what you earn per customer over time minus your costs to acquire the customer. It's pure economics: revenue minus costs. You did your main homework by finding the product-market fit and developing your irresistible offer. So you found your possible revenue stream. Now it's time to find the ways to increase your average profit per sales even if it is just a few percent. In chapter 26 we've talked about how to Get ready to up-sell, cross-sell and down-sell. This is exactly what you need in this case. So, if you don't have at least a few up-sell and cross-sell ideas to test, you might be willing to check that chapter once again.

While looking for possibilities to get extra revenue and extra profit per sale, you might design an up-sell strategy of upgrading your product from economy class to business class, luxury, premium, personalized, or even custom solutions. You could also create a cross-sell strategy by adding products or services that go along with your main offer. And don't forget that one of the most important things you can test in your business is the price you charge for your products or services. Due to psychological factors of how people perceive price, it's possible that changing only the price (increasing or decreasing) might result in a higher profit (we've talked about profit margin and pricing in Chapter 13: Evaluating profit and growth potential).

The good thing about finding the ways to improve your economics (increase customer lifetime value) is that it requires almost no extra cost, except perhaps for running some market experiments. Your mind and time are the main resources needed for successfully increasing average customer lifetime value.

Find the ways to increase conversion rate

There is a saying that every visitor who comes to your site or store and doesn't buy is trying to tell you something about your business. The same can be applied to all stages of your sales funnel where other actions might be counted as conversions (for example, subscribe, download, watch a video, or sign up for a trial). Potential customers rarely give you their feedback or instructions what you can improve. They just quit your website or shop and your conversion rate stays low or even starts decreasing. Conversion is an important area for profit-hacking for startups because sales funnels tend to get longer and more complicated as the business grows. The dull advertising of "Buy my stuff!" doesn't work anymore.

As you already know, A/B testing is the core component of hacking your conversions. Don't expect miracles to happen just because of one successful change. Instead, be prepared for continuous A/B testing which is one of the core elements of *Evolutionary Redesign*.

Evolutionary Redesign is the art and science of strategically using A/B tests to ensure that design updates lead to increases in conversions and revenue. This approach works best when the brand itself is not broken; in other words, there is a market fit, but better performance is targeted. In this situation, startups will run A/B experiments to look for improvement in core products, value propositions, and communication messages. The Evolutionary Redesign is usually preferable to so-called radical redesign where you completely change the entire brand, product, or core value proposition all at once.

Many studies report that if the company is selling online or at least generating leads, the following are the most important pages on the website and should be considered for A/B testing:

- Landing page — Generated leads are directed here
- Plans and pricing pages — Main value proposition is communicated
- Demo or quote request pages — User activation
- Contact page — If website generates leads, contact information is what you want visitors to be looking for

- Cart page — If products are sold online, it indicates strong intention to buy the product, but yet it's not a purchase (actually there are startups who have up to 70% cart abandon rate)
- Checkout pages — Final step in the online purchase process.

These pages directly impact your bottom line. Visitors on these pages are only a step or two away from converting to being paid customers or at least subscribers. Review them and continuously work on improving them. There are plenty of things that can be tested, but you should analyze your key metrics and focus on those tests which have the greatest potential impact. Here are just a few examples of what you might consider for testing to increase conversion on particular pages:

- Addressing a specific problem or need
- Addressing a specific segment
- Structure and layout of your main or special offer
- Call to action tagline and button
- Actions the visitor needs to take to convert
- Pictures and videos

 Find out what your next alteration should be

You should work with all three domains—*leads, sales conversion, and customer lifetime value*—regularly to keep your business optimized. There is no rule of thumb as to which domain to focus your main attention and which test to run next. You should evaluate your situation strategically and decide on which domain to focus on first. Which of them requires most of your attention in order to achieve your next major milestone? Decide what's most important to you and allocate your resources accordingly, as shown in Table 47. This is a strategic decision for your focus for the next month (it's advisable to review your situation and re-allocate resources monthly).

Table 47. Resource allocation for profit growth initiatives

	Traffic	Conversion	Economics
Time	10%	60%	30%
Money	40%	50%	10%
Other resources	?	?	?

The resource distribution plan in Table 47 tells that most of the time you intend to devote to improving conversions (60%) and economics (30%), but most of the money should be allocated to conversions (50%) and traffic (40%).

When it comes down to a tactical level concerning which particular initiative to test, the PIE framework (Potential, Importance, Ease) introduced by Steven Daar (2014) comes in handy. For startups, I would recommend a slightly modified PIE framework, where *importance* is replaced by *investments*. So your first task is to make a list of possible changes that you think might positively influence your lead generation, conversion rate, and customer lifetime value. Next, decide which of them to focus on using the PIE framework. To do this, evaluate each initiative by putting a score from 1 to 10 according to each of these three criteria:

1. **Potential.** How much potential is there for increasing lead generation (traffic), conversion rates, and average customer lifetime value? If potential changes might result in extreme changes, you should put a grade 10. If the expected outcomes are miserable or doubtful at all, you should put just a 1. It's obvious that there is no sense wasting time and energy on low-ranking initiatives.

2. **Investments**. How much would it cost for you to run a test and implement changes if needed? The more investments that are needed, the smaller the score you should put for this possibility. Initiatives which require additional funding and more resources than you have should be evaluated at low scores like a 1 or 2. If you don't need to spend anything and you can implement changes with the resources you already have, such initiatives can be rated as a 10.

3. **Ease**. How much effort will it take to test and implement? The less work and effort needed, the higher the score you should give. If it requires a lot of time and effort to test an initiative, you should put a low score, even if the potential might be high with a low investment required.

To make it simple, just complete Table 48 for each of your ideas (giving a grade from 1 to 10) for profit-hacking and check the total score. In the example, Idea 2 had the highest value and should be implemented first.

Table 48.   Profit hacking idea evaluation example

	Idea 1	Idea 2	Idea 3
Potential result	5	7	3
Low investment	8	8	2
Easy to do	4	5	9
Total score	17	20	14

If you'd like to go into more detail about estimating the potential revenue increase, you can try this online calculation spreadsheet or download it and use it on your own computer. It allows you to estimate sales revenue by changing traffic, average revenue from one-time and repeated sales, as well as changing conversion rates for different stages of the sales funnel. This allows you to see on which stage of the sales funnel you should focus most of your time and resources.

Table 49. Revenue estimations based on traffic, conversion, and revenue per sale

Action in sales funnel Stage		Conversion		Potential Customers		Target	
		Overall	Con-verted	Lost	Con-verted	Lost	
Stage 1	Visiting the website	100.0%	100.0%	100,000	-	100.0%	100,000
Stage 2	Signup for free trial	15.0%	15.00%	15,000	85,000	30.0%	70,000
Stage 3	Activating free trial	80.0%	12.00%	12,000	3,000	15.0%	15,000
Stage 4	Buying the product	20.0%	2.40%	2,400	9,600	4.0%	11,000
Stage 5	Repeat purchase	40.0%	0.96%	960	1,440	1.5%	2,500

Potential customers at first stage (traffic)	100.000
Average revenue from one-time sales	250
Average revenue from repeated purchase	75
Current one-time sales	600.000
Current repeated sales	72.000
Target one time sales	1.000.000
Target repeated sales	112.500

Just by changing conversion, traffic, and revenue per sale, you can see what effect that would have on your sales funnel and your final financial results. For example, we see that the signup rate for the free trial in the example (*Table 49*) is only 15% and the conversion rate for buying a product is 20%. If we make some changes in the main offer, website design, or e-mail campaigns with the goal of increasing signup trials by 5% and buying conversion by just 2%, that would give us extra $280,000 in one time sales and $27,000 in repeat sales (Table 50).

This calculation spreadsheet also helps you to set targets for each conversion stage and see what revenue from one-time and repeated sales you are aiming for. In the example (Table 50), it shows that if you achieve your target conversion rates, you'll earn $1,000,000 revenue in one time sales and an additional $112,500 in repeated sales. Experiment with this spreadsheet and see what would be realistic in your case and what the impact would be on your revenue.

Table 50. Updated revenue estimations based on traffic, conversion, and revenue per sale

Action in sales funnel Stage		Conversion		Potential Customers		Target	
		Overall	Con-verted	Lost	Con-verted	Lost	
Stage 1	Visiting the website	100.0%	100.0%	100,000	-	100.0%	100,000
Stage 2	Signup for free trial	20.0%	20.00%	20,000	80,000	30.0%	70,000
Stage 3	Activating free trial	80.0%	16.00%	16,000	4,000	15.0%	15,000
Stage 4	Buying the product	22.0%	3.52%	3,520	12,480	4.0%	11,000
Stage 5	Repeat purchase	40.0%	1.41%	1,408	2,112	1.5%	2,500

Potential customers at first stage (traffic)	100.000
Average revenue from one-time sales	250
Average revenue from repeated purchase	75
Current one-time sales	880.000
Current repeated sales	105.000
Target one time sales	1.000.000
Target repeated sales	112.500

 Recommended reading

1. Steven Daar. *Profit Hacking: The Web Entrepreneur's 3 Part Formula For Maximizing Success*
2. Leigh Caldwell. *The Psychology of Price: How to use price to increase demand, profit and customer satisfaction*

32. Marginal users & magnets to get them

WHY IT IS NEEDED

Not every customer who visits your website or physical store is willing to buy immediately. In fact, it takes time to build trust and prove your value. In some industries, it takes less time to build trust, while in other cases building trust can require up to a few month or more before you are able to sell to the customer. The more your business is innovative and strange, the more skeptical most people will be towards you. So get used to the fact that you'll have to spend some time building trust. Another fact to be noted is that a very high percentage of visitors never return to a website.

If you have already developed your sales funnel, it means you know what action you want potential customers to take when they visit your website, physical store, or have interaction with you in any other way. You may want them to buy a product, pay for a service, sign up to your pre-order list, become your beta user, come to your special event, etc. But what you do if they quit your website or physical store without completing your desired action? They basically quit your sales funnel even without entering it. Whatever your initial goal is, you have a chance to increase your conversion rate by focusing your attention on marginal users and setting up compelling lead magnets for them.

When it comes to driving growth, people who are already using your product are not the ones you have to worry about the most. Yes, they are important, but they already know and trust in you and your product. What you need to focus on is the marginal user, the potential customer or user that is close to making a purchase decision, but doesn't make it without additional encouragement. Simply stated, you know there is a certain number of potential customers who are not yet using your product or who don't know even about it, and there are paying customers. If you make a list of your paying customers, the marginal users would be those who you would write down somewhere outside the margin. They are not paying yet, but they are close enough and might convert at any time.

A lead magnet is a tempting offer that provides a very specific value to highly a targeted customer segment (marginal users, in this case). In other words, when you offer your lead magnet, you give an ethical bribe or gift (call it what you like it) in exchange for their contact information. The main goal of such lead capturing is to secure the marginal users' contact information so that you can get them into your sales funnel and start building a relationship and trust. So instead of doing nothing and continuing to lose your website visitors who don't buy and never return back, offer them a tempting lead magnet as soon as they visit your website and once again when they are trying to leave. Different studies report that well-developed lead magnets can result in up to 20 to 60 % conversion depending on the industry and some other variables. So, just imagine what a tremendous effect that could bring to your startup if your average sales conversion is just 2% or even less. According to Marketo, Forrester, and CSO Insights, companies that excel at lead nurturing generate 50% more sales at 33% lower cost per lead (Jean Marie Bonthous).

HOW TO DO IT

 Identify your most important marginal users

In order to create effective lead magnets, you must first identify your marginal users, those potential customers who are the most likely to convert into paying customers. One of the quickest ways is to look for the answers in your target customer's persona or segmentation that we did in Chapter 3: Segmentation and potential market size, as well as in your sales funnel and customer journey map (especially focusing on customer touchpoints). You should be able to identify where your marginal users are and get some insights about how you could reach them. Try to figure out what potential customers do and feel in each stage of your sales funnel, what do they want, need, or dream about? Decide on how your products or services can satisfy those needs.

Online marketing traditionally suggests developing different lead magnets for each stage of your sales funnel. Therefore, it's quite common to identify your marginal users (hottest potential prospects) at the beginning of your sales funnel (for example, they might be first-time visitors to your website). You also need to think about who you should target at the end of your sales funnel, for example, when you've employed every marketing effort you can but these potential customers still didn't buy. So, who are they and what do they really want? You should also consider any sales funnel stage in between. Identify at which stages of the sales funnel potential customers might be already close enough to make a purchase decision or, on the contrary, at what stage are you losing most potential prospects without having a chance to reach them again. Who are these people and what would encourage them to buy your product?

Figure 47. Main types of marginal users

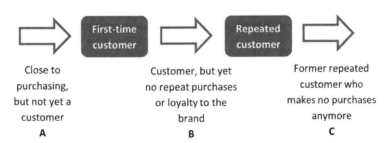

For any early stage startup business, I would pay attention to at least two main groups of marginal users. First, you should really be concerned about bringing as many potential customers to your sales funnel as possible. Therefore a lead magnet for marginal users who get in contact with you, your product, or brand for the very first time is a must (A in Figure 47). Once you have a well-tested lead magnet for this group of marginal users, it's time to check those customers who already bought from you but who didn't become loyal or repeat customers (B in Figure 47), and those who were your repeat customers, but who don't make purchases anymore (C in Figure 47).

The main part of this task is to set criteria for how you can identify the different types of marginal users. Once you have that done, let's get down to creating lead magnets to hook them.

 ### Decide on lead magnet type

The best-performing lead magnets add great value to the potential customer by satisfying their specific need or solving their problem. These lead magnets appeal to the target audience because they provide a much-needed service, valuable information, guidelines on how to solve a problem, and so on. The best lead magnets do not seek to answer all of a customer's questions, but very specific ones. Lead magnets can be of different forms, but all of them can be delivered or at least ordered through your website. Here are a few of the most common types of lead magnets that you might consider adopting for your startup:

- *Cheat sheets* are well-designed short tips, lists, or worksheets that help customers solve a specific problem. But, be aware, even though it looks easy to prepare a cheat sheet (it is short and simple), this lead magnet used by itself is less effective. Therefore, think about how you could reinforce a cheat sheet. Combining it with any additional type of lead magnet (for example, a free video training or an ebook) could bring significant results.

- *Free training* can include videos, workbooks, courses sent by email or done on specific platforms, or any combination of these. If your marginal users have problems that require multiple steps to get to a final solution, free training might be an ideal lead magnet. If you could show step-by-step training on how to solve at least a small piece of a general problem, it could be a very effective lead magnet to attract those potential customers who really want to solve the main problem. The lead magnet will give them real value (by solving a small piece of the problem) and will generate more trust towards your products and services.

- *Free templates* might generate lots of targeted leads, you just have to be sure your templates support what you are selling and don't replace it. Templates as a lead magnet can be used in many startup businesses because they can consist of nearly anything you can imagine, from spreadsheets to videos. I used templates as a lead magnet to promote this book, and I started collecting leads before I had written a single chapter. Without spending anything on advertising, I collected more than a thousand qualified leads. If people are downloading templates that are useful for developing a startup business, they might be also interested in reading my book about startup marketing. So when my book was ready to be published, I already had a solid list of marginal users. Maybe you were one of them and I sincerely thank you for that.

- *Swipe files* contain good ideas and examples of things that your marginal user could use in practice. For example, a swipe file of texts for a SaaS business email automation campaign (we'll talk about marketing automation in Chapter 35: Marketing automation strategies and tools) could include 10 to 20 different email text templates for various scenarios, and those templates could be used nearly by any SaaS business with slight changes.

- *Toolkits* can be a little more complex to produce because they are filled with resources that usually include one or two e-books and a worksheet, a video, or a checklist.

If you are short of ideas what value you could share for free with your marginal users, take a look at these additional types of lead magnets:

1. Free product or service
2. Free tickets to live events
3. Product samples
4. Product giveaways
5. E-books
6. Audiobooks
7. Checklists
8. Worksheets
9. Workbooks
10. Test or quiz
11. Case study
12. Free consultation
13. Coupon for special deal
14. Free shipping
15. Audio CDs
16. Mini-courses
17. Video courses
18. Audio courses
19. Email courses
20. Webinar with live Q&A
21. Webinar replays
22. Cheat sheets
23. Guides
24. Mind maps
25. Process flow diagrams
26. Resource lists
27. Tip lists and sheets
28. FAQ sheets
29. Planners
30. Specific calendars
31. Action plans
32. Spreadsheets
33. PowerPoint download
34. Starter kits
35. Scripts
36. Industry reports
37. Predictions and forecasts
38. Infographics
39. Calculators
40. Generators
41. Recorded video events
42. Transcripts
43. Branded, promo materials
44. Acceptance to Facebook group or any other members area
45. Access to library
46. Mobile games and apps
47. Recipes and other kinds of regular advice
48. Original research data
49. Certification program
50. Lotteries and contests

Create magnets to hook your marginal users

The main point here is that you must give customers a reason to provide you with their contact information. Most people today are overloaded with emails, newsletters, and all kind of promotions. Therefore, if you want to earn a potential customer's trust and get their contact details, your lead magnet must offer significant value to those people you want to reach. Simply inviting people to sign up for your newsletter no longer generates the results it once did. The same can be said about primitive and plain lead magnets: creating a lead magnet just to have one won't make much sense nor benefit your business. Remember, the value you share in your lead magnet can differentiate your marginal users. The only potential customers who will take your lead magnet are those to whom it is meaningful (for example, if somebody signed-up for the trial version of your software, it's obvious that this person probably has a need for this or similar software, and that makes him a valuable lead).

If your products or services require more consultation and care before someone decides to buy, you should apply the multiple-step lead generation approach. This means that you propose a so-called soft offer with no obligation from customer's side and later (when the customer moves along your sales funnel) you introduce additional lead magnets that deliver even higher value, but require a bit more effort or commitment from the potential customer (for example, to complete more fields in your contact form or to provide credit card details). This step-by-step approach helps build the relationship and trust by encouraging a potential customer to make small commitments and eventually, purchase your product.

No matter what marginal user group you are targeting and if you are using a multiple-step lead generation approach or just a single lead magnet, to create an effective lead magnet it must contain:

- *Promise*—explaining what you are offering in exchange for their contact details
- *Clarification*—making it clear why you created the lead magnet and who it's designed for
- *Key points (bullet points)*—summarizing and emphasizing the value of the lead magnet
- *Call to action*—clear and concise instructions about what action the potential customer should take

Once you've created your lead magnet, it's time to implement the process, which works as follows:

1. *A target customer visits your website and sees your free, highly valuable lead magnet.* Be sure to place your lead magnet in the most visible part of your website and make sure that visitors see the promise of your lead magnets.

2. *A potential customer enters his contact information into an opt-in form on your website to get access to your lead magnet.* Be sure to capture and store those contact details automatically. Setting up an opt-in form is much easier than you think and most email marketing platforms provide solutions that you can integrate them into your website.

3. *You set up an autoresponder message via your email marketing platform to automatically send your new subscriber a link to download or access your lead magnet.* There are many options and they range in pricing and functionality. Probably one of the best choices for early stage startups would be a free account on MailChimp, which provides services for free until your list reaches 2000 contacts. By the way, the freemium model worked as a great lead magnet for MailChimp! One year after adopting this lead magnet (freemium model), MailChimp had grown their user base five times over, from 85,000 in September of 2009 to 450,000 in September 2010. The company was adding more than 30,000 new

free users and 4,000 new paying customers each month; and MailChimp's profit (not revenue), meanwhile, had grown 650% (Erik Devaney, 2017).

4. *Your target customer almost instantly receives an automated email message with the link to access your lead magnet.* You don't need to do this manually, your email marketing platform or any other email autoresponder solution does it for you.

5. *You start building a relationship with your target customers and earning their trust.* This step can also be mostly automated (see Chapter 35: Marketing automation strategies & tools), but the most important thing is not to start bombarding your potential customer's email with promotion and sales offers. If you do that, you risk losing most or even all of your generated leads.

 Test your magnets and update sales funnel, if needed

Even before implementing the process workflow that we have just discussed, I recommend that you show your lead magnet to at least ten different people who fall under your target customer persona. Ask them how they view your offer from their perspective. Is it clear and appealing? If none of them is interested, well... you already know that you haven't found a market fit yet and you will need to do some changes in your lead magnet before employing it in your sales funnel on a large scale.

Here is a brief checklist for an efficient lead magnet. Run through it on your own, as well as with those first ten interviews, and finally check how it performs in the sales funnel.

- *Does your lead magnet appeal exclusively to the target audience?* Focus on developing a lead magnet that is interesting for your marginal users, not everyone. Otherwise, you'll be wasting your time and resources in the next stages of your sales funnel. The goal is to generate leads that are as targeted as possible instead of attracting just a curious crowd.

- *Does your lead magnet have a high perceived value?* Perceived is the key word here. It doesn't matter how valuable you perceive the lead magnet to be. The main question is how your potential customers perceive the value you are proposing. The good news is that an effective lead magnet doesn't have to cost much. It just has to be something of value to your audience. The higher perceived value of your offer, the more you can ask in exchange. While most lead magnets are used for collecting email addresses if the offer is really valuable you can ask potential customers to do more. For example, LinkedIn gives away $50 coupons for advertising services. Even though Linkedin incurs no direct costs, the perceived value to the target audience is quite high. Therefore, Linkedin asks you to create a company page and provide your credit card details so that you can be charged if your advertising exceeds $50. So, make sure your lead magnet has a high perceived value.

- *Is your lead magnet offer specific and relevant to the product or service you are willing to sell?* A great offer isn't just good for the person who receives it; it must be useful for your startup, too. Especially in the case of lead generation, you want your offer to tie into the product or service you're selling. That way, it will help advance the sale, and maybe even inspire or at least educate your target audience to take specific actions.

- *Is it easy to understand and take action on?* Make it simple. Don't add a lot of conditions or steps. Your lead magnet should seek an immediate response and action from the viewer. If possible, stick with one step: click here to download, type in this discount code, register here, call this number, etc. The simpler the better!

- *Is it visually appealing?* Lead magnets with great designs are more likely to increase your conversion rates and compel visitors to opt in for your offers.

- *Does it help create and facilitate a long-term relationship with your target customers?* Too many businesses are trying to pitch and sell at the very first contact with the customer. As we've already discussed, earning trust and building a relationship helps to open the door to the long lasting business without being pushy and annoying.

 Recommended reading

1. Kendra Lee. *The Sales Magnet*: *How to Get More Customers Without Cold Calling*
2. *Danavir Sarria 101 Lead Magnet Ideas For Every Stage Of Your Marketing Funnel*

33. Marketing material for viral growth

WHY IT IS NEEDED

Many startups are talking about word of mouth advertising and hoping for viral growth. But viral effect happens very rarely, especially if there is no consistent, targeted action from the startup. So, how can you increase your chances? How can you make your product or brand go viral?

My global research on startups showed that more than two-thirds of the early stage startups (67.5%) wanted help with scaling their business. Nearly four out of five (78.9%) of the startups had already launched their products. But only 1 in 10 (10.6%) of all startups who took part in the research had prepared marketing material to support their viral growth. That means that 7 out of 8 startups don't have their marketing material ready for viral growth but they still expect a miracle to happen! Why? There is a simple explanation. Most startups don't know what to do or how to do it effectively. So, in this chapter, we'll talk about five types of marketing material for viral growth (and I sincerely hope you can find one to adopt for your business).

HOW TO DO IT

Create a viral landing page

This is a must-have for any business, even if it doesn't sell online. The primary goal of an ordinary landing page is to collect visitors' contact information to initiate marketing automation campaigns or to do a manual follow-up and lead the potential client to eventually purchasing the product or ordering the service. There is no reason to ignore the opportunity to collect potential customers' contact details and implement a follow-up strategy as a part of your sales funnel/pipeline.

Usually, landing pages are designed to capture leads, that is, to make as many visitors as possible submit their contact details in exchange for some valuable gift. You may have noticed that most landing pages also have built-in sharing and invitation buttons, but that's not what makes them viral. If you want to create a landing page that could go viral and be promoted word of mouth through social networks, you must give a reason and as well as a convenient way to do so.

People like to share things that make them look cool. Discovering something that solves a serious problem or is fascinating might initiate the "*Aha!*" moment and increase their willingness to share it with their friends. In general, there are three main requirements for your landing page to become viral:

1. The pitch on the landing page has to be worth signing up for
2. There must be a significant nudge to share it with friends
3. It has to be straightforward and easy to share

If you're interested, you could read the article by Gerry Dimova (2015), where she covers a couple of real case studies about creating viral landing pages for startups.

 Draft and share at least a few infographics

According to Jesse Mawhinney (2016), content with relevant images gets 94% more views than content without images. Also, infographics are liked and shared on social media three times more than other any other type of content. Knowing this, you should consider hiring a freelancer (on Fiverr, for example) who will create a professional infographic for $50 or less.

- Select an important topic that is relevant to your target audience.
- Find the right data and analyze it. Your goal is to find an answer or insight which might be useful and exciting.
- Create a story based on your findings. Don't just spit out all the facts you've found. Try to bind them in a story line, for example, that shows the problem and possible solutions.
- Telling your story visually is the task for the graphic designer, who you can find on many freelancing websites, usually for a reasonable amount of money.
- Polish the design and the story. It should be smooth, nice, and catchy.
- Distribute via your marketing communication channels (for example, social networks, landing page, email campaigns). But don't forget about appropriate directories and blogs where you can upload your infographics (for example,

InfographicJournal.com, InfographicsShowcase.com, InfographicsArchive.com and others).

Once you have your infographics ready, you might want to check the article by <u>Neil Patel</u> (2012) where he provides additional advice about how to boost your viral growth by sharing your infographics.

Create as many as possible useful or emotional videos

Dave Loyd (2015) forecasts the 74% of all Internet traffic in 2017 will be video. Furthermore, using the word *video* in an email subject line boosts open rates by 19% and click-through rates by 65%. Considering this and the fact that today online video streams easily on the high-speed Internet, video needs to be included in your content marketing mix. Creating a video is not hard: it can be direct-to-camera video, a video capturing your screen, or it can be sourcing videos from YouTube that enhance your story. But not every video goes viral, and there is no secret recipe for how to create a guaranteed viral video. Thus, most viral videos (we are talking about startup videos, not just random videos created for amusement) should meet these conditions:

- There is an emotional story (but not a depressing one), or the video itself initiates emotions.
- There is value in the video, a solution of a particularly painful problem (we already talked about the fact that people want to look cool thus are prone to share the solutions they find).
- The branding and advertising are kept minimal and subtle.
- A marketing plan stands behind the video (whether it's paid or free promotion, there should be a plan for how the link to the video will be distributed).
- Quality and length of the video must be compatible with your target customer time commitment (how much time and attention they are likely to spend in the typical situation).

 ### Let your targets customer play with a quiz

Let's take Shoe dazzle as an example. They sell women's shoes. The way they started to sell shoes was quite innovative and created a significant viral effect. If you want to look what they have to offer or want to get their exclusive deal, you are invited to take a quiz. It's a comfortable, enjoyable, and pleasant quiz, especially knowing that once you do the quiz, you'll find out your style profile and will be offered only those shoes which fit your style.

Figure 48. Shoe dazzle quiz example

STYLE PROFILE

TAKE THE QUIZ AND DISCOVER YOUR STYLE PROFILE IN JUST A FEW MINUTES

1. Which shoe is the most you?

2. What's your go-to black style?

Source: Shoedazzle.com

So if a shoe seller can find the way to use a quiz for viral growth, then it is a must try for you as a startup assuming you have an innovative product or a service. Quizzes are a great way to introduce innovations. While the product is new, potential customers are unaware of it and don't search for it. But if you create a quiz that reveals how this innovation solves a well-known problem (for example, women trying to decide which shoes fit their style best), it could initiate *Aha!* or *Wow!* moments and your target audience will be sharing your quiz like crazy.

 Be generous and share some giveaways

Generally speaking, the giveaway is any kind of added value (free seminar, manual, book, tickets to events, starter package of your product, and so on). Who doesn't want to get free stuff if it's useful? Who doesn't want to look cool sharing that useful stuff for free? As my global research on startups showed, most early stage startups share their giveaways in exchange for contact information on their landing page (which, by the way, in most cases was not a viral landing page). The giveaway is usually some marketing material that is worth sharing. You must come up at least with a simple strategy for how to initiate the virality of your giveaway. Here are a few ideas:

- Create a giveaway for a particular blog or another channel that reaches your target audience and let the owner of the channel share it with his audience.
- Offer a free account on your platform or community (if you have one) to thought leaders and ask them to share their experience with the public.
- Reach out to group leaders on social networks (Linkedin, Facebook, Meetup, or any other social network where your target customers are active) and ask them if they'd share your giveaway with their group members
- Use marketing tools like Maitre App or Pay with a tweet to fuel up viral sharing of your giveaways or any other content.

Some call Maitre App a revolution in viral marketing. It's very simple solution to what previously required massive investment or coding skills. Maitre App not only helps to collect your website visitors' emails but also encourages them to share your content with their friends if they want to get a reward. Also, it allows you to use engagement emails to remind your subscribers to share their referral link and increase virality. Such emails can be triggered by special events, like when a subscriber (actual or potential customer refers) a new person or they lose their position in the list.

Figure 49.   How Maitre App works

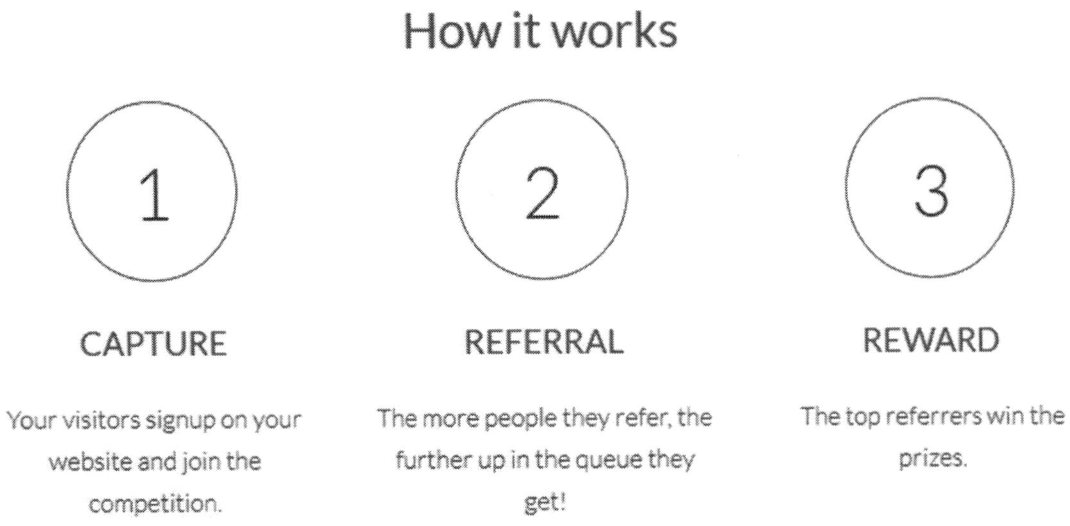

How it works

1	2	3
CAPTURE	REFERRAL	REWARD
Your visitors signup on your website and join the competition.	The more people they refer, the further up in the queue they get!	The top referrers win the prizes.

Source - maitreapp.co

Pay with a tweet does what it says—allows visitors to access your content after they share your link and message via their social network account (Twitter, Linkedin, Facebook, G+, and few others). This tool would be best to use with those visitors whose emails you already have (for example, they signed up for a free or trial version of your product and you can offer an additional giveaway, meaningful discount, or some exclusive features or benefits in exchange for them sharing your link and message via social network).

You already know about the top five types of marketing material that can boost your startup's viral growth. But before creating any marketing material, be sure, you are providing something people want, and that is worth talking about. Otherwise, none of tips and tricks will help you. On the contrary, you could get anti-advertising by creating a negative viral effect.

Trying to leverage another company's or person's audience is another condition you should keep in mind. If you can find any way to leverage someone else's audience, then you will be taking advantage of a traffic shortcut and will well-positioned to creating a viral effect. That's the essence of viral growth. But to use someone else's audience, you must provide valuable and exciting content to share.

 Recommended reading

- Gerry Dimova. (2015). *How to create a viral startup beta landing page + 2 case studies*
- Jesse Mawhinney. (2016). 37 *Visual Content Marketing Statistics You Should Know in 2016*
- Neil Patel (2012). *5 Ways to Get Your Infographic to Go Viral*
- Dave Loyd (2015). *SEO for Success in Video Marketing*

34. Key leverage points and partnerships

WHY IT IS NEEDED

In today's economy, it's more difficult than ever for anyone, especially a small business, to go it alone. It costs more to pay for all your own advertising, find all your own customers, and do everything else using only your own resources. There's an alternative: cooperating with and forming strategic alliances with other businesses. This enables you to pool resources, share customers, spread the cost of marketing, and do it in a way in which all parties win. A partnership with another company can be simple and limited or very involved and complex.

Partnerships in marketing can be employed by virtually any business when it can find partners interested in mutually beneficial cooperation. Fundamentally, it involves pooling resources—whether those resources are knowledge, expertise, distribution infrastructure, brand recognition, reputation, or simply money—to achieve a result that would be more costly to obtain independently. Startups are eligible for business partnerships from the very beginning. Actually, a lot of successful startups made a major leap in progress not just by boldly attracting investments, but by creating strategic partnerships. So, it doesn't matter where your startup is in the development cycle, you can and should look for possible partnerships that will boost your business.

HOW TO DO IT

01 **Identify Key Leverage Points**
Find out where even a small amount of your effort can generate significant results

02 **Identify Possible Partners**
Decide on the best partnerships and make a list of potential partners

03 **Prepare a Win-win Partnership Offer**
Before scheduling a meeting with partners, be sure you have a win-win proposal

04 **Reach Out to Potential Partners**
Stay focused and persistent, but don't be stubborn; explore alternatives instead

 Identify key leverage points relevant for you

Usually, there are at least a few possible leverage points in any business and yours is not an exception. Leverage point means a place where even small amounts of effort can generate significant results. Most starting entrepreneurs can't see leverage points at the beginning, but once they notice and create at least one of them, it becomes nearly a habit to exploit them. If you manage to identify and use leverage points in your startup, you'll quickly notice a meaningful increase in your key metrics of growth and profits. Here are a few areas where you could start looking for possible leverage points:

1. *Marketing leverage* is the ability to control and generate large profit increases from low-cost or no-cost marketing methods. Marketing automation and sales

funnel optimization are the most popular domains of startup marketing. We've already talked about many things that could at least slightly increase conversion in your sales funnel. These also might be leverage where the implementation doesn't require too many resources. For example, one-time offers and point of purchase incentives might be a leverage point for nearly any startup. It takes no extra expense to generate a second or third purchase if you implement an up-sell or cross-sell strategy. Increasing the frequency of customer purchases is another example of leverage because if you have customer contacts, know his interests, or at least purchase history, you can make him a customized offer without even spending anything on advertising.

2. *Customer service and FAQ automation* might be another pool of possible leverage points. Remember what we've talked about in terms of customer touchpoints and think about how a minor change in each of the touchpoints could result in a major effect on your business. A number of startups use a FAQ (Frequently Asked Questions) section on their website to provide answers to the most common questions in order to save their time avoiding explaining the same issues to each client. Well, that is a good solution, but not a great one, at least not from a marketing perspective. Effective marketers see FAQs as a leverage point to overcome any objections potential customers might have. Raising the right questions and answering them shows potential customers that you have nothing to hide, that many other people had similar doubts and reservations about buying or using the product, but here are the clear and honest answers to these questions. Some startups from my research reported that just by applying this type of approach to FAQs has helped to increase conversion by 5 to 18%.

3. *Big data leverage* allows you to do analysis that identifies purchase patterns of your customers. It might lead you to identify much more accurate targeted segments (or even niches) and create customized offers for them. But you should consider this domain of leverages only when you have a huge amount of data. Otherwise, results aren't accurate and valuable.

4. *Sales force leverage* helps get more out of your sales team without expanding it or spending additional costs. The main principle is to identify the right sales process and improve the effectiveness. This is usually done through outlining a consistent sales process and then setting sales objectives around those activities or the ones related to specific sales goals. According to Shelley Cernel from SalesForce (2015), companies that follow a defined workflow are 33% more likely to be high performers. The next step is to properly train your sales team. Continuous training can yield up to 50% higher net sales per sales rep, especially if the sales team is equipped with such tools as sales playbooks, training materials, persona-based selling tips, etc. Startups never stop learning, therefore this cycle should be repeated continuously: identify which sales tactics are

effective, build them in your sales processes, and teach your sales team to use these tactics.

5. *Partnership leverage* basically mean that you are using other peoples' resources at low or no cost at all and you might be trying to get money, connections, specific skills or business operations, time, and any other resources.

 Find with whom you would like to partner

There are dozens of ways to cooperate with other businesses. One of most common practices (although in some countries, it's illegal) is to trade mailing lists with other businesses. It is forbidden by customer rights protection laws in some countries, but there is a civilized and polite solution. If you can't exchange mailing lists, you can rent them by sending official emails with your name from your mailbox and combining promotional information of your partner. Most often examples include:

- *The partnership of non-competitive businesses.* This could include a tow service, auto-repair shop, and car-rental business teaming up to offer end-to-end service to the same customer.

- *Destination partnership.* For example, hotels, restaurants, and tourist-oriented businesses pool resources to market their location to prospective travelers.

- *Technology partnership.* These are often formed to promote a new device or concept. In many cases, innovative technology startups often face greater competition from companies that represent the existing and established alternative technology. A partnership allows these startups to create a greater market presence to displace the old technology and ensures that they get to establish the standards for the production of the new technology.

- *Partnership to expand into new markets.* This is particularly useful since independent expansion requires a huge investment of resources and the development of new distribution channels. This is especially useful for tapping into overseas markets, whereby a company in one country can offer a product through another company already established in another country, thus tapping into the new market immediately. This principle also works for domestic expansion.

Research prospective partners, taking into account the likelihood of a return on investing in such a relationship:

- What can these companies provide to you?
- What could you provide to them?
- Do they have a partnership with other companies, and how have they fared?

- Are they stable and follow similar values as yours?
- Do they have a compatible management style?

If you run a web design business and want to find more potential leads, try partnering with a web hosting company or online marketing agencies. Any partnership which benefits both companies is a great idea and a great way to grab the attention of new potential clients. It's also a great way to boost your targeted marketing. Just make a list of potential partners to serve the same customer segments but don't compete with you.

Todo.ly is an online to-do list and task manager. The founders had a goal to reach millions of new users and make *Todo.ly* widely available as a web application. They succeeded in securing a partnership with Google Chrome and were able to leverage their 200 million user database to help them achieve their one-year growth goal in just three weeks:

- 1000% increase in average daily traffic
- 780% increase in user base
- 400,000 new tasks each month

The key was that the Chrome platform was brand new and the *Todo.ly* application was submitted three to four months prior its launch date. As the *Todo.ly* app was exactly what Google was looking for to add to the Chrome Webstore, they have contacted the founders and asked for an integrated two clicks login through Google OpenID. *Todo.ly* has implemented that and became featured from day one. There was a huge marketing campaign around the Chrome Webstore, TV spots, prints, and press conference.

Peter Varadi, the founder of *Todo.ly*, shared his advice based on his personal experience: "*Look for new waves of technology, new platforms that are expected to be used by a massive number of people and try to be on that platform as one of first.*" In *Todo.ly* case, it was clearly visible that Chrome had 200 million users already and when they launched their webstore, they would obviously put it front of all their users. Google needed web apps to fill their webstore for the launch and they opened the app submission process a few months earlier. That was a timely opportunity for *Todo.ly* to jump in. What could be your new wave and chance?

 Prepare a win-win partnership offer

David Abingdon (2005) recommends paying attention to eight major facets on which companies can work together:

1. Sharing costs of advertising and other marketing
2. Logistics (i.e., airlines carry overload parcels for international couriers)

3. Packaging (milk cartons carry the advertisements for other products and businesses)
4. Product design (IBM computers use to recommend only Microsoft software)
5. Selling (buy only X brand washing powder with this model of washing machine)
6. Service (carpet fitter recommends carpet cleaner)
7. Geographic proximity (business furniture retailer sends customers across the street to buy business office supplies, such as paper, pens, etc.)
8. Pricing (buy a dinner for four at the Italian restaurant and get a discount on a haircut)

The effective partnership involves coordinating the strengths of different companies in order to meet a market demand. This requires significant pre-planning, as well as an ongoing effort to maintain the new business relationship. At first, the marketing team usually identifies the business opportunity that could potentially be met through a partnership as a win-win solution.

Once a company (or multiple companies) for a partnership is found, each stakeholder must establish plans and expectations up front. Whether or not the partnership involves creating a new business entity (as in a joint venture), both businesses need a clear understanding of what each partner is expected to do, and how management decisions will be made in collaborative efforts. Spelling out commitments and expectations increases the amount of mutually beneficial exchange that can take place between partners. Employees of both partners must be on board with the program, understanding both what they're providing and what value they're receiving from the partnership.

While partnership in marketing can be mutually beneficial, it can also be tricky at times. Here are some pitfalls to avoid:

- *Win-lose agreements*—avoid agreements that benefit one party more than the other
- *Leader-leader*—determine how exactly decision-making will be made or shared
- *Failure-blame*—if an event doesn't get the attendance promised, don't point fingers at the organizers
- *Prejudicial allocation of real estate*—if one partner gets the event booth by the door and another gets the back corner, find a way to compensate

There is a great example of strategic partnerships in *Viral Loop: The Power of Pass-It-On* by Adam Penenberg (2010). Initially, the "Am I Hot or Not" website was hosted in a data center. The more bandwidth they consumed, the more they would have to pay. It was quite a reasonable approach for an early stage startup without a huge volume of consistent traffic. But soon after successful launch, it was estimated that, at the current volume of daily visitors, the website "Am I Hot or Not" would cost $ 150,000 in bandwidth in the very first year. The project was huge and had virally-growing traffic, but no revenue model and no income at all. The more successful the project was, the more likely it could go bankrupt.

The *Guardian*, the *New York Times*, and news outlets from around the world found "Am I Hot or Not" irresistible and it granted it free media coverage, which added additional traffic spikes as well as higher retention. Founders of "Am I Hot or Not" cold-called the head of Rackspace business development to propose a trade. "I know you guys want to go public and it's great to get your name out," Hong, one of the founders of "Am I Hot or Not," said. "Your whole value proposition is that you can help companies scale by outsourcing. If you can help us, we will have all these upcoming interviews, and we can be a poster child for you." The Rackspace executive agreed, and every day that week Hong called to request more machines. By its eighth day, the site was fielding 1.8 million page views per day.

He approached Ofoto about an affiliate deal, telling an executive how he had dispatched people to Yahoo to upload photos. Hong could just as easily sent them to Ofoto, and by hosting them, Ofoto would have the lead in offering additional services. The agreement he struck meant that Hong had moved something from costing money to making it free to actually generating a profit.

They were featured in *People*, *Time*, and *Newsweek* and by the end of the year, they were on *Entertainment Weekly's* It List. They were also profiled in the *New Yorker*.

Reach out to potential partners and be persistent

Most partnerships are mutually beneficial, so before scheduling a meeting, be sure you have a win-win proposal. Persistent actions are as important as reaching potential investors during fundraising. Look for possibilities to network at appropriate conferences and trade shows and meet partners face-to-face. Use personal referrals and active follow-up on your most valuable potential clients. If you have to reach out to potential partners by email, focus your introductory e-mail on what's in it for them (this might include traffic, money, new customers, or gaining competitive advantages, depending on how the partnership works). Always explain your startup's vision clearly and highlight why partnering with your new company is beneficial for them. Persistent actions mean a lot. You shouldn't give up if most of you potential partners say "No" or simply ignore your offer. If it is a win-win proposal, you'll eventually find significant partners if you just put forth enough effort.

I want to share my personal experience with partnerships. I was working as CMO (Chief Marketing Officer) in an international logistics company, but I wanted to start my own marketing consulting practice. I created a website and needed to attract targeted visitors. At that time SEO was quite a new thing, because not every business understood it's importance, so I decided to take a chance on it. I wanted to find as many link-exchange partners as possible. These are companies that provide services to other businesses who would be willing to put my link on their website if I would put their link on my website. Basically, it means no costs to any of us, we are not competitors, and even if the website visitor doesn't click on the link, Google will see it anyway and will rank our websites higher. When I approached potential partners with this proposal, roughly only 2 out of 10 agreed to exchange links, but when it came to implementation, I lost a third of these partners because to some of them thought it was too difficult or it took too much time and effort. But I didn't stop until my website got into the top the three of Google search results by almost all of my main keywords. Even though I was just starting out as a marketing consultant, my website was listed first compared to well-established marketing experts who had 15 or 20 years of experience. I got more leads, worked on them attentively, and converted them into sales. After just a few month, national business magazines and portals started asking my opinion about various aspects of marketing, and I became a nationally known marketing expert. And all of it started from my persistent, targeted actions to create beneficial partnerships.

 Recommended reading

1. David Abingdon. *Out of the Box Marketing*
2. Richard Gibbs, Andrew Humphries. *Strategic Alliances & Marketing Partnerships: Gaining Competitive Advantage Through Collaboration and Partnering*
3. Penenberg *A.L. Viral Loop: The Power of Pass-It-On*
4. Gherasim A. (2011). *The Creation Of Partnerships - Essential Objective In Industrial Marketing.* Economy Transdisciplinarity Cognition. 2011, Vol. 14 Issue 1, p391-401

35. Marketing automation strategies & tools

WHY IT IS NEEDED

Your marketing database might be your most valuable asset, but it is only as valuable as you make it. You've put a lot of work into generating leads (Chapter 32: Marginal users and magnets to hook them), so don't waste it. Companies that invest in marketing automation see 70% faster sales cycle times (Jean Marie Bonthous, 2016), 80% of marketing automation users saw their number of leads increase, and 77% saw the number of conversions increase (*John Koetsier, 2015*).

Marketing automation platforms enable you to create and manage customer interactions with greater speed and customization, send different messages to different customer segments, automatically launch email campaigns to individual prospects based on their action, or other triggers that you choose. Marketing automation enables customer-segmented communication tracks to provide content and messaging based on the potential customers' behavior, interest levels, and demographics. Automation can range from setting up single email campaigns to designing entire sets of emails and multi-channel content to enrich and expand customer interactions while building trust and strengthening the relationship. Manual processes could never scale to meet the demands of these sophisticated and targeted lead nurturing methods.

Several books have been written on this topic. I recommend looking at *Intro to Marketing Automation: Maximize Your Advertising ROI* by Dr. Todd Kelsey and *Automation Domination: A Business Owner's Guide To Dominating Your Market Online* by Todd McPartlin. Those authors did a great job introducing marketing automation essentials and practical tips. But, for now, let's take a look at how marketing automation could make your startup business scale faster and what you need to do.

HOW TO DO IT

01 Identify What Could Be Automated
Look broader and don't limit yourself with an email workflow only

02 Outline Your Automation Strategy
Draft your strategy and plan an automation workflow for each stage of the sales funnel

03 Choose Marketing Automation Tool
Don't hurry to buy or subscribe without comparing different tools to your needs

04 Create Automation Workflows
Stick to the rule of build-measure-learn and remember that content relevance changes

Find out what could be automated in your situation

Marketing automation is more than an email workflow engine. Your marketing automation workflow steps can include updating of contact attributes, importing of data into your CRM, management of subscriptions, and more. Customer contact attributes can even be used in the personalization of your website content, enabling you to design a visitor experience according to their specific interests. This tactic provides an additional communication channel with your customers.

Review your sales funnel and customer journey map and ask yourself, "What would I like to automate in order to save my time and grow my business faster?" At this point, don't limit yourself by wondering if there is a technical solution to do the automation. Just list your ideas about what should be automated to scale your business. This might include:

- Sending email campaigns
- Quickly building micro websites and landing pages
- Tracking website activity analytics
- Creating and distributing forms and surveys
- Client membership management
- Updating lead records in CRM (lead segmentation and scoring)
- Providing hot lead data to your sales team
- Getting reminders sent to yourself and team members
- Sharing your content online/offline
- Automating activities in social networks
- Monitoring efficiency of online advertising
- Sending SMS
- Others

 Outline your marketing automation strategy and workflows

To get started, draft your strategy and plan your automation workflow for each sales funnel stage on paper. Why it is this so important? The technology itself doesn't engage and convert prospects. It's having the marketing plan in place that makes it all happen. Have you heard of the 40/40/20 rule of direct response marketing? Even though some people think it is old school, you should review it anyway before investing in marketing automation. The rule says that the success of a campaign (in this case, marketing automation campaign) is based:

- 40 % on targeting the right audience (identifying your marginal users and successfully using your lead magnets to attract them)
- 40 % on the offer you make (your lead magnet offers, main irresistible offer, cross-sell, up-sell, down-sell offers)
- 20 % on your creative execution (copywriting, design, right timing)

A marketing automation workflow is a series of automated actions that are initiated based on advanced pre-defined triggers related to a person's behaviors or contact information. It means that you have a possibility to outline the typical behavior scenarios of your potential customers and bring your main offer in front of them when they are most likely to buy. But, to do that, you need to know who you are contacting, what you are communicating and delivering to them, and how to communicate with them in the most appealing manner.

The most basic marketing automation workflow could be:

1. To build an email list of potential customers (leads) to whom your product might be highly valuable and get them into your sales funnel
2. To develop a relationship and build trust with those leads by delivering them value without asking them to buy anything (the more that the largest part of your sales funnel is automated, the more chances you have of scaling your business fast)
3. To convert those leads into paying customers at some point
4. To keep your customers happy about their choice and initiate word-of-mouth advertising (remember the viral loop when your current customers refer your business to their friends and bring new leads into your sales funnel).

Once you are clear about your marketing automation strategy, it's time to plan actual workflows based on triggers. Here are the top ten most frequently used marketing automation campaign triggers, but you can always add new ones that are more relevant to your business situation.

1. *Content download trigger* is used for topic-oriented lead nurturing. Usually, it is directly related to lead magnets; once the potential customer downloads a lead magnet, a particular marketing workflow starts.
2. *Achieving certain lead scores and activity triggers* usually launch campaigns targeted to highly engaged persons who are interested in a product or topic, but are not yet ready to buy. For example, an invitation to a webinar, opportunity to join a special group on social networks, or a quiz might be good tools to grow their interest in your product and their trust in you.

Figure 50. Example of marketing automation workflow

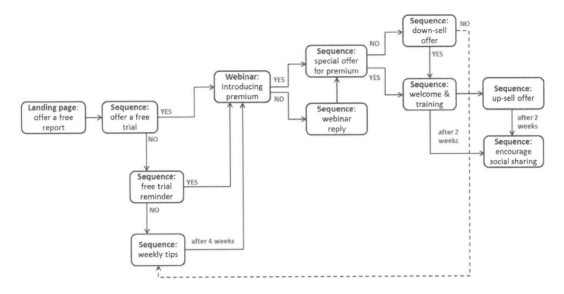

3. *Achieving high lead score trigger* is used to increase sales readiness. If you set up a lead scoring system on your website or CRM (if it is integrated with your marketing automation platform), once a potential customer reaches a certain score, automatically offer them the activity you identified as being key (for example, sending them your irresistible offer).

4. *Shopping cart abandonment trigger* is used to identify potential customers that were ready to buy but didn't finish their purchase. You can automatically contact those website visitors and

   - remind them of their purchase they might have forgotten.
   - Offer a special discount or bonus to loyal and long-term buyers
   - Ask for feedback on why they didn't finish the purchase (even if you won't sell this time, you might get valuable insights how to improve your whole sales funnel)

5. *Past purchases and sales cycle triggers* are used for up-selling, cross-selling, and cycle-based selling campaigns. We talked about those strategies in Chapter 26: Get ready to up-sell, cross-sell, and down-sell.

6. *Sales cycle stage trigger* usually initiates after sale support automation. Start automatically building a positive relationship with your customers once they have bought your product. Provide great after-sales support, like sharing useful training material and videos, informing them about product updates, sending personalized holiday greetings (you can automatically put your customer's name in the pre-build template and everyone will get a personal and warm greeting from you).

7. *Inactivity of leads* can be set as a trigger to wake inactive leads or remove them from your CRM. If somebody was interested in your product a while ago but didn't buy it, send them an exclusive offer to re-engage them. You'll get one of two benefits: you'll wake up the potential client and close the sale or will remove this lead from your list and thus save your marketing automation resources.

8. *High or low Net Promoter Score (NPS) trigger* is used to automatically launch word-of-mouth fostering campaigns (motivate your happy customers to spread the news about you) or problem-solving campaigns (figure out what is wrong with your product, service, or overall customer experience if this person gave you a low NPS value).

9. *Event registration trigger* initiates automated communication to event participants, for example, reminders, special content sharing, sending invoices, event updates, etc.

10. *Company manual download or video watch trigger* can be used for employee training campaigns. This kind of trigger is mostly used by large companies that have many employees, but during my global research on startups, I found many startups who are already in the market use this trigger for training their affiliate partners and value-added resellers or sales agents.

 Evaluate marketing automation tools and choose the one that best fits your needs

Chose the marketing automation platform that best fits your needs. Don't hurry to buy or subscribe yet, unless it is a free account like the one offered by MailChimp. There are five key tasks to do before you make a decision to implement a marketing automation platform:

1. *Estimate your technical needs but don't over-complicate it*. What would be the best and what is the minimum you could start with. How well does the platform scale as you increase the size of your database or the number of transactions? How does the platform scale to support new channels/mediums? As you grow, your sales funnel and marketing plan might become more advanced and include new technical solutions. Will your chosen marketing automation platform support them?

2. *Evaluate integration possibilities with your other tools and systems.* If you know what integrations you are looking for, great! If not, you might want to look at integrations with other systems you use within your company. There is a lot of value in integrating all the systems that touch the customer's journey. The visibility you get into the customer and the potential for reducing the number of manual touch points make it well worth it.

3. *Determine your budget and create a shortlist of platforms.* Is there an onboarding cost? Many vendors charge an onboarding cost. How does your cost change as you scale up? Your initial cost might be low, but what will it jump to when you renew?

4. *Read reviews and customer feedbacks, especially outside of the platforms itself.* Reading testimonials on vendors website will give you some clue as to what to expect from the platform. But if you search for reviews in forums and third party websites, you might find out additional pros and cons that are not necessarily shared by the vendors.

5. *Watch videos and demos, conduct a free trial (if one is available) and check customer support.* Evaluate the tool by using it for at least one campaign so that you know firsthand how it delivers on its promises, and how well it matches your needs.

After comparing at least few marketing automation platforms, you should be able to answer the main question: will this help to build and scale your business? Before making your final decision, think about if it will help you to close more business, do it faster, and save your money.

 Create, measure and update your marketing automation workflows

While creating your workflow content and messages, remember that it must be high quality, useful, and valuable for your customers. Otherwise, your messaging and content will quickly be treated as spam. Most prospects convert into leads based on interest in a particular product or area of concern. Marketing automation content should relate closely to those interests until the prospect indicates a desire to move on to other products or topics.

Though you shouldn't start your active sales pitch too early, it is important that your marketing automation processes and objectives are aligned with the sales process, especially if your main sales are not done online. I've seen many startups make this mistake. Their marketing communication is well automated and planned for ahead of time, but there is no connection with the sales team (in the best case, the sales team gets hot leads in the CRM). If you have employed marketing automation, try to align it and update it according to the sales process.

The build-measure-learn rule also works well here. Use A/B tests everywhere you can in your marketing automation (for example, email subject line, email copy, etc.) to increase conversion of your workflow and keep it up to date. Remember that the relevance of your automated content might have a short lifespan. Don't forget to check your automated content and triggers, and periodically review them to ensure that messaging and content are appropriate and aligned with your target customer segments.

Recommended reading

1. *Dr. Todd Kelsey. Intro to Marketing Automation: Maximize Your Advertising ROI*
2. Todd McPartlin. *Automation Domination: A Business Owner's Guide To Dominating Your Market Online*

There is no magical growth hack that would stick and stay constant forever. At least none of the thousand startups I analyzed boasted about found a magical growth hack. Growth hacking is a never-ending process. But when you know how to measure your growth and pay attention to what really matters, it's much easier to focus your efforts on the right things that help in scaling your business. Unfortunately, sporadic actions won't yield sustainable results in the long run. You need to work on business growth consistently and methodically. Review this chapter and do these exercises from time to time and you'll notice that you are getting closer to your goal of building a profitable and scalable business.

Keep the Pace

You now know the whole methodology of *Startup Evolution Curve*. But unfortunately, that's not enough. You must now take consistent, targeted actions. I know the feeling when your mood is elevated, your motivation is high, and you have so many great ideas after reading the book. You should have come up with at least a few ideas that will help you to develop your startup faster. Write them down.

These are top five ideas that I found most useful after reading this book:

1. _____

2. _____

3. _____

4. _____

5. _____

Conditions change rapidly, especially in the startup environment. If you created or found something meaningful, rest assured that it won't stay valuable forever. You must use your momentum and never stop building your startup business until you succeed! If you hit the wall, don't worry. All startups have tough moments and difficult challenges to solve. Join the community of like-minded entrepreneurs on the Linkedin group "Startup Evolution Curve" and share your experiences, challenges, and questions that you have. I've created this group especially for this purpose: to share the experience, useful resources, and to support each other.

Lack of funds should not be a reason for procrastination until you find investors. Work on your idea now! You already know what you can do even without money! Most of the tasks from Stage 1: Feasibility study as well as from Stage 2: Hypotheses and Experiments don't require much money, just your time, creative thinking, and devotion to do what's needed, even if it's not as exciting as you'd like. So, grab a cup of coffee or tea, relax, clear your mind and write down where you will focus your efforts.

I will focus my efforts on these main tasks in each stage:

	Feasibility Study • _____ • _____ • _____
	Hypotheses and Experiments: • _____ • _____ • _____
	Fundraising: • _____ • _____ • _____
	Product Launch: • _____ • _____ • _____
	Growth Hacking: • _____ • _____ • _____

Considering all this, my goal for the next month is:

_____

_____

_____

Here are my main tasks for each week in order to reach the monthly goal:

Week 1	
Week 2	
Week 3	
Week 4	

If you want to develop your startup faster, visit www.EvolutionCurve.com

- Download the templates mentioned in this book and start using them absolutely for FREE. It will save your time and will help to focus your thoughts on necessary aspects.
- Signup for your FREE video training course on how to create an irresistible offer and win your first clients even if you don't have a product yet!
- Be among the first to know about my new books and master class video courses. I'll let you know when these are available for free or with heavy discounts.

If you liked this book and have found useful ideas, please leave your review. It's really simple and would help me a lot! I would appreciate your help. Go to the Startup Evolution Curve detail page on Amazon.com and click *Write a customer review* in the *Customer Reviews* section. It would be awesome if you could share even a single sentence about what you've found most valuable in this book and to whom you would recommend it. If you'd like to get in contact, my direct email is startup@evolutioncurve.com

Thank you in advance and good luck building your startup!

References

Top 10 books on startup development I highly recommend to read:

1. Alexander Osterwalder, Yves Pigneur, Gregory Bernarda, Alan Smith. Value Proposition Design: How to Create Products and Services Customers Want (Strategyzer)

2. Eric Ries. The Lean Startup: How Today's Entrepreneurs Use Continuous Innovation to Create Radically Successful Businesses

3. Steve Blank, Bob Dorf. The Startup Owner's Manual: The Step-by-Step Guide for Building a Great Company

4. Alexander Osterwalder, Pigneur Yves. Business Model Generation: A handbook for Visionaries, Game Changers, and Challengers

5. Patrick Van Der Pijl, Justin Lokitz, Lisa Kay Solomon. Design a Better Business: New Tools, Skills, and Mindset for Strategy and Innovation

6. Ash Maurya. Scaling Lean: Mastering the Key Metrics for Startup Growth

7. Philip Kotler, Gary Armstrong. Principles of Marketing

8. Jay Conrad Levinson, Jeannie Levinson, Amy Levinson. Guerrilla Marketing, 4th edition: Easy and Inexpensive Strategies for Making Big Profits from Your Small Business

9. David Goldsmith. Paid to Think: A Leader's Toolkit for Redefining Your Future

10. Carlos Espinal. Fundraising Field Guide: A Startup Founder's Handbook for Venture Capital

References

- Abingdon David. Out of the Box Marketing. Thorogood Publishing Ltd. (September 27, 2005)

- Baehr Evan, Loomis Evan. Get Backed: Craft Your Story, Build the Perfect Pitch Deck, and Launch the Venture of Your Dreams. Harvard Business Review Press (October 27, 2015)

- Barnes Cindy, Blake Helen, Pinder David. Creating and Delivering Your Value Proposition: Managing Customer Experience for Profit. Kogan Page; 1 edition (October 3, 2009)

- Belsito Mike. Startup Seed Funding for the Rest of Us: How to Raise $1 Million for Your Startup - Even Outside of Silicon Valley. March 5, 2015

- Blank Steve, Dorf Bob. The Startup Owner's Manual: The Step-by-Step Guide for Building a Great Company. K&S Ranch; 1 edition (March 1, 2012)

- Blank Steve. Startups Should Never, Ever Rely On Consultants To Figure Out What Their Customers Want. http://www.businessinsider.com/startups-should-never-ever-rely-on-consultants-to-figure-out-what-their-customers-want-2010-5

- Bonthous Jean Marie. 28 Remarkable Lead Management & Marketing Automation Statistics. http://seamlesssocial.com/28-remarkable-lead-management-marketing-automation-statistics/

- Chernev Alexander. The Marketing Plan Handbook, 4th Edition. Cerebellum Press; 4 edition (November 1, 2014)

- Cremades Alejandro. The Art of Startup Fundraising: Pitching Investors, Negotiating the Deal, and Everything Else Entrepreneurs Need to Know. Wiley; 1 edition (March 31, 2016)

- Croll Alistair, Yoskovitz Benjamin. Lean Analytics: Use Data to Build a Better Startup Faster (Lean Series).

- Cutler Kim-Mai. Lessons From A Study of Perfect Pitch Decks: VCs Spend An Average of 3 Minutes, 44 Seconds On Them. https://techcrunch.com/2015/06/08/lessons-from-a-study-of-perfect-pitch-decks-vcs-spend-an-average-of-3-minutes-44-seconds-on-them

- Daar Steven. Profit Hacking: The Web Entrepreneur's 3 Part Formula For Maximizing Success. Kindle Edition. December 14, 2014

- Davis Mark Peter. The Fundraising Rules. CreateSpace Independent Publishing Platform (March 22, 2013)

- Devaney Erik. Monkey Business: The Story Behind MailChimp's Wild Growth. http://blog.drift.com/how-mailchimp-grew?utm_campaign=Submission&utm_medium=Community&utm_source=GrowthHackers.com

- DeWolf K.A. Bootstrapping Entrepreneur: 100 Free Online Tools for Startups and First-Time Entrepreneurs. September 20, 2014

- Dib Allan. The 1-Page Marketing Plan: Get New Customers, Make More Money, And Stand out From The Crowd. Successwise (January 25, 2016)

- Diehl Gregory. Brand Identity Breakthrough: How to Craft Your Company's Unique Story to Make Your Products Irresistible. Identity Books; 1 edition (May 9, 2016)

- Dimova Gerry. How to create a viral startup beta landing page + 2 case studies. https://sansmagic.com/how-to-create-a-viral-startup-beta-landing-page-2-case-studies/

- DocSend & Tom Eisenmann. What we learned from 200 startups who raised $360M. https://docsend.com/view/p8jxsqr (2015)

- Donlon Jessica. The Marketing Score Blog. 18 Marketing Performance Metrics that Matter. http://www.themarketingscore.com/blog/bid/220074/18-Marketing-Performance-Metrics-that-Matter

- Espinal Carlos. Fundraising Field Guide: A Startup Founder's Handbook for Venture Capital. Reedsy. Kindle Edition. August 11, 2015

- Feld Brad, Mendelson Jason. Venture Deals: Be Smarter Than Your Lawyer and Venture Capitalist. Wiley; 3 edition (November 22, 2016)

- Flynn Pat. Will It Fly?: How to Test Your Next Business Idea So You Don't Waste Your Time and Money. SPI Publications (January 31, 2016)

- Frost Phil. How to Identify Your Online Marketing Leverage Points. https://www.mainstreetroi.com/how-to-identify-your-leverage-points/

- Garza Joe. 50 Bootstrapping Hacks for Every Stage of Your Startup. Founders Institute https://fi.co/posts/17831

- Gherasim A. The Creation Of Partnerships - Essential Objective In Industrial Marketing. Economy Transdisciplinarity Cognition. 2011, Vol. 14 Issue 1, p391-401

- Gibbs Richard, Humphries Andrew. Strategic Alliances & Marketing Partnerships: Gaining Competitive Advantage Through Collaboration and Partnering. London: Kogan Page. (March 1, 2009)

- Gibson Marcus, Gianforte Greg. Bootstrapping Your Business: Start and Grow a Successful Company with Almost No Money. CreateSpace Independent Publishing Platform (January 16, 2013)

- Goldsmith David. Paid to Think: A Leader's Toolkit for Redefining Your Future. BenBella Books (October 1, 2013)

- Graham Paul (September 2012). Startup Equals Growth, in Graham's Essays on entrepreneurship

- Graham Paul. Do Things That Don't Scale. http://paulgraham.com/ds.html

- Greer Allen. Don't Do A Redesign! Learn Why Evolution Beats Revolution. https://blog.kissmetrics.com/dont-do-a-redesign/

- Harenstam Fredrik, Thuriaux-Aleman Ben, Eagar Rick. (2015.05.27). Systematizing Breakthrough Innovation: Study Results. http://www.innovationmanagement.se/2015/05/27/systematizing-breakthrough-innovation-study-results/

- Holiday Ryan. Growth Hacker Marketing: A Primer on the Future of PR, Marketing, and Advertising. Portfolio; Reprint edition (September 30, 2014)

- *Innmind* (2016). How many startups are there in the world. http://innmind.com/articles/262

- Joseph Jim. The Experience Effect: Engage Your Customers with a Consistent and Memorable Brand Experience. AMACOM (May 3, 2010)

- Joyner Mark. The Irresistible Offer: How to Sell Your Product or Service in 3 Seconds or Less. Wiley; 1 edition (September 5, 2005)

- Kalbach James. Mapping Experiences: A Complete Guide to Creating Value through Journeys, Blueprints, and Diagrams. O'Reilly Media; 1 edition (May 5, 2016)

- Karjaluoto Eric. Speak Human: Outmarket the Big Guys by Getting Personal. smashLAB Inc (October 31, 2009)

- Kelsey Todd. Intro to Marketing Automation: Maximize Your Advertising ROI. RGB Press (August 2, 2015)

- Kendra Lee. The Sales Magnet: How to Get More Customers Without Cold Calling. KLA Press; 1st edition (January 29, 2013)

- Kim W. Chan, Mauborgne Renée A. Blue Ocean Strategy, Expanded Edition: How to Create Uncontested Market Space and Make the Competition Irrelevant. Harvard Business Review Press; (January 20, 2015)

- Kocialski Cynthia. Perfect Pricing in One Simple Lesson: Find Your Pricing Edge, Attract More Customers, and Earn More Profit. October 22, 2014

- Koetsier John. Marketing Automation, how to make the right buying decision. VB Insight. http://venturebeat.com/2015/05/05/marketing-automation-best-bets-80-of-companies-increase-leads-77-increase-conversions/

- Kotler Philip, Armstrong Gary. Principles of Marketing. Pearson; 16 edition (January 9, 2015)

- Leigh Caldwell. The Psychology of Price: How to use price to increase demand, profit and customer satisfaction. Crimson Publishing (November 2, 2012)

- Levinson Jay Conrad, Levinson Jeannie, Levinson Amy. Guerrilla Marketing, 4th edition: Easy and Inexpensive Strategies for Making Big Profits from Your Small Business. Mariner Books; 4 Upd Exp edition (May 22, 2007)

- Loyd Dave. SEO for Success in Video Marketing. https://blogs.adobe.com/digitalmarketing/search-marketing/seo-for-success-in-video-marketing/

- Maurya Ash. Running Lean: Iterate from Plan A to a Plan That Works. O'Reilly Media; 2 edition (March 9, 2012)

- Maurya Ash. Scaling Lean: Mastering the Key Metrics for Startup Growth. Portfolio (June 14, 2016)

- Mawhinney Jesse. 37 Visual Content Marketing Statistics You Should Know in 2016. https://blog.hubspot.com/marketing/visual-content-marketing-strategy

- McPartlin Todd. Automation Domination: A Business Owner's Guide To Dominating Your Market Online. iML Publishing (September 17, 2013)

- Michael E. Porter. How Competitive Forces Shape Strategy. March 1979. Copyright © 1979 by the Harvard Business School Publishing Corporation; all rights reserved.

- Olsen Dan. The Lean Product Playbook: How to Innovate with Minimum Viable Products and Rapid Customer Feedback.

- Osterwalder Alexander, Pigneur Yves, Bernarda Gregory, Smith Alan. Value Proposition Design: How to Create Products and Services Customers Want (Strategyzer). Wiley; 1 edition (October 20, 2014)

- Osterwalder Alexander, Yves Pigneur. Business Model Generation: A handbook for Visionaries, Game Changers, and Challengers. John Wiley and Sons; 1st edition (July 13, 2010)

- Osterwalder A. The Business Model Ontology. A Proposition in A Design Science Approach. Universite De Lausanne Ecole Des Hautes Etudes Commerciales.

- Parasuraman, A. (1997). Reflections on gaining competitive advantage through customer value. Journal of the Academy of Marketing Science, 154-161

- Patel Neil (2012). 5 Ways to Get Your Infographic to Go Viral. https://www.quicksprout.com/2012/06/11/5-ways-to-get-your-infographic-to-go-viral/

- Patel Neil, Taylor Bronson. The definitive guide to growth hacking. https://www.quicksprout.com/the-definitive-guide-to-growth-hacking/

- Patrick Van Der Pijl, Lokitz Justin, Solomon Lisa Kay. Design a Better Business: New Tools, Skills, and Mindset for Strategy and Innovation. Wiley; 1 edition (September 13, 2016)

- Penenberg A.L. Viral Loop: The Power of Pass-It-On. Sceptre (2009)

- Poland Stephen R. Founder's Pocket Guide: Startup Valuation (Founder's Pocket Guide Book 1). 1x1 Media (August 16, 2014)

- Porter Michael E. Competitive Strategy: Techniques for Analyzing Industries and Competitors. Free Press; 1 edition (June 30, 2008)

- Reason Ben, Løvlie Lavrans, Flu Melvin Brand. Service Design for Business: A Practical Guide to Optimizing the Customer Experience. Wiley; 1 edition (December 14, 2015)

- Ries Al, Trout Jack. Positioning: The Battle for Your Mind. McGraw-Hill Education; 1 edition (January 3, 2001)

- Ries Al, Trout Jack. Marketing Warfare. McGraw-Hill Education; 1 edition (November 22, 1997)

- Ries Eric. The Lean Startup: How Today's Entrepreneurs Use Continuous Innovation to Create Radically Successful Businesses. Crown Business; 1 edition (September 13, 2011)

- Romans Andrew. The Entrepreneurial Bible to Venture Capital: Inside Secrets From the Leaders in the Startup Game. McGraw-Hill Education; 1 edition (August 16, 2013)

- Rumelt Richard. Good Strategy Bad Strategy: The Difference and Why It Matters. Crown Business; 31625th edition (July 19, 2011)

- Schroeder Bernard. Fail Fast or Win Big: The Start-Up Plan for Starting Now. AMACOM; 1 edition (February 18, 2015)

- Sean Ellis. (2009). What is a Perfect Startup Launch? http://www.startup-marketing.com/category/launch/

- Shelley Cernel. (2015). How to Improve Sales Productivity: 7 Helpful Hints http://www.knowledgetree.com/blog/2015/05/how-to-improve-sales-productivity/#

- Stickdorn Marc, Hormess Markus Edgar, Lawrence Adam, Schneider Jakob. This Is Service Design Doing: Applying Service Design and Design Thinking in the Real World. O'Reilly Media; 1 edition (May 5, 2017)

- Stickdorn Marc, Schneider Jakob. This is Service Design Thinking: Basics, Tools, Cases. Wiley; 1 edition (January 11, 2012)

- Suster Mark. Upfront VC analysis 2016. http://www.slideshare.net/msuster/upfront-vc-analysis-2016/11-11Public_Tech_Markets_are_obviously

- Thiel Peter, Masters Blake. Zero to One: Notes on Startups, or How to Build the Future. Crown Business; 1 edition (September 16, 2014)

- Vasconcellos e Sa Jorge. Strategy Moves - 14 Complete Attack and Defense Strategies for Competitive Advantage. Pearson Education Limited, 2005

- Waleed Esbaitah. Growth of Real Estate Crowdfunding in 2016. Crowd Fund Beat. http://crowdfundbeat.com/2016/04/05/growth-of-real-estate-crowdfunding-in-2016/

- Webb Nicholas J. What Customers Crave: How to Create Relevant and Memorable Experiences at Every Touchpoint. AMACOM (October 13, 2016)

- Weinberg Gabriel, Mares Justin. Traction: How Any Startup Can Achieve Explosive Customer Growth. Portfolio (October 6, 2015)

- Wilhelm, Alex (2014). What The Hell Is A Startup Anyway? Posted Dec 30, 2014. Link: https://techcrunch.com/2014/12/30/what-the-hell-is-a-startup-anyway/

- Wilmerding Alex and Aspatore Books Staff. Term Sheets & Valuations: A Line by Line Look at the Intricacies of Term Sheets & Valuations (Bigwig Briefs). West (June 21, 2009)

- Wind Yoram (Jerry), Findiesen Hays Catharine. Beyond Advertising: Creating Value Through All Customer Touchpoints. Wiley; 1 edition (February 15, 2016)

About the author

"I help early stage startups to become fundable and financially self-sustainable."
That's how Dr. Donatas Jonikas defines his mission and passion.

Dr. Donatas Jonikas holds a Ph.D. in Economics and a Master's in Marketing Management. He is also a reserve lieutenant with infantry platoon commander qualifications. Being a scientist, a marketer, and a military commander makes him an extraordinary mentor for startups where so much uncertainty exists in every step. Donatas believes that knowledge and skills alone are not enough to achieve your goal, rather you must take the correct actions at the correct time. Donatas developed and helped to implement winning marketing strategies for more than 50 companies in different countries and industries around the globe. He has shared the stage with many of the world's foremost industry experts in startup conferences, hackathons, entrepreneur events, and competitions.

Made in the USA
San Bernardino, CA
13 February 2018